RELIGION AND THE FAMILY

Religion & the Family

Edited by RONALD A. SIMKINS
and GAIL S. RISCH

Creighton University Press | Omaha, Nebraska

© 2008 by Creighton University Press.
All rights reserved.

No part of this book may be reproduced or transmitted in any form or by any means, electronic or mechanical, including photocopying, recording, or any information storage and retrieval system, without permission in writing from the Publisher, except in the case of brief quotations embodied in critical articles and reviews.

Library of Congress Cataloging-in-Publication Data
Simkins, Ronald.
　Religion and the family /
　by Ronald A. Simkins and Gail S. Risch.
　p.　cm.
　ISBN 978-1-881871-49-1
　1. Family—Religious life—United States.
　2. United States—Religion.
　I. Risch, Gail S., 1951– II. Title.
　BL625.6.S56 2005　　201'.7—dc22
　2005025678

EDITORIAL
Creighton University Press
2500 California Plaza
Omaha, Nebraska 68178

MARKETING &
DISTRIBUTION
Fordham University Press
University Box L
Bronx, New York 10458

Association of Jesuit University Presses

Printed in the United States of America

Contents

Acknowledgements   vii

Introduction
    RONALD A. SIMKINS & GAIL S. RISCH   ix

Religion and Family in America:
A Socio-Historical Reconnaissance
    CHARLES L. HARPER   1

Sacred Kinship: *Creating and Extending Family among the Lakota of Pine Ridge*
    RAYMOND A. BUCKO, S.J.   28

Competing Portraits of the Israelite Family
    RONALD A. SIMKINS   46

Reshaping Family in Egypt:
The Islamist Discourse
    JOHN C. M. CALVERT   68

The Sacramental Texture of Family Life:
A Contemporary Roman Catholic Perspective
    WENDY M. WRIGHT   87

Kids Caught in the Crossfire:
Reflections on the School Wars
    BETTE NOVIT EVANS   102

Religion, the Family, and the Public School
during Non-School Hours: *Good News v. Milford*
    R. COLLIN MANGRUM   135

Culture Wars, Family Wars? *The Political
Mobilization of Clergy on Family Issues*
    SUE E. S. CRAWFORD   172
    MELISSA M. DECKMAN
    LAURA R. OLSON

The Impact of Religiosity on Marital Stability
    LISA A. RILEY   198

The Shape of Family and Family Values:
"*The Bible Tells Us So*," or Does It?
    SUSAN A. CALEF   223

An Early Christian Debate on Marriage
and Family: *The Jovinianist Controversy*
    DAVID G. HUNTER   247

Faith, Praxis, and Practical Theology:
At the Interface of Sociology and Theology
    MICHAEL G. LAWLER   262

Acknowledgements

The essays in this volume were originally delivered at a symposium on Religion and the Family sponsored by the Center for the Study of Religion and Society at Creighton University (April 5–6, 2002). The symposium consisted of fourteen scholars representing a wide range of disciplines—biblical studies, theology, spirituality, history, anthropology, sociology, political science, and law—addressing the complex and changing relationship between religion and family. The result was an engaging conversation on the fluid composition of the family and the ways in which the changing family has shaped religious understandings and experiences.

The present volume presents the substance of that symposium. A significant contribution of this volume is its interdisciplinary approach to the topic. Each of the essays addresses the interrelationship of religion and family, but the questions that each author brings to the topic are shaped by her or his academic discipline. Individually, the essays make substantive contributions to their fields; collectively, the papers present a new, complex picture of the relationship between religion and family.

Most of the contributors to the volume are at Creighton University, representing the wide range of academic departments with an interest in religion and family. David Hunter is at Iowa State University. He was invited to participate in the symposium based on his work in early Christianity. Laura Olsen, from Clemson University, and Melissa Deckman, from Washington College, were unable to participate in the symposium, but collaborated with Sue Crawford in her study of clergy.

Introduction

RONALD A. SIMKINS
AND GAIL S. RISCH

Religion and family have a symbiotic relationship. In the pre-modern world, religion, along with economics and education, was embedded in the family and in political structures. People did not talk about religion as something separate and apart from the kin group or the polity. Rather, religion was an expression of family or political life, and a change in the latter was reflected in a change in the former. New forms and functions of the family gave rise to new religious expressions. Only with the complex society of the modern industrialized world, a rather new state of affairs that emerged in the eighteenth century, does a separation of family, education, economics, government, and religion surface. Yet, as the essays in this volume demonstrate, the relationship between religion and family remains intertwined.

Family has been and continues to be a surprisingly evolving reality, and each permutation carries with it a new constellation of religious ideas and practices. Until the early nineteenth century most middle-class Europeans and North Americans defined family based on a common residence under the authority of a household head, rather than on blood ties. During the same period, the elite class understood family as the larger descent group from which claims to privilege and property derived. Not until the nineteenth century did the word family commonly describe a married couple with their co-resident children, distinguished from household residents or more distant kin. By the turn of the twentieth century, the restriction of the word to the immediate, co-residential family was so prevalent that the adjective "extended" had to be added when people referred to kin beyond the household.[1] Social changes brought about a similar evolution of marriage. Before the Hardwick Act of 1754, clandestine or informal marriages were common in England (30–50% of all marriages by some estimates). The Church of England recognized as married those couples who consented to be married and whose family acknowledged their union; community acceptance, rather than religious ritual, was primary. With the passage of the Hardwick Act, common-law marriages were abolished and only those marriages conducted under the supervision of the church were considered legitimate. Although the marriage ceremony witnessed by clergy gradually became the norm, many people were unable to afford the full formal ceremony or refused to recognize the authority of the church and so continued to participate in informal marriages. The enactment of the Marriage Act of 1837 finally provided an alternative means of legitimation through a civil ceremony—and these marriages were recognized by the church. Religion was enmeshed in the family so that as definitions of the family and marriage shifted over time, religion was shaped accordingly. But the converse is also true. Religion has shaped our understanding of the family. Most weddings in the United States, for example, are conducted by clergy and take place in a religious institution, regardless of the religious devotion or piety of the couple.

In contemporary American culture, the erroneous assumption of universality has virtually reduced family to its "lowest common denominator—married couple and children"[2]—which has been identified, especially by the Christian Right, with the family "instituted by God." Just as God gave Eve to Adam and blessed them "to be fruitful and multiply," so the only legitimate, divinely sanctioned family is defined in terms of the heterosexual couple and the procreation of children. Reflection on the reality of family in both past and present societies, however, challenges this ideologically laden notion of the "traditional" family and its religious underpinnings. Whether tradition refers to several hundred years or to merely two or three generations, it is always, to varying degrees, adapted and transformed as it is passed on. The tension around family diversity is acutely illustrated by the polarized "family values" debate that emerged over a decade ago and continues to undergird political and religious discourse related to family issues. While a significant body of social scientific research reports on what some perceive as a decline of the family and marriage, and thus the failure of religion to maintain traditional forms, others interpret data regarding changes in family forms as part of a broad and comprehensive restructuring of familial institutions for the good of society.³ In either case, the symbiotic relationship between religion and family is implicit.

The complex relationship between religion and family on the American scene is discussed in the opening essay by Charles Harper, "Religion and Family in America: A Socio-Historical Reconnaissance." Through three major periods of American history, Harper traces the rise, transformation, and resurgence of familialism—a dominant social and religious ideology. The traditional form of familialism emerged during the colonial and early national period as a set of cognitive and normative assumptions that encouraged "premarital sexual restraint, dedication to one's partner in a lifelong marital covenant, procreation, and the raising of children who are subject absolutely to parental (especially paternal) authority." The family, according to the assumptions of familialism, was an institution ordained by God in Eden, and thus its form and function had religious implications.

The rise of modernism and secularism in the late nineteenth and early twentieth century led to a transformation of the traditional familialism. According to Harper, the individuation that accompanied these broad social and intellectual movements, along with the often-resulting alienation and anomie, exposed the inadequacies of familialism. As the family adapted to the changing landscape, religion served to redefine familialism in the new contexts through the Social Gospel, Fundamentalism, and Catholic Social Action. The last half of the twentieth century was a period of turbulent change from the suburbanization of the 1950s, through the counter-cultural movements of the 1960s and 1970s, to the abandonment of the mainline churches in the 1980s and beyond. The American family was also changing rapidly with dramatic increases in cohabitation, divorce, remarriage with "blended families," and out of wedlock births. Because a perceived irrelevance of traditional forms of religion or a general lack of religiosity, traditional familialism was unappealing to many. Yet, while new forms of familialism thrived with the upsurge of marginal religious movements in the 1970s, Protestant fundamentalism and evangelicalism injected new life into the traditional forms. Despite the change of family and religion through American history, "a stable characteristic of the American experience is the remarkable persistence of the ideology of religious familialism that specifies family in fairly traditional forms with religious sanction."

Religion and family are variegated and complex human institutions that only can be adequately defined in their particular socio-historical expressions. As a result, the relationship between religion and family is necessarily complex, and one from which numerous social, cultural, legal, and moral issues emerge. It is helpful, therefore, to consider the religion-family relationship in light of three general paradigms: religion and family are indistinguishable, religion and family are separate but linked, and religion and family represent conflicting domains. The relationship between religion and family within these paradigms ranges from family embodying or actualizing religion, to family serving or facilitating religion, to family obscuring or challenging religion.

In the first paradigm, religion and family converge; they are inextricably linked in such a way that one has no role or content apart from the other. People and groups within this paradigm understand, experience, and speak of family and religion as virtually a single entity. The reality here is that family and religion are inter-penetrative; understanding and experiencing one necessarily and simultaneously understands and experiences the other. Either religion is embedded in the family, or the family is the symbol of religion. The essays in this collection by Bucko, Simkins, Calvert, and Wright represent this paradigm.

In "Sacred Kinship: Creating and Extending Family among the Lakota of Pine Ridge," Raymond Bucko, S.J., presents an anthropological and personal exploration of the *Hunka*, the Lakota adoption ceremony. The *Hunka* is a means through which the family is strengthened and extended by transforming strangers into kin and sanctifying existing relationships. The ceremony involves a number of religious elements including the symbolic use of corn and a sacred pipe, the erection of a special ceremonial lodge, the exchange of gifts, public prayers and feasts, and it must be conducted by a religious leader. The *Hunka* creates a new reality with moral, religious, and social obligations; the adopted kin must act as a kin. For the Lakota, "kinship is a sacred as well as a human matter that requires prayer, humility, and the leading of a moral life expressed through reciprocity with the divine and the human."

Ronald Simkins argues in his essay, "Competing Portraits of the Israel Family," that the presentation of the family in the Hebrew Bible is based not on divine sanction but on the political economy of ancient Israel. Religion and family in the biblical tradition is shaped by two distinct portraits of the family. One portrait of the family emphasizes the conjugal relationship between a husband and his wife and includes their children (the nuclear family), whereas a different portrait is characterized by an extended family consisting of brothers, sisters, uncles, cousins, and more distant kin of the clan (*mishpahah*). Rather than complement one another, however, these portraits represent competing interests for the loyalty of the man who was at the center of the Israelite family. The biblical texts that reflect the pre-monarchic period or were composed during the post-monarchic period present an image of the family in which the man's loyalty and obligation belonged to his kin. The biblical texts that were produced by the monarchy, however, emphasize the conjugal bond to the expense of kin relations because such relations tended to undermine the patron-client relations that were the basis of the political economy of the state. In other words, religion and family in the biblical tradition was the battleground in which the conflict inherent in the political economy of ancient Israel took place.

Whereas the essays by Bucko and Simkins illustrate the embeddedness of religion in the family, the essays by Calvert and Wright demonstrate how the family can serve as a symbol or microcosm of religion. In "Reshaping Family in Egypt: The Islamist Discourse," John Calvert addresses how Egyptian Islamism has reconceived the family in response to the challenges of modernity. Traditional Islamic understandings of the family—especially regarding issues of marriage, divorce, and succession—were challenged by Egyptian society's encounter with the economic forces and cultural influences stemming from Europe and the United States. Although the Western technological and organizational expertise offered positive developments, other aspects of Western culture functioned to undermine the unity and structure of the traditional family. Most symptomatic were the entry of women into the workplace and the erosion of patriarchal authority in the home. In order to distance Egyptian culture from the West, Islamists redefined the family in terms of the private roles of men and women, infusing them with Islamic content. The family was conceived as a microcosm of the *umma*, the worldwide community of believers, and as a conceptual marker that distinguished between the materialism of the West and the spiritual realm of traditional Islamic social forms.

Wendy Wright's contribution to understanding the relationship of religion and family is quite personal. In "The Sacramental Textual of Family Life: A Contemporary Roman Catholic Perspective," she presents her experience of pregnancy and then parenting a teenaged daughter as a model of a spiritual journey that seeks to find God in the ordinary fabric of daily life. Although the Catholic tradition has often seen the natural family and the mundane as a barrier to participation in the "true" spiritual family, the Christian Humanism implied in Salesian and Ignatian spirituality opens up the whole created world, including the family, to be "perceived as revelatory of divine life and as God-directed." Wright's dialogue between the Christian spiritual tradition and her own lived experience of family life demonstrates the sacramental qualities of the family in which the mundane relationships and interactions of daily life can stir the imagination to perceive glimpses of divine life.

The second paradigm of the relationship between religion and family suggests that family, while remaining separate from religion, has a crucial role in a person's or group's understanding and practical realization of religion. Reality from the perspective of this paradigm maintains a reciprocal and complementary relationship between family and religion; the two have distinguishable yet permeable boundaries. Examples of this paradigm are represented by the essays by Evans, Mangrum, Crawford, Deckman, and Olson, and Riley.

Historically, religion and family have been integrally linked with education. The family was responsible for education and religion was often the subject of education. In the contemporary secular state, however, education has been placed under the auspices of the government and the role of religion in education has consequently been the flashpoint of much, often heated debate. At the core of the debate is the relationship between religion and family. According to Bette Novit Evans, "many religious parents think public school teachings threaten the faith of their children, undermine their moral values, and undercut the rights of parents to transmit their religious heritage to their children." In her essay, "Kids Caught in the Crossfire: Reflections on the School Wars," Evans explores the dynamics of the conflicts over public education. She argues that schools are major battlefields because they are deeply symbolic to Americans. They serve many of the same functions of religion: They symbolize the larger community, they are a common source of socialization, they impart a common body of knowledge and values, and they offer comprehensive explanations of the world. After surveying how the Establishment and Free Exercise Clauses have been used in constitutional challenges to restrain or support the role of religion in public education, and analyzing many of the current issues of contention, Evans ends her discussion by assessing the impact of the school wars on public education and religion. She concludes that "the school wars may be a very healthy phenomenon because conflict over values is really the heart of pluralism," and thus offer a healthy education to our children.

R. Collin Mangrum, in his essay, "Religion, the Family, and the Public School during Non-School Hours: *Good News v. Milford*," gives a legal analysis of a specific example of the school wars and discusses the implications for religion and family. The relationship between religion and family is largely expressed in the private setting of the home or in religious institutions. *The Good News Club v. Milford Central School* case, in which a nondenominational Christian youth organization was denied access to school facilities after hours, raises the constitutional issue of the freedom to express the religion-family relationship in the public forum: To what extent do American constitutional principles entitle families to have their children receive moral training from a religious perspective on public school premises after hours? Mangrum gives careful analysis to the U.S. Supreme Court's decision in which the majority declared that the Milford School District had discriminated against the religious viewpoint of the Good News Club in violation of Free Speech Clause of the First Amendment. In other words, the family's right to religious speech is protected in the public forum like all other speech. "Families who are concerned over public school's secular curriculum constitutionally may choose to have the curriculum supplemented if the school has established a limited public forum wherein other after-school activities are justified as teaching moral lessons."

The school wars might be interpreted as part of a larger "culture wars" thesis, which suggests that the political debates that are transforming American politics feature two opposing camps fighting to define the cultural views about family and morality. In such a culture war, the role of the clergy would appear to be crucial. Do clergy fall into two opposing camps on such issues as gender equality, family rights for gays and lesbians, and the state's role in reducing divorce rates? Are clergy more interested in family politics or other political issues? How do liberal clergy treat these issues in public differently from conservative clergy? Do the clergy's civil discourse fit the expected patterns of the culture wars thesis? Sue Crawford, Melissa Deckman, and Laura Olson, in their essay, "Culture Wars, Family Wars? The Political Mobilization of Clergy on Family

Issues," present their findings to these questions based on a large survey of the clergy of the Disciples of Christ, a mainline Protestant denomination. The study found that although the clergy are concerned about many culture war issues, they are most concerned about social justice issues, and their pattern of public discourse did not fit the expectations of the culture wars thesis. "Although Disciples clergy are divided over many culture war issues, their divisions seem to result in different priorities for civic speech rather than wars over set issues."

Because both religion and family are institutions that emphasize values and provide a context of socialization, it is not surprising that research has found a link between religious characteristics and marital stability. For example, studies have shown that couples in which the husband and wife participate in the same religion have a lower rate of divorce than couples that do not share religion. In "The Impact of Religiosity on Marital Stability," Lisa Riley reports on a recent study addressing the question: What are the factors that increase the likelihood of remaining in a marital relationship? Unlike many earlier studies that relied on only a single factor to measure a person's religiosity, this study determined religiosity by a variety of measures, including religious homogamy, participation in joint religious activities, level of religious differences, and the use of marriage preparation. One significant finding is that a couple that remains in an interchurch marriage does not have a greater likelihood of marital instability when other variables are included. Rather, such factors as a lower level of joint religious activity or higher level of religious differences, rather than an interchurch marriage itself, might foster marital instability. Who then has the greatest likelihood of marital stability? "If one waits to get married until s/he is older, attends marriage preparation, has one's family's approval of his/her spouse, marries someone with a similar level of education, participates with one's partner in religious activities, has few religious differences, . . . then one's chances of remaining married is very high indeed."

In the third paradigm of the religion-family relationship, religion transcends the perimeters and definition of family, or family is a deterrent or barrier to religion. Persons and groups within this paradigm understand and experience family and religion as distinct spheres of reality—the physical versus the spiritual, or the mundane versus the transcendent—which are often in conflict with one another. The essays by Calef and Hunter in this volume represent this paradigm.

Susan Calef, in her essay, "The Shape of the Family and Family Values: 'The Bible Tells Us So,' or Does It?" attempts to place what Jesus said and did with respect to the family in its proper historical and social context. Responding to the numerous "family values" advocates who hold up the "biblical family" as traditional and normative, Calef argues that the Bible presents multiple images of the family, many far from idyllic or edifying, and that Jesus' view of the family is neither traditional nor comforting. Instead, Jesus saw his mission to set family members against one another. His call to discipleship meant abandonment of family and renunciation of family property. Jesus himself seems to have been at odds with his own family, even renouncing his blood ties to them. "In his own person Jesus modeled an unconventional, even iconoclastic, relation to the institutions of family and household of his time and culture. He did not marry; he did not conceive children; he did not assume the headship of a patriarchal household." Yet, Jesus does not appear to be anti-familial. His teachings support families, and he takes action on behalf of family members. Moreover, Jesus redefines the family in eschatological terms: the kingdom of God entails a new family, not based on blood relations but on doing the will of God. "Biological family ties and harmonious family relations are not ultimate values, according to the Jesus of the Gospels. Rather, blood kin ties and obligations are subordinated to a higher priority, the reign of God, and the new eschatological family of disciples dedicated to that reign."

Although Jesus' view of the family has had little impact on current "family values," even on those who uphold the "biblical family" as the norm, Jesus' radical renunciation of blood ties had a significant impact on early Christianity. Celibacy became, especially with the rise of asceticism, a model of Christian discipleship. By the fourth century, however, celibacy had become a divisive factor in the Church: it was thought to be superior to married life. Recognizing the faulty basis of this hierarchy, Jovinian claimed that married and celibate Christians were equal in merit and would receive an equal reward in heaven. Although Jovinian's teaching received much support, he was condemned as a heretic. In "An Early Christian Debate on Marriage and Family: The Jovinianist Controversy," David Hunter examines Jovinian's theological views and those of his primary critics: Pope Siricius, Bishop Ambrose of Milan, and St. Jerome. He argues that "the controversy around Jovinian was not so much about the Christian family itself, as about the use of celibacy to construct hierarchy and, specifically, clerical authority in the late fourth century." Nevertheless, the controversy had significant implications for the Christian understanding of the family: family life was mundane and inferior to the ascetic life.

In the concluding essay of this collection, Michael Lawler argues that the realities of the family have theological import. In his essay, "Faith, Praxis, and Practical Theology: At the Interface of Sociology and Theology," he contends that sociology has an important part to play in manifesting and interpreting what the Church *actually* believes and what the Church *ought to* believe, and appeals to the theological realities of *sensus fidei* and *reception* in a discussion of Catholic moral doctrine. Lawler shows the significance of the process of *reception* by which members of the Church assent to a teaching and confirm that it is good for the whole Church and in agreement with the apostolic tradition. He uses classic examples of *non-reception* to illustrate the development and re-reception of traditional teaching about usury, slavery, religious freedom, and membership in the Body of Christ, and that a *sensus fidei* of virtually the whole Church is crucial to the process of development. While the Church itself praises the use of sociological research and states that "sufficient use should be made . . . of the findings of the secular sciences, especially psychology and sociology," Lawler suggests that sociological research, in fact, has documented what the majority believes, the *sensus fidei*. In respect to the Church's teaching on birth control, for example, sociological research has documented the non-reception of *Humanae Vitae*'s prohibition of artificial contraception as well as the re-reception of the procreative model of marriage in its interpersonal form among both theologians and married couples. This suggests a contemporary example of "dramatic development of doctrine in the Church," in line with the developments that took place in the doctrines on usury, slavery, religious freedom, and membership in the Body of Christ. Lawler's presentation of the interface of sociology and theology argues convincingly that empirical research can provide the data about what *is* the current situation as well as the *sensus fidei* that can inform theological reflection and dialogue about what *ought to* be the belief of the Church.

Notes

1. See Stephanie Coontz, "Historical Perspectives on Family Diversity," in *Handbook*

of Family Diversity, David H. Demo, Katherine R. Allen, and Mark A. Fine, eds. (New York: Oxford University Press, 2000), 20–28.
2. Frank P. Furstenberg, Jr., "The Future of Marriage" in Family in Transition, Arlene S. Skolnick and Jerome H. Skolnick, eds. (New York: Longman, 1999), 148.
3. Janet Z. Giele. "Decline of the Family: Conservative, Liberal, and Feminist Views," in *Family in Transition*, 449–72.

RELIGION AND FAMILY

Religion and Family in America:
A Socio-Historical Reconnaissance

CHARLES L. HARPER

The standing of religion in America has always been tied to the forms and functions of the family. The reasons are not hard to specify.

> Both provide values; both provide a context where one is valued (more than elsewhere) as whole persons rather than on the basis of specific contributions . . . both provide a framework for seeing oneself as a good person . . . independent of the success that one has in acquiring money, fame or power. Both are "private spheres" in contrast to work or politics . . . and as such are felt to be spheres of individual autonomy and dignity, free of the constraints of one's job or government imposes.[1]

The interactions between religion and family and their connection with the rest of society involve the full range of social stability and change processes. These include existing patterns that are shaped by circumstances and history, innovative responses to broad societal change and problems, conflict about particular goals, and accommodation that enables disparate or antagonistic parts to maintain differences while coexisting in society.

The Colonial and Early National Period

Families and religion have been joined from the earliest stages of European contact in America. Historians have documented that the first English settlers of North America used their religious convictions to arrange both the major themes and the minute details of their domestic lives. Moran, for instance, commented that the metaphor of church as family "seems to have dominated Puritan thought so completely as to suggest that the Puritans' religious experiences in some way duplicated their domestic experiences."[2] Furthermore, the relationship was symmetrical, since the Puritans "not only clothed piety with ideas taken from household experience but also invested family life with religious values. Each sphere supplied codes for interpreting acts played out in the other sphere."[3]

This pattern of fluid reciprocity between religion and family continued well after the founding of the United States.[4] Among Protestants and Catholics alike it began to take a somewhat different form: the fusion of the heavenly and the homespun became a carefully constructed cult of domestic Christianity.[5] This movement tried to make the home, according to one advocate, "a bright temple filled with the light of God's presence, blessed and protected by God's visiting angels, and fragrant with the odor of paradise."[6] Under this conception of religion, every home would be established as an unconsecrated house of worship, and every family would be transformed into an unofficial congregation.

The cultural configuration produced by the convergence of the mundane activity of the domestic world with a reverence customarily reserved for religion, is the ideology called familialism, which counted the family as one of the "two institutions that have come down to us from Eden to perpetuate some of its purity and peace." (The other, incidentally, was Protestant-style observance of the Sabbath.)[7] In its more concrete formulations, familialism encourages premarital sexual restraint, dedication to one's partner in a lifelong marital covenant, procreation, and the raising of children who are subject absolutely to parental (especially paternal) authority.[8] This was belief and public culture, but family reality had a darker side. Strongly patriarchal families meant firm discipline; beatings and such authority often went hand in hand. Native Americans were appalled at the routine physical harshness of white settler parents, particularly fathers.[9] Demos argues that outright child abuse was rare, but that many fathers had abundant outlets for considerable nastiness.[10]

Even so, the dominance of familialism suggests that over time, religion and the family came to occupy contiguous cultural "spaces" on the private side of the American social experience. The abundant attention that churches bestowed through their rhetoric and programs about the condition of the family in society is not coincidental. The affinity between the two institutions, both "victims" of the process of privatization, expressed itself in the emergent ideological configuration common to both. Broadly speaking, familialism is a set of cognitive and normative assumptions that interprets the family as the crucial social institution, for both the individual and society as a whole.[11]

There were few Roman Catholics or Jews in America during the colonial period, but in the early national period they began to come in what would later become large waves of immigrants. There was a yeasty mix of marginal religious movements in America like the Shakers, the Oneida community, Anabaptists like the Amish, and the successful Latter Day Saints, who were to become a major faith in America and the world. Such movements were controversial and notorious because they were outside the American religious mainstream and because they posed challenges to the Protestant establishment by experimenting with communal economics and forms of sexuality and family outside the boundaries of American culture.

The Late Nineteenth and Early Twentieth Century

By the 1880s America was undergoing profound social transformations: industrialization, urbanization, and the absorption of waves of immigrants who increasingly were not English speaking Protestants. By 1900 at least half of all Americans were no longer farmers or small town dwellers; urban populations swelled and industrial factories, along with mines, railroads and huge banks and corporate enterprises, came to dominate the American political economy. Culture was also changing. The growing number of workers in the sweatshops and mines of early industrialism provided receptive audiences for popular Socialist and Marxist ideas, which paralleled the spread of Darwinism and evolutionary thought. American worldviews were penetrated by secularism and scientific thought, and emerging technologies in industry, transportation, communication, and medicine had profound implications for what Americans believed and how families lived.

By the beginning of the twentieth century, the era of modernity was well underway. Modernity meant the growth and abstraction of social relations, the pulling away from the solidarity, concreteness, and sense of relationship with others in small communities and families where one's work was nearby. The other side of the coin was individuation, which weakened the supportive community that sustained individuals and replaced it with the megastructures of modern society. This left individuals more alone and in need of belonging than ever before. The prospects of alienation and anomie (normlessness) increased. Secularization provided alternative answers and explanations previously regarded as God-given and directed. Religious explanations were limited and science and reason came to explain more of what people wondered about.[12] Innovative reactions to profound changes emerged, as Americans struggled to reshape the religion-family connection to address particular needs and problems. Not surprisingly, many people experienced such changes as threats to their lives.

One response to modernity was the Social Gospel movement, which embraced the realities of modernity, and also attempted to address the festering social problems connected with industrialization, urbanization, and immigration. It grew from both external circumstances and on-going theological reflection, from the soil of Protestant evangelicalism, the abolition movement, and the teachings of influential ministers and reformers like Washington Gladden and Walter Rauschenbusch. In their view, Christianity should actively work to alleviate the suffering brought by the emerging modern world. Rauschenbusch began his ministry in a notorious New York slum, "Hell's Kitchen," where he was visited by workers who were "out of work, out of clothes, out of shoes, and out of hope."[13] The need for a more socially conscious religion generated Christian Socialism. This movement omitted the atheistic and revolutionary elements of Marxism became influential among many who could not accept socialism as a complete ideology or political system. If sin and salvation were both social and personal, then system, structure, and the individual needed to be changed.

The Social Gospel was an influential cultural movement rather than a religious movement with its own organizations, and as such, it intersected with other social reform movements of the late nineteenth and early twentieth century. Gladden, for instance, urged Christians to support the efforts of African Americans and organizations like the N.A.A.C.P. in addressing racial problems. The social gospel strongly supported the rights of workers to organize and an end to exploitive labor conditions. The concerns of the social gospel overlapped with the Progressive movement, which was a much more influential social movement that began the public regulation of early industrial capitalism. Social Gospel advocates included influential scholars, including Thomas Dewey and George

Herbert Mead.[14] Jane Addams, who founded urban settlement houses to address the needs of poor urban and immigrant families, is the best currently known woman reformer associated with the Social Gospel. Many woman reformers were associated with the powerful turn-of-the-century Temperance movement. In these reform efforts there is an explicit attempt to reshape the religion-family connection. Whereas the dominant Christian evangelical tradition had emphasized right behavior and individual salvation, the Social Gospel movement sought to protect workers, families, women, and children marginalized by the operation of society. To some, the Social Gospel seemed like a departure from a simpler gospel, but to supporters, it seemed like an extension and growth of the historic Christian faith. While the Social Gospel is no longer an identifiable cultural movement, its remnant "markers," accommodating modernity, social and economic justice, and seeking the "kingdom of God" on earth through societal transformation, continue to shape seminary education and the social teachings of mainline Protestant denominations (e.g., Methodist, Episcopalian, and Presbyterian).

Fundamentalism was a second innovative reaction to modernity. Conservative and evangelical Protestantism had dominated in America since the early years of the nation and were not new, but fundamentalism was. Concerned by the Social Gospel and the constellation of changes that came with modernity, conservative church leaders held a series of conferences that resulted in the publication in 1912 of twelve influential volumes entitled, The Fundamentals: A Testimony to the Truth.[15] These volumes proposed essential doctrines for Christianity, such as the literal inerrancy of the Bible, the virgin birth of Jesus, his bodily resurrection from the dead, and the imminent second coming of Christ. Other related doctrines inferred from these were the deity of Jesus, the sinful nature of humanity, salvation through God's grace, and the bodily resurrection of believers on the "last day." They paid much attention to the refutation of errors such as the theory of organic evolution, the analysis of biblical texts using methods of secular scholarship ("higher criticism"), and to "heretical" religions like Roman Catholicism, Judaism, Mormonism, and spiritualism.

The Fundamentalist movement became a more influential and self-conscious social movement as social implications of modernity became more apparent. These included the arrival of large numbers of immigrants who were "different" in the late nineteenth century, particularly

Jews and Roman Catholics, and urbanization and industrialization that eroded the farming, small town, and small business social patterns that had dominated the first century and a half of the nation's existence.[16]

Faced with such complexities that impacted both religious and family life, proposals to bring back the "old time religion" of Christianity (real or imagined) along with the traditional family, meant the reaffirmation of the ideology of familialism. It proved enormously appealing and grew with a flurry of activity following World War I. By the 1920s the spellbinding evangelist Billy Sunday convinced many that true Christianity had to combat a clever satanic plot, consisting of Kaiserism (the war had just ended), Bolshevism (the revolution had just occurred), evolutionism, modern biblical scholarship, and liberal theology—all evil in their own right.[17] In addition to supporting Prohibition and the teaching of evolution in public schools, the problems of families and the liberalization of sexuality were implicated in this laundry list of threats. William Jennings Bryan ran for the presidency three times, partly to promote the Fundamentalist agenda, which peaked in 1925 when the highly publicized Scopes trial took place and partly because of a negative public and media reaction along with organizational conflicts within the movement.[18] Fundamentalism has returned in contemporary America with great vigor.

Roman Catholic Social Concerns were a third mode of response to modernity in relation to religion and the family that was both similar to and different from those previously examined. Thus far, I have noted Catholics only as immigrants who created problems for Protestants during the early national and industrial periods. In the Protestant-dominated early national period, Roman Catholics suffered the effects of minority status, and were suspect for many reasons. Their loyalty to the Pope was viewed as divided loyalty and made them appear to be questionable, as did sending their children to religious schools, large families, and prenuptial agreements to raise a child as a Catholic in rare interfaith marriages.[19] Equally important, they were predominantly urban working-class people living in immigrant ghettos or enclaves, in which Catholicism sheltered them from a hostile social world. Suspicion turned to politically organized bigotry in the nineteenth century in a nativist movement (the American Protective Association) that opposed Jews, Catholics, and all who were not "Old American." Spurred by economic hard times, the nativist movement mushroomed in cities, commanding nearly a million members in 1896.[20]

Roman Catholic social concerns were shaped by these circumstances, by Catholic clergy, and by a series of complex papal doctrinal pronouncements about the relationship between the church and the modern world. Catholic Social Action, even as much as the Protestant Social Gospel, came to view labor conditions in emerging industrial capitalism as important to the church-society relationship, as well as to social justice and the well being of individuals, communities, and families. In 1886, Cardinal Gibbons of Baltimore saved the Knights of Labor from papal condemnation. In 1891 the encyclical Rerum Novarum was the "magna carta" of a more liberal form of Catholicism that in some ways accommodated growing modernity. It defended the dignity of labor, but rejected socialism, and similar doctrines. It argued that problems could be solved by the application of religious ethics. In 1894 the Archbishop of St. Paul was notable for his participation as a peacemaker in two great railway strikes in the Northwest.[21]

Some Catholics, such as John Ryan, a young teacher fresh from doctoral studies at Catholic University of America, were not as suspicious of socialism. In 1906 he argued in his book, A Living Wage: Its Ethical and Economic Aspects, that "the average family of that day . . . could not live decently on less that six hundred dollars a year and that at least 60% of adult male wage earners received less than this sum."[22] One is reminded of Water Rauschenbusch's experience in his "Hell's Kitchen" New York pastorate. To the common position that only religion would solve the labor question, Ryan responded that "Most certainly it will not be solved . . . without religion . . . but neither will religion suffice in the absence of a detailed application of moral principles to the relations of employer and employee."[23] In short, he proposed minimum wage legislation and that the state was morally bound to compel employers to pay living wage whenever it could. An outpouring of Catholic literature on social justice concerns followed Ryan's book, and shortly after World War I, the bishops legitimated this by establishing the National Catholic Welfare Council.

As with the other adaptations to modernity, concern for the welfare of families was clearly implied by Catholic social concerns. The ideal family, for example, was described in a "Catholic sociology" text written in the 1930s as existing for procreation, the basic social institution, the primary economic unit, a religious school, and intended by God to be monogamous.[24]

Catholic social concerns were like Protestant fundamentalist reactions

Religion and Family in America | 7

in their concern for strong (and, as they claimed, "traditional") families and the corrosive effects of secularization, but different in promoting unionization and in their concern for maintaining the faith in ethnic enclaves. As time went on, and particularly after World War I, Protestants and Catholics were engaged in a process of social accommodation. In fact, as early as the turn of the century, one optimist wrote, "Old feuds between Protestant and Catholic have ceased to be as important as their united battles against moral decay."[25]

In sum, the period was a long period of concerns and fears about the corrosive effects of modernization and secularization, with various responses and currents of conflict unleashed by mutual distrust among Americans (not to mention a great depression and two World Wars). American religion was obviously transformed by movements about the Social Gospel, Fundamentalism, and Catholic Social Action.

American families were also transformed. By the late nineteenth century the role of American fathers had moderated the harsh disciplinary patriarch of earlier times. Fathers began providing children with allowances and education. "Fathering" became active, demanding, and expensive. Work in an urban-industrial context impacted family role division, and along with breadwinning, fatherhood encouraged an assertive kind of masculine guidance. Yet men were urged to restrain their tempers and develop an active loving demeanor. Many fathers found themselves caught in a tension between general standards of assertive manhood and the special virtues required for intimate family life. Families continued to be patriarchal in terms of power, but they became matricentric as mothers increasingly became the "center of family life," replacing the eighteenth century patriarch as the molder of future generations.[26]

Notwithstanding such changes, families and religion both thrived as social institutions as did the connections between them.[27] The clearest evidence for this assertion is from the sample surveys and observational studies of communities. In 1929 and again in 1937 (during the great depression), pioneer researchers studied Middletown (as they called Muncie, Indiana), taken to be a "bellwether" community to represent America. Residents believed the family to be the institutional bedrock of a God-fearing community. Ideally, the family was monogamous, fertile, permanent, and child valuing. The Middletown research was so important, that the community has been restudied several times, and I will return to it later.[28]

The Last Half of the Twentieth Century

After the turmoil and deprivations of World War II, Americans wanted a return to "normal life" and had pent-up desires for better lives and families, including children, better material lives, and new houses. They also had the cash (which could not be spent during the war) to support those needs. Along with new "standardized" housing developments and subsidized freeways, these desires resulted in vast suburbanization. To accommodate the families with many small children (later to be termed baby boomers) suburbanization meant not only new houses, but also new churches and booming church attendance. Demonstrating again the durable connection between family and religion, suburban families turned to churches for moral guidance in raising young children and many other family matters. Large numbers of women had taken wartime jobs, but when the men returned, they were encouraged by family and pediatric experts of the times, including Dr. Benjamin Spock, to return home and find true happiness in domestic roles as homemakers caring for their husbands and children.

By the 1950s it was clear that the postwar recovery and suburbanization were not producing times of restored calm and traditional life. Complex change continued, stimulated by many causes, but particularly by the vast increase in geographic, social, and economic mobility among Americans. Secondary and higher education became more common, standardized, and secular. The mass media, particularly television, invaded traditional life, families, and religion with often disturbing information, ideas, aesthetics, values, and popular culture. Emerging anti-Communism and the cold war produced broad fears and anxieties about World War III and a nuclear holocaust. Social critics and sociologists worried about the emergence of growing anomie and rootlessness in a "mass society." Middle class families worried about the problems of adolescents, juvenile delinquency, and teen culture (remember Elvis, hot rods, and rock and roll?).

By the 1960s the nation had rediscovered its racism, along with embarrassing poverty and poverty-stricken ghettos amidst much celebrated affluence. A great depression did not return, but alternating inflationary and recessionary periods meant that women increasingly needed to work to help support their families, and many younger educated women resented being cast into a "homemaker-mother only" role by society (including their religions). Betty Friedan's manifesto, The Feminine Mystique, became a widely read devastating critique of that role for American women.[30] Pervasive civil rights and feminist movements called into question the reality of America as a "land of opportunity for all persons," as implied by national rhetoric. Feminism, in particular, called into question the desirability and justice of traditional patriarchal family systems, which religions of all kinds had a long history of supporting. Furthermore, America became drawn into a long, unpopular, and ultimately unsuccessful war with a third world country, Vietnam.

The confluence of the anti-war movement, racism, and sexism produced the counterculture of the 1960s. That movement, both political and cultural, was incubated in the university experience of relatively privileged upper middle class young adults, rather than among their working class peers. It was associated with unconventional lifestyles (remember hippies?), recreational drugs, loosened sexual norms, and many criticisms of conventional jobs and family along with experimentation with communal lifestyles. In its political manifestations it became an undogmatic "new left" that opposed the war and most forms of established authority, including parental and religious ones.

All this was confusing, particularly to the postwar young families (now not so young), who had given birth to the baby boomers who became the demographic basis of the counterculture. Equally disturbing was that the United States seemed to become less a land of opportunity for anyone who wanted to work hard. Its celebrated free markets became progressively dominated by huge corporate behemoths, and as these became more productive, automated, and computerized, they required less human labor of all kinds. Thus, the expected upward mobility experienced by America's middle and working classes in the early postwar period began to sputter and measurably stagnate in the middle 1970s. Indeed, a host of scholars documented what can be described as a net downward mobility among America's working and middle classes. Consider the titles of the most widely read renditions of this picture: Falling From Grace and Fear of Falling.[30]

After the great depression and World War II, nothing was more typically American than the expectation that children, once grown and in careers of their own, would eventually surpass their parents' financial well-being and quality of life. However, growing family incomes increasingly resulted not from higher wages, but by people—especially women—working longer hours and forgoing benefits and "family time." Such affluence was precarious, and any downturn in the economy produced less such "extra work" and precipitated family hardships.³¹

Threats of downward mobility made the "American dream" nourished by generations of Americans, the mass media, and public rhetoric, increasingly illusory. Stagnation and downward mobility wreaked havoc on families by destroying the economic foundations of family life, often stretching emotional bonds to the breaking point. It meant housing was less affordable, less discretionary money, and a harder time supporting customary middle class consumption styles.

For many reasons, the "American family" also seemed in a disorderly process of change. Cohabitation among young adults grew to be regarded almost as a normative experience for many young adults. Divorce carried less social stigma, was legally easier, and divorce rates grew rapidly. Remarriage among the formerly married became more common, and many struggled with the legal and cultural ambiguities of "blended families." Out of wedlock births also increased significantly, particularly among low-income groups and African Americans. Singlehood became an acceptable lifestyle for both males and females. As dual income families became statistically common and ideas about gender equity came to permeate American life, the patriarchal family structure so celebrated by American familialism seemed increasingly unworkable as well as unappealing to many Americans. Indeed, the normative family for many came to be seen as a process of negotiated boundaries, relationships, and role-making, rather than the role-taking in historic models. Predictably, religions responded to these confusing and turbulent postwar realities.

Religious Responses in the PostWar Era

In the immediate postwar years, Roman Catholic leaders attempted to perpetuate the norms and structures that had served them well before the war. For instance, Roman Catholic teachings about family continued to support a mother-homemaker role for women and jobs for men. Consider the following, cited at length from a widely used Catholic religion text for high school seniors, published in 1946 and revised in 1957:

> What shall it be, a career or marriage? This is the silly question many women whom God has not called to the convent ask themselves. As if the grandest career . . . were not the art of being a perfect Christian mother! Indeed, Pope Pius XII has said: "Every wom-

an is made to be a mother—a mother in the physical meaning of the word, or in the more spiritual and exalted, but not less real, sense."
... as most women ultimately choose (motherhood) they have an obligation in conscience to prepare themselves for the proper fulfillment of its duties: the care of a house, the rearing of children, the selection and preparation of food, and all the rest.

[Rather than women working outside the home] ... would it not be better for many women to get married earlier, without having worked or started on a career [and without having built up habit that make husbands discontented, homes unhappy, divorces frequent, and society restless?]. Would not men's wages be higher if women did not compete with men for jobs?

[For families in difficult circumstances] ... as Pope Pius XI said in his encyclical on Christian Marriage, the general remedy lies not in "a job for every wife nor in degrading ... government relief or subsidy, or local charity, but in a "living family wage" for every husband and prospective husband (italics in the original).[32]

Obviously, all this became difficult in the world of dual income families and the change previously described.

Maintaining the "ghetto enclave" church within a society hostile to Catholicism was also difficult. American Catholics, whose patriotism was decisively demonstrated by their participation in the national war effort (twice), became increasingly educated, upwardly mobile, assimilated. Increasingly less "different" working class people, Catholics entered the mainstream of American social life, rather than needing to be protected from it. Jewish leaders were similarly concerned by assimilation and a declining salience of Jewishness among the most successful American Jews. As Catholics and Jews became more like other Americans, social (if not religious) barriers to intermarriage weakened. Growing intermarriage was a particular problem for Jewish leaders, who feared that the much smaller population of American Jews could virtually disappear through intermarriage.[33] It is a deep irony that American Catholicism and Judaism, having developed institutional defense mechanisms to protect their followers from oppression as minorities, now faced unfamiliar and vexing threats to survival as they became increasingly successful and accepted. Both had survived and protected ghetto enclaves, but how could they survive assimilation and secular success?

For Catholics, the movement from a stigmatized sect-like church to an American "denomination" was accelerated both by the election of John Fitzgerald Kennedy to the presidency and the reforms of the Second Vatican Council, called by John XXIII in the early 1960s. By many estimates, the latter was one of the most significant events for world Catholicism in the last 100 years. Rather than an outright rejection of modernity and secularism, Vatican II reforms sought to make the church more relevant to the modern world. It instigated sweeping reforms like the adoption of vernacular language rather than Latin for the mass, a streamlined liturgy, and legitimated greater participation of the laity in both liturgy and parish management, thereby significantly reducing the social distance between clergy and laity. It began to speak of the "People of God" in a more inclusive sense.

But perhaps most significant was the "freedom of conscience" document established by the Council, which meant that Catholic pronouncements about marriage, family, and sexuality had less binding power to counteract the engulfing tides of American culture and normative social patterns. The Church's support for families with a patriarchal division of labor and patterns of authority, and the strict prohibition of "artificial" contraception, became less compelling, if contravened by individual conscience, as they often were by the most successful and assimilated upper middle class American Catholics.[34] Gone was the "ghetto church" and gone for many was a church in which clerical authority and tradition always trumped matters of conscience.

While these changes resonated with many, particularly the more assimilated middle class Catholics, others came to see the Vatican II reforms as an accommodation to American culture that produced a dilution of what it meant to be a Catholic. As Steinfels put it:

> The prevailing individualism, the tempting congregationalism of American Protestant Christianity, and the pragmatic rationality of our economic and business systems are increasingly congenial to the mindset of American Catholics. All of these represent enticing alternatives . . . [to the] understandings that lie at the heart of Catholicism.[35]

These were not just the musings of a genre of Catholic intellectuals. By the 1970s, both women's religious orders and the priesthood seemed in precipitous decline, while mass attendance and some Catholic sacraments (like confession) seemed to decline.[36] Interpreters of these changes have been debating ever since about whether they were due to the Vatican II reforms accommodating postwar modernity or the subsequent conservative retrenchment that began in 1968 with *Humanae Vitae*, which flatly prohibited all means of artificial contraception for Roman Catholics. This more conservative mood, emanating from the Vatican, continues today. Perhaps both affected complex Catholic religiosity, but did so differently for diverse socioeconomic groups and birth cohorts.[37]

Turning to Protestant responses, "mainline" or more liberal Protestant denominations like Presbyterians, Episcopalians, and Methodists had presided over and benefited from the postwar boom of suburban church building and piety, and supported postwar trends and movements. They generally supported grievances expressed about race, gender, and economic justice. Indeed, delegations of Methodists, Episcopalians, and Presbyterians, as well as Roman Catholics, were prominent in the "marches to the South" to demonstrate for voter rights for African-Americans. Not only were they prominent in civil rights demonstrations, but also their lobbying clout was critical in the passage of anti-discrimination legislation that came to fruition in the Johnson Administration in the late 1960s and early 1970s. They embraced the cause of feminism (most fully ordaining women by the 1970s), and sympathized with the anti-war movement. Such Protestant denominations broadened their concerns with oppression in the world, and embraced disarmament (especially nuclear disarmament) and movements for self-determination and freedom from world capitalist "exploitation" of third world nations and people. This was consistent with social ethics as taught in Protestant seminaries, inspired by the remnants of the Social Gospel movement and by their ecumenical participation in the National and World Council of Churches.

These responses, however, mostly represented "official" ones from their seminary scholars, denominational hierarchies, and from many pulpits, but they often left more confusion "in the pews" than they did a loyal and mobilized laity. Efforts to redress the grievances of African-Americans, Native Americans, and other minorities triggered latent racism and fears among (mostly) white suburbanites having no real lived experience with minority Americans. Closer to home, middle aged parents often found church leaders seeming to side with their unruly sons and daughters (sojourners in the counterculture) against their parental authority and their ability to transmit role models. Church leaders also sympathized with feminists, who had agendas for family (gender equality) and child-rearing (gender neutral) that were confusing, to say the least, to those nourished in more traditional families.

Mainline Protestantism fully supported family planning and artificial contraception, and endorsed the legalization of abortion as in Row v. Wade. Even such liberal Protestantism could not fully sanction homosexuality, but neither could it resoundingly condemn it, or fail to recognize their social oppression or the justice claims of an increasingly articulate presence of gays in American life. Many denominations experimented and continue to experiment with homosexual marriages and openly gay ordained clergy. Finally, supporting liberation movements in the third world, often clothed in the rhetoric of anti-capitalism and anti-Americanism magnified the discomfort of many with church leaders. It seemed to many that such denominations did a better job of afflicting the comfortable, as many of their parishioners were, rather than comforting the afflicted in their congregations.

These trends lead to what Dean Kelly and a host of other sociological observers noted: by the 1980s the established churches seemed to be losing ground, in terms of their cultural pre-eminence, membership, attendance, and financial contributions.[38] The apparent decline in American religiosity most obviously affected the liberal Protestant denominations, but it affected also American Catholicism and Reform Judaism, which had also embraced the social and cultural mainstream of American life. The turmoil in the social mainstream had implications for the dominant ways of being a "religious American."[39] Some of the Roman Catholic postwar responses were about problems that were uniquely Catholic, but by the late 1960s Catholicism and Mainline Protestant churches seemed to have similar problems: an aging population, and aging leadership, and a decrease in the intensity of religiosity among their younger members.[40]

An apparent upsurge of marginal religious movements in the 1970s was another religious response to the trends and turmoil of the postwar years. In retrospect it is not clear whether they in fact proliferated or were merely "discovered" by the media and the public, but there was a new genre of such movements or "cults" by the mid 1970s. They differed from America's historic marginal religions in one important way: most overwhelmingly appealed to young adults, particularly those from upper-middle class, relatively privileged backgrounds.

Like the historic marginal religions they challenged the boundaries of American life and culture. For instance, the asceticism of the Hare Krishnas challenged the dominant materialism in American culture, while the economic communalism of the Unification Church challenged ruling economic individualism. Like the older marginal religions, the "new religious movements," as scholars called them, often challenged the meaning of sexuality, gender roles, and the time-honored forms of the family.

Among the new religions of the 1970s, perhaps none gave as much importance to family symbolism as did the Unification Church (commonly known as the "Moonies" after the surname of the movement's founder, Korean evangelist Sun Myung Moon). It turned familistic imagery into theology and family life into the vital link between God and humanity. Members referred to themselves as brothers and sisters in the "united family." Moon and his wife are honored as "true parents" in this figurative extended family, and all members, in turn, were counted as the couple's "spiritual children."[41] Surveys of unmarried Moonies found them to look forward to marriage, with many eventual children, and with relationships governed by conservative values. The establishment of God-centered families was not merely for the salvation of individuals, nor a foundation upon which the community and nation could be built. "It was the essential salvific link between the sinful past and the prophetic millennium."[42] With such an emphasis, the Moonies seem unlikely to be cast as ominous threats to the American way of family life. Yet their critics in the pervasive "anti-cult" movement of the times perceived them to be a force that splintered existing families by isolating adult children from their parents. They were accused of exerting a domineering control over choices of spouses and the scheduling of weddings, and so monopolizing the time and energies of members as effectively to estrange them from non-member parents, siblings, and other relatives. More broadly, the Moonies and other "cults" were perceived as taking young adults out of the mainstream of American life.

Because the Unification Church appeared to duplicate—if in somewhat darker hues—the picture of a happy extended family, some researchers hypothesized that this was its chief appeal to recruits, in a time when marital discord, separation, divorce, single parenthood, and domestic abuse seemed more common. In this view, as conditions supporting stable families progressively deteriorated, the secure inner confines of familialistic "new religions" beckoned. Those attracted should, therefore, be particularly young adults from compromised families of origin. However, neither impressionistic evidence, nor participant observation, nor more rigorous empirical data have confirmed this hypothesis.[43] Persons who joined the new marginal religions appeared to have been relatively satisfied with their family of origin. They reported pleasant feelings toward their families, uneventful passages through adolescence, and often outright admiration for their parents. It was not the deprivation of familial closeness and warmth that propelled young adults into new religions but rather the idealistic urge to guarantee them into adulthood. As sociologist Eileen Barker wrote in a magazine for English Catholic Clergymen:

> It is . . . a strange twist of fate that many of the children have been susceptible to the Unification Church not in spite of, but because of, their parents' attempt to inculcate such ideals as love, duty, service, devotion and truth.[44]

As refracted in the mass media, cults have faded from public view. However, the "cult scare" of the 1970s shifted into another about "Satanism" in the 1980s, and this, in turn, passed into scares about militias, White supremacists, groups perpetrating hate crimes, and internal terrorists (Remember Waco and the Oklahoma City bombing?). In spite of the small number of people involved, marginal movements continue to be frightening, to have obvious connections with religion, and to challenge the cultural, family, and religious parameters of American life.

Undoubtedly the most widely noted reaction to the complexities of accumulating postwar change and turmoil was the return of Protestant fundamentalism and evangelicalism to center stage in American life. They had been "in the shadows" since their dénouement shortly before the great depression. Except for their luke-warm engagement with postwar anti-Communist crusades of the 1950s, they were mainly concerned with individual salvation rather than public issues, and widely perceived as rural, anti-intellectual, and passe. But as the fates of liberal Protestantism and Catholicism seemed to enter a dark period, the fortunes of fundamentalism and evangelicalism flourished, so that by the 1970s, they had become a re-energized New Christian Right with a vast constituency. The politicized New Christian Right was a protagonist in what both traditional and progressive camps billed as the next "cultural war."[45] To the extent that it really existed, that culture war was first and foremost about the family.

Few social movements in American history can rival the New Christian Right in the emphasis that its ideology placed on reordering family life by restricting intimate relationships to traditional models. According to Jerry Falwell, famous pastor, evangelist, and founder of the now-defunct Moral Majority, the family is the God-ordained institution of marriage of one man and one woman together for a lifetime . . . [The family's] continued health is a prerequisite for a healthy and prosperous nation. No nation has ever been stronger than the families within her. America's families are her strength and they symbolize the miracle of America.[46]

Such conservative Christians looked to the family not only to serve as the cherished repository of the earthly purpose and spiritual peace for which people strived, with God's help, but also to perform a function of social control. The Christian family was supposed to be always vigilant for any signs of virtue's erosion against the encroaching tides of licentiousness. That could flow from imperfectly subdued internal passions or from without, such as high level conspiracies in the elite media. It could flow from Federal Government agencies, particularly the Internal Revenue Service, the National Endowment for the Humanities, or the Department of Education.[47]

Since public schools were seen as the compromised purveyors of secularism, moral relativism, and often pre-empting parental prerogatives, Christian activists created a private "home schooling" movement that has grown to significant proportions. Though the Constitution offers broad guarantees of parents' right to direct their children's' education, and the Supreme Court has repeatedly upheld those guarantees in cases involving, for example, the Old Order Amish and other religious minorities, in practice home schooling was fairly uncommon. In 1983 it was only explicitly permitted in four states, but by 1993 it was legal in all 50 states, though subject to varying degrees of state regulation. Home schoolers, reflecting their fundamentalist composition, provided a coherent critique of mainstream education and child-rearing patterns. It also challenged current dual income family systems, in that women were admonished to be committed full-time to their children, including a teaching role. Thus, from the ambiguities of the times, normative familistic ideology returned with a vengeance. One commentator noted that Christian evangelicals ordinarily believed that "the family is the principal force for order in society. Strong traditional families are the main check on the passions of a sinful human race."[48]

Critics have alleged that ironically, given such a draconian theology, the New Christian Right is anti-family. It is, for example, common wisdom among social service providers that fundamentalists have extraordinarily high rates of domestic violence. Common wisdom perhaps, but to my knowledge, it is largely undocumented. Research suggests that New Christian Right families were, in actual practice, not simply sources of harsh judgement, or intrusions of heartlessness into those aspects of behavior and personality that call for understanding and a healing spirit. An impressive body of research found flexibility, negotiation, and a vibrant give-and-take in everyday life in the godly homes of conservative Christians.[49]

Similarly, critics questioned the effects of the home schooling movement, both in terms of educational outcomes and whether it amplified social alienation and lack of involvement in mainstream social institutions. On the first point the evidence is clear. Home schooled kids have been dominating national spelling and geography bees, and several surveys showed them scoring higher on standardized tests, including the SAT, than public school kids. While researchers have few concerns about the academic competence of home schoolers, they have raised questions about the long-term consequences of the movement for social cohesion. For example, Lisa Lombardi's response to Margaret Talbot's favorable review of home schooling research suggested that while her sister's home schooled elementary-aged children can indeed read well and do numbers, they will know nothing about geology [or] evolution or natural selection, which are the cornerstones of modern biology, from ecology to genetics and gene mapping. They will speak only English. They will have been taught that their way of belief and behavior is the only way, with no exposure to other cultures, other beliefs, except to be told that those ways are wrong. And that includes not only other systems such as Islam and animism but also Catholicism and, indeed, other kinds of Protestantism, which are also anathema [sic] to my sister. Those children will know a great deal about the Second Amendment and nothing about the First, which guarantees freedom of, and freedom from, religion. They will be taught that the United States is a Christian, rather than a secular, nation.[50]

Aside from such abstract concerns about social and cultural cohesion, researchers have focused more concretely on social involvement. They found that home school kids are not isolated from their peers, and make friends in church groups, scouts, little leagues, etc. In fact, some researchers found that home schooling families are more enmeshed in their communities than public school families (they were more likely to vote, participate in community service activities, and use public libraries). Most researchers have concluded they do not divert people from civic life.[51]

I argue that these facts mean, that in actual practice—at least regarding family and education—the New Christian Right shows many signs of accommodation to the social realities of America, in spite of its strong rhetorical challenges to American social institutions. This is also the case for liberal Protestantism and Roman Catholicism (in the liberalism of Vatican II as well as its more recent conservative turns), and many argue that the same can be said of the 1970s New Religions.

Durable Connections and Change

Through it all, familialism remained a dominant social and religious ideology, and there is evidence that, notwithstanding the turbulent postwar years, a strong connection between religion and family continues. The restudy of Muncie, Indiana, ("Middletown") published in 1982, is a prime example of this continuing relationship. There was some change. Fewer adolescents, for instance, reported friction with parents about expectations for church attendance. But as in 1924 married women in 1978 reported that they attended church partly because they saw some gains for their children in doing so. In fact, references to this benefit were more common than in 1924, and the respondents in 1978 were less likely to stress social or business-related motives for attending church.[52] Married couples who were members of religious congregations in the United States continued to exhibit a high degree of religious homogamy, generally between 82 and 93 percent, although survey data suggested that mixed matches were becoming more common for all categories of married people.[53] Studies examining the intersection of religion and family revealed that religious norms continue to influence the manner and timing of marriage, the bearing of children, as well as attitudes under which marriage ought to be dissolved.[54]

As common knowledge suggests, religion influences reproduction and fertility. Religions approach fertility in distinctive ways: Roman Catholics desire and produce the largest families, followed by Protestants and Jews, in that order. Since the baby boom years, however, the difference in childbearing between Catholic wives and others has narrowed. Impressed by the pervasiveness of this convergence, some observers of fertility trends suggested, "the appearance of traditionally higher 'Catholic' fertility appears to have all but disappeared." [55] In spite of the unambiguous prohibition against "artificial" birth control in the 1968 encyclical *Humanae Vitae*, Catholic women of childbearing age who used contraceptives other than the "rhythm" method increased significantly between 1965 and 1970. Westhoff and Bumpass observed, "the papal encyclical has not retarded the increasing defection of Catholic women from this teaching."[56] Catholics adopted a range of contraceptive techniques at about the same rates as did other Americans. Although other researchers did not dispute this, they nevertheless contended that the perceived demise of "Catholic fertility" and the general convergence of fertility patterns across the United States were unwarranted. Catholic couples still reported higher fertility.[57]

Finally, there is continuing evidence about the efficacy of religious socialization that takes place within families as well as in the more formal religious educational settings. In the simplest terms, the religious values of pre-adolescent, adolescent, and college-age children usually resemble those that their parents have endorsed.[58] A frequent finding is the salient influence of mothers in the process of shaping religious orientations, particularly of male children.

Discussion

How can one find theoretical and conceptual sense in this somewhat rambling socio-historical reconnaissance? Let me do so by returning to some of the rubrics with which the paper began, about processes of stability and change. A stable characteristic of the American experience is the remarkable persistence of the ideology of religious familialism that specifies family in fairly traditional forms with religious sanction. It persists today. As all ideologies, familialism masks reality as well as reveals it. As families have adapted to progressive waves of modernity, they have probably become less patriarchal and certainly more varied, less predictable, and with greater legitimacy given to what the ideology of familialism recognizes as only distorted "fragments and hybrids" (e.g., single parent families, stepfamilies, gay families).

The notion that America is a particularly religious nation among industrial nations is another aspect of stability that masks change. American "exceptionalism" is undoubtedly true in some senses, described and documented by a host of scholars. But in spite of its comparative vibrancy today, American religion has been transformed: it is certainly more diverse, ecumenical, and inclusive (as waves of immigrants continue to be incorporated). It is in many senses intertwined with secular knowledge and institutions, with less distinct boundaries from the social world. Consider how churches use secular psychology in their pastoral work, and how even conservative religions use sophisticated media and marketing techniques. Moreover, consider how, in spite of powerful legal norms about the "separation of church and state," in 2002 America had a Presidential administration advocating and willing to fund "faith-based" solutions to social problems. Undoubtedly some traditional forms of religiosity have declined, while churches are permeated by a matrix of inchoate "spirituality" that is both an opportunity and a worry for denominational leaders.[59]

Beyond ideological persistence and some trends that they mask, it is temping to posit a cyclical model of change, for as progressive waves of modernity shaped America since the beginning of the industrial era, contentious reform movements arose in both religion and family life. In their conservative and fundamentalist manifestations these reform movements sought to "turn back the clock" with a longing for that "old time religion" (real or imagined) as well as for what Stephanie Coontz called the "family of Western nostalgia."[60] Others partly or wholly embraced modernity, such as Protestant Social Gospelers, Catholic Social Concerns, and marginal religious movements—both old and new. In the last half of the twentieth century both Mainline Protestantism and Roman Catholicism have embraced modernity with reservations and today are in the process of backpedaling, attempting to reclaim what was conceded to secularism and, more importantly, to recover lost constituencies. Furthermore, for all of its fire and brimstone, the realities of fundamentalist family life and home schooling, as well as the political engagement and media savvy of

Christian conservatives, suggest considerable engagement with the realities of modern life. In other words, all such diverse reactions to powerful structurally driven change eventually result in accommodation—both to each other in a finite social world, and to the imperatives of modern life. In that social life, religion and family continue to be closely bonded, and both in processes of disorderly change and institutional adaptation.

Ironically, the robust character of the religion-family bond may reduce the impacts of each in a broader world that sorely needs their moderating influences.[61] In a small-scale survey that needs replicating, Tamney and Johnson found that almost 60% of Americans thought their religion affected how they treated their families, but only 37% claimed it was similarly related to their jobs, and only 10% said that it affected for which political candidates they voted.[62]

Notes

1. Stephen Hart, "Religion and Change in Family Patterns," *Review of Religious Research* 28 (1986), 51–52.
2. Edmund S. Morgan, *The Puritan Family: Religion and Domestic Relations in Seventeenth-Century New England*, revised edition, enlarged (New York: Harper and Row, 1966), 166
3. Gerald F. Moran, "The Puritan Family and Religion: A Critical Reappraisal," in *Religion, Family, and the Life Course: Explorations in the Social History of Early America*, Gerald F. Moran and Maris A. Vinoviskis, eds. (Ann Arbor: University of Michigan Press, 1992), 13.
4. Alan Booth, David R. Johnson, Ann Branaman, and Alan Sica, "Belief and Behavior: Does Religion Matter in Today's Marriage?" *Journal of Marriage and the Family* 57 (1995), 661–71.
5. Kevin J. Christiano, "Religion and the Family in Modern American Culture," in *Family, Religion, and Social Change in Diverse Societies*, Sharon K. Houseknecht and Jerry G. Pankhurst, eds. (New York: Oxford University Press, 2000), 43–78.
6. Quoted in Colleen McDannell, *The Christian Home in Victorian America, 1849–1900* (Bloomington: University of Indiana Press, 1986), xiii.
7. Ibid., 1.
8. William V. D'Antonio, "The Family and Religion: Exploring a Changing Relationship," *Journal for the Scientific Study of Religion* 19 (1980), 89–104.
9. P. Filence, "A Man's Place: Masculinity in Transition," *Journal of Social History* 14 (1989), 323–25.

10. J. Demos, *Past, Present, and Personal: The Family and the Life Course in American History* (New York: Oxford University Press, 1986).
11. Christiano, "Religion and the Family in Modern American Culture," 46–47. See also Peter L. Berger, "Religious Institutions," in *Sociology: An Introduction*, Neil Smelser, ed. (New York: John Wiley, 1967), 373.
12. Peter L. Berger, *Facing Up to Modernity* (New York: Basic Books, 1977), 71–80.
13. Ronald C. White and C. Howard Hopkins, *The Social Gospel: Religion and Reform in Changing America* (Philadephia: Temple University Press, 1976), xv.
14. Randall Collins, *The Sociology of Philosophies: A Global Theory of Intellectual Change* (Cambridge: Harvard University Press, 1998), 682.
15. *The Fundamentals: A Testimony to the Truth*, vols. 1–12 (Chicago: Testimony Publishing House, c.1919).
16. Ronald L. Johnstone, *Religion in Society: A Sociology of Religion*, sixth edition (Upper Saddle River, NJ: Prentice Hall, 2001), 159–60.
17. Erling Jorstad, *The Politics of Doomsday* (Nashville: Abingdon, 1970), 24.
18. Norman F. Furniss, *The Fundamentalist Controversy* (New Haven: Yale University Press, 1954), 56.
19. Johnstone, *Religion in Society*, 317.
20. Arthur, Schlesinger, Sr., "A Critical Period in American Religion 1875–1900," in *Religion in American History: Interpretive Essays*, John M. Mulder and John F. Wilson, eds. (Englewood Cliffs, NJ: Prentice Hall, 1978), 313.
21. Schlesinger, "A Critical Period in American Religion 1875–1900," 312.
22. Cited in White and Hopkins, *The Social Gospel*, 220.
23. Ryan, quoted in White and Hopkins, *The Social Gospel*, 224.
24. E. J. Ross, *Rudiments of Sociology* (New York: Bruce Publishing Company, 1934), 39–41.
25. H. D. Sedgwick, Jr., "The United States and Rome," *Atlantic Monthly* 84 (1899), 445–58.
26. Ellen Rothman, *Hands and Hearts* (New York: Basic Books, 1984), 116.
27. Houseknecht and Pankhurst, *Family, Religion, and Social Change in Diverse Societies*, 47.
28. Robert S. Lynd and Helen Lynd, *Middletown: A Study in American Culture* (New York: Harcourt Brace, 1957; Robert S. Lynd and Helen Lynd, *Middletown in Transition: A Study in Cultural Conflicts* (New York: Harcourt Brace, 1982).
29. Betty Friedan, *The Feminine Mystique* (New York: W. W. Norton, 1963).
30. Katherine Newman, *Falling From Grace: The Experience of Downward Mobility in the American Middle Class* (New York: Free Press, 1988); Barbara Ehrenreich, *Fear of Falling: The Inner Life of the Middle Class* (New York: HarperPerennial, 1989).

31. Uctelle, L. and N. R. Kleinfeld "On the Battlefields of Business, Millions of Casualties," *New York Times* (March 3, 1996).
32. Right Rev. Msgr. Clarence E. Elwell, Rev. James T. O'Dowd, Rev. Anthony N. Fuerst, Frank J. Sheed, and Very Rev. John J. Voight, *Toward the Eternal Commencement: Our Quest for Happiness, Book Four, for the senior year*, revised edition (Chicago: Mentzer, Bush, & Company, 1957), 238–41.
33. Edward S. Shapiro, *A Time for Healing: American Jewry since World War II* (Baltimore, Johns Hopkins University Press, 1992).
34. Thomas E. Dowdy and Patrick H. McNamara, eds., *Religion: North American Style* (New Brunswick, NJ: Rutgers University Press, 1996), 113. See also Andrew Greeley, *The Catholic Myth: The Behavior and Beliefs of American Catholics* (New York: Macmillan, 1990).
35. Margaret O'Brien Steinfels, "The Laity," *Commonweal* 120 (1993), 8–20.
36. Helen Ebaugh, *Out of the Cloister* (Austin: The University of Texas Press, 1977); Richard Schoenherr and Laurence Young, *Full Pews and Empty Alters: Demographics of the Priest Shortage in U.S. Catholic Dioceses* (Madison: University of Wisconsin Press, 1994).
37. Andrea Willams and James Davidson, "Catholic Conceptions of Faith: A Generational Analysis," *Sociology of Religion* 57, 3 (1996).
38. Dean Kelly, *Why Conservative Churches are Growing* (New York: Harper and Row, 1972); Robert Wuthnow, *The Restructuring of American Religion* (Princeton: Princeton University Press, 1988); Wade Clark Roof and William C. McKinney, *American Mainline Religion* (New Brunswick: Rutgers University Press, 1987).
39. Will Herberg, *Protestant, Catholic, Jew* (Garden City: Doubleday Anchor Books, 1960).
40. Dowdy and McNamara, *Religion: North American Style*, 114.
41. Christiano, "Religion and the Family in Modern American Culture," 62.
42. Joseph Fichter, S.J., "Family and Religion Among the Moonies: A Descriptive Analysis," in *Families and Religions: Conflict and Change in Modern Society*, William D'Antonio and Joan Aldous, eds. (Beverly Hills: Sage, 1983), 293.
43. Fichter, "Family and Religion Among the Moonies"; Eileen Barker, "Free to Choose? Some Thoughts on the Unification Church and Other Religious Movements, II," *Clergy Review* 65 (1980), 392–98; Suart A. Wright and Elizabeth S. Piper, "Families and Cults: Familial Factors Related to Youth Leaving or Remaining in Deviant Religious Groups," *Journal of Marriage and the Family* 48 (1986), 15–25.
44. Barker, "Free to Choose?" 396–97.
45. James Davidson Hunter, *Culture Wars: The Struggle to Define America* (New York: Basic Books. 1991).

46. Jerry Falwell, *Listen, America!* (New York: Bantam Books, 1981), 104.
47. Christiano, "Religion and the Family in Modern American Culture," 66–67.
48. Julia Corbett, "The Family as Seen Through the Eyes of the New Religious-Political Right," in *Religious Television: Controversies and Conclusions, Communication and Information Sciences*, Robert Abelman and Stewart M. Hoover, eds. (Norwood, NJ: Ablex, 1990), 290.
49. Christiano, "Religion and the Family in Modern American Culture," 66; Nancy Tatum Ammerman, *Bible Believers: Fundamentalist in the Modern World* (New Brunswick: Rutgers University Press, 1987); Patrick McNamara, "The New Christian Right's View of the Family and Its Social Science Critics: A Study in Differing Presuppositions," *Journal of Marriage and the Family* 47 (1985), 449–58; Corbett, 285–94.
50. Lisa Lombardi, Letter to the Editor, *The Atlantic Monthly* 289 (February 2, 2002), 15.
51. Margaret Talbot, "The New Counterculture," *The Atlantic Monthly* 288, 4 (2001), 136–43; Mitchell L. Stevens, *Kingdom of Children: Culture and Controversy in the Homeschooling Movement* (Princeton: Princeton University Press, 2001).
52. Theodore Caplow, Howard M. Bahr, Bruce Chadwick, Reuben Hill, and Margaret Holmes Williamson, *Middletown Families: Fifty Years of Change and Continuity* (Minneapolis: University of Minnesota Press, 1982).
53. Andrew Greeley, "Religious Intermarriage in a Denominational Society," *American Journal of Sociology* 75 (1970), 949–52; Norval D. Glenn, "Interreligious Marriage in the United States: Patterns and Recent Trends," *Journal of Marriage and the Family* 44 (1982), 555–66; Matthijs Kalmijn, "Shifting Boundaries: Trends in Religious and Educational Homogamy," *American Sociological Review* 56 (1991), 786–800.
54. Darwin L. Thomas and Marie Cornwall, "Religion and Family in the 1980s: Discovery and Development," *Journal of Marriage and the Family* 52 (1992), 983–92.
55. Charles F. Westhoff and Elise F. Jones, "The End of 'Catholic' Fertility," *Demography* 16 (1979), 209–17.
56. Charles F. Westhoff and Larry Bumpass, "The Revolution in Birth Control Practices of U.S. Roman Catholics," *Science* 179 (January 5, 1979), 42.
57. William D. Mosher and Gerry E. Herdershot, "Religion and Fertility: A Replication," *Demography* 21 (1984), 185–91.
58. Johnathan Kelly and Nan Dirk De Graaf, "National Context, Parental Socialization, and Religious Berlief: Results from 15 Nations," *American Sociological Review* 62 (1997), 639–59; Scott Myers, "An Interactivew Model of Religiosity Inheritance: The Important of Family Context," *American Sociological Review* 61 (1996), 858–66.

59. Charles L. Harper and Bryan F. LeBeau, "Social Change and Religion in America: Thinking Beyond Secularization," http://are.as.wvu.edu.
60. Stephanie Coontz, *The Way We Never Were* (New York: Basic Books, 1992). See also Arlene Skolnick, *The Intimate Environment: Exploring Marriage and Family* (Boston: Little Brown, 1996).
61. Christiano, "Religion and the Family in Modern American Culture," 69.
62. Joseph Tamney and Stephen Johnson, "Consequential Religiosity and Modern Society," *Review of Religious Research* 26 (1985), 360–78.

Sacred Kinship: *Creating and Extending Family among the Lakota of Pine Ridge*[1]

RAYMOND A. BUCKO, S. J.

The oft spoken aphorism "the family that prays together stays together" might well be translated into contemporary Lakota as "the family that prays together increases." While anthropologists define three modes of increasing a family size—birth, marriage, and adoption—Western culture's relative disuse of and ambivalence about adoption has placed it as a peripheral concern, ancillary and exceptional rather than central and habitual to family life. The Lakota, a northern plains Indian group also known as the Sioux and, in the nineteenth century, the Dakota, have a long tradition of ritual adoption known in their language as the *Hunka*.

In order to set the context for discussion of adoption in Lakota culture, it is essential to understand the centrality of family, or, more properly, kinship; for the Lakota, kinship is more broadly drawn and conceived than in Western, European-based culture. The most eloquent spokesperson in this regard is the Yankton Sioux anthropologist Ella Cara Deloria:

> Kinship was the all-important matter . . . By kinship all Dakota people were held together in a great relationship that was theoretically all-inclusive and co-extensive with the Dakota domain. Everyone who was born a Dakota belonged to it; nobody need be left outside . . . In the last analysis every other consideration was secondary—property, personal ambition, glory, good times, life itself. Without that aim and the constant struggle to attain it, the people would no longer be Dakota in truth. They would no longer even be human (Deloria 1944: 24–25).

Deloria states principles that remain essential to the Dakota, which includes, for her, all the Sioux groups, the eastern Dakota and western Lakota. First, to be a relative is to be human, to be part of a group. Second, no one need be left outside this group. Thus for the Lakota and Dakota, adoption is a way to both humanize and literally familiarize the world. There is an essential binary opposition in the Lakota cultural and social system between *Lakota/Dakota* (ally/friend) and *Toka* (stranger/enemy), but this opposition is creatively mediated by the *Hunka*, a ceremony that transforms strangers into kin in a sacred manner. The last important element of Deloria's definition is all-important. She asserts that while kinship is primary to what it means to be a Dakota, she also admits that this structure is one that requires, "a constant struggle to attain it." An anthropological definition becomes an existential imperative: to be a relative is to act as a relative; to be kin is not to simply occupy a social position and carry a social title. The dynamism of Dakota kinship is that one can be assigned titles or change titles in the system based on a ceremony, the *Hunka*, which is a culmination of a series of reciprocal social interactions that are publicly recognized, sanctified, and intensified by elevation to the level of kinship.

Deloria also points out that the Lakota verb wacekiye means either "to address a relative" or "to pray" (Deloria 1944: 28–29). Spiritual and familial kinship are linked as one. Lakota end all prayers with the phrase, "*Mitakuye Oyas'in*" (for all my relatives), praying for all who are related, in recognition of universal kinship. As we will see in this paper, the *Hunka* ceremony is a religious ritual that extends the Lakota kinship network.

Origins of the *Hunka*

The ethnographic literature provides a variety of explanations for the origin of the *Hunka*, all of them embedded in a religious context. The earliest material we have on the *Hunka* is a series of interviews and personal observations collected by James Walker, a physician on the Pine Ridge Reservation from 1896 to 1914. Clark Whissler of the American Museum of Natural History asked Walker to collect anthropological data, and Walker himself recognized the importance of a cultural understanding of the Oglalas for the success of his medical work. In 1905 Wissler specifically asked Walker to investigate the *Hunka* ceremony (DeMallie and Jahner 1980: 16).

Walker records a story of the first *Hunka* told by No Flesh. A head chief had four sons, all of whom where killed in battle while performing noble deeds. When they died, the chief gave away everything he had, even his wife's clothing. The chief then went to seek a vision. *Tate*, the Spirit of the Wind, sent his youngest son, *Yamni*, the Spirit of the Whirlwind, to bring the chief a message. He was to travel north until he reached a tipi, to go inside, and to bring back with him what he found there. The chief told the people of his vision and journeyed north. On the fourth day, he found a tipi, went inside and found a baby boy and girl. He brought them back and claimed them as his son and daughter. A shaman asked the chief what the last word was that the whirlwind said to him. The chief replied, *Hunka*. The shaman explained that the boy and girl were *Hunka* and that he was *Ate* (father). The boy and girl grew up well. When the chief was an old man, the shaman told him to put on a great feast with presents for his people explaining: "When one's heart is good towards another, let them be as one family" (No Flesh 1980: 195). Therefore, if one wanted to do a great favor for another, he or she should choose the other as an *Ate* or *Hunka* (No Flesh 1980: 193–195). No Flesh dates this event to the time before the Sioux became a unified people (No Flesh 1980: 193).

Two other of Walker's teachers, George Sword and Afraid of Bear, date the origin of the ceremony according to their tribal winter counts (native histories note each year's most significant event). The origin of the *Hunka*, according to No Ears, dates to when the people lived in the "Land of the Pines," an ecological reference associated with the North. The winter count for the year 1805 (1804–1805) is remembered by Afraid of Bear as "When They Waved Horses' Tails over Themselves" (Afraid of Bear 1980: 201), and as "When They Waved Horses' Tails over Each Other" by Sword (Sword 1980: 198). Afraid of Bear believes that until that year the *Hunka* ceremony could be performed by anyone; a man from the spirit world came to say that the ceremony had to be done in a proper way (Afraid of Bear 1980: 201). Sword also dates the "present form" to this date, indicating that it was not the institution of adoption itself but the ritual performance that was new (Sword 1980: 198).

John Blunt Horn told Walker that in the year marked by the winter count as "When Many Pregnant Women Died" (1799), the *Hunka* was stopped for five years because the people believed that the improper conduct of this ceremony caused the tragedy (Blunt Horn 1980: 203). Five years later, when a man wanted to make a *Hunka*, the medicine men counseled together and learned from the spirits how to perform the ceremony correctly. From 1804 on, the ceremony was conducted in a new way and only by those who knew the secrets of the spirits concerning the proper conduct of the ceremony (Blunt Horn 1980: 204).

From 1911 to 1914, Ethnomusicologist Frances Densmore worked among the Lakota of the Standing Rock Reservation, as well as the Sisseton and Wahpeton living in Sisseton, SD (Densmore 1918: 1). She indicates that the winter count for 1801, *Awica alowanpi* (truthfully singing winter), is the first year this ceremony was held by the Standing Rock Sioux (Densmore 1918: 69). James Howard reanalyzed this winter count along with others and showed that there are two winter count dates marked by *Hunka* ceremonies, 1798–1799 and 1801–1802 (Howard 1960: 351–352). Despite discrepancies between different winter counts, the fact that this event was chosen as the most significant occurrence of a specific year indicates its importance.

High Eagle, one of Densmore's teachers, associates the ceremony with the virtue of the White Buffalo Calf Maiden, with the sacred pipe that she gave to the people, and with the *Hunka* Wand. This wand, a ritual device used in the ceremony, was probably a pipe stem at one time (DeMallie 2001: 807). High Eagle states that the ceremony honors children in a profound way and links a man to the father of the child for whom the adoption is performed as brothers (Densmore 1918: 70). He explains the use of corn in the ceremony through a story about a childless couple who prayed for a child in a sweat lodge and were given corn as their child (Densmore 1918: 72–73). This origin story was later corroborated by William Horn Cloud (Lewis 1990: 82).

Black Elk provides a different origin story for the *Hunka* and links the ceremony to the White Buffalo Calf Maiden. Black Elk states that this Sacred Woman gave the Lakota five new rites and blessed two rites they already had (sweat lodge and vision quest) (Brown 1953: 1). Black Elk's narrative of the origin of this ritual, which the Maiden promised would be revealed to them in the future, involves a vision received from Wakan Tanka (the Great Mystery) by Matohoksila (Bear Boy). Bear Boy has a vision of corn, which he had never seen before, and subsequently finds a patch of corn and brings it back to his people. The Lakota and the Arikara were at war at this time. The corn belonged to the Arikara and the pipe to the Lakota. Black Elk then describes in great detail the peace made between these two nations through the *Hunka* ceremony using these two ritual devices, corn and pipe (Brown 1953: 101–115).

Etymology of Term *Hunka*

George Sword points out that the term *Hunka* is a foreign term from another Indian language but offers no translation for it (Sword 1980: 198). No Flesh's story of the origin of the *Hunka* states that a medicine man asked the chief, who was given the ceremony by a spirit, for the last word the spirit gave him; the chief replied "*Hunka*." This word becomes the name both of those adopted in the ceremony and of the ceremony itself (No Flesh 1980: 194). Missionary Stephen Return Rigg's dictionary of the Dakota (eastern Sioux) language defines the term *Hunka* as:

> a parent or ancestor; an elder brother is often so called—*miHunka*; one who has raised himself or herself in the estimation of the people so as to be considered as a kind of benefactor or parent of all; the son is sometimes called from his munificence (Riggs 1890: 157).

Riggs does not give an etymology of the word *Hunka* itself. His next entry in his dictionary is the term *Hunka dowanpi*, which he defines as "a rite or ceremony of the Daktoas." Literally this terms means "*Hunka* sing." Sing is a common term in contemporary Lakota for a religious ceremony. Riggs goes on to include a more detailed description of this ceremony provided by Reverend W. J. Cleveland, a missionary at the Rosebud Agency. Cleveland explains the Lakota version of the ceremony:

> When a person, because he thinks highly of them, or for other good reason, intends in a measure to adopt the children of another, or to become "ate" (father) to them, or be regarded by them as a relative in Dakota fashion, he makes the "*Hunka* lowanpi" for and in honor of the children. The children thus become "*Hunka*," and are always after known as such by a red strip across the side of forehead and cheek, which they are permitted to wear as a badge. The number of these stripes shows how many times the wearer has been made "*Hunka*" (in Riggs 1890: 158).

Reverend John P. Williamson omits the term *Hunka* in favor of a literal translation of Western notions of adoption. His translation of the noun "adoption" in Dakota is *cincayapi icupi* (Williamson 1992: 3), which literally means "they take so that they have children." For the verb "to adopt" he uses *tawaye kta icu*, "he/she will take his family (household)"

(Williamson 1992: 3). Both terms refer exclusively to adoption when both parents are dead, a situation that is only part of the larger institution of adoption as practiced by the Dakota and Lakota.

Jesuit missionary linguist Eugene Buechel includes a brief entry in his dictionary for the *Hunka lowanpi*: "A rite or ceremony of the Dakotas. The Making of Relatives." He also translates the term *Hunka* as "an ancestor" (Buechel 1970: 188). The phrase, "the making of relatives," is the term contemporary Lakota use when referring to the *Hunka* in English (Powers 1991: 100). It is also the term used by Black Elk in his description of the *Hunka* (Brown 1989: 101). Edward Curtis, known for his photographs of Indian life, collected ethnographic portraits of Native rituals. In his passages on the *Hunka* he translates the term as "a term of respect for one's parents or ancestors," and refers to the ceremony itself as "the foster-parent chant" (Curtis 1970: 71).

The *Hunka* Ceremony

George Sword, one of Walkers principal teachers, provides extensive details about the *Hunka* ceremony (Sword 1980). According to Sword the ceremony is intended to make Indians kin to each other. Whites are sometimes adopted and there are different types of the ceremony, which vary according to the means and social status of the participants. The intended adoptee must agree to be adopted. If this is a child, her/his parents must agree to the arrangement on behalf of the child. The adopter chooses the relationship: one can adopt another as a parent, a grandparent, a child, or a sibling. To do the ceremony "properly," Sword says a religious leader must conduct it; friends must be invited; a feast must be provided; and presents must be given. While friends can contribute to the effort, in more notable adoptions the adopter provides everything. The greater the feast, the greater the honor paid to the adoptee and the greater the prestige of the adopter. If one is poor or unpopular the "ceremony would not amount to much" (Sword 1980: 199). Sword does not give details of the ceremony beyond the necessary preparations involved, but adds that he has personally been made a *Hunka* multiple times.

When the ceremony is performed correctly, Afraid of Bear contends, the spirits are pleased. He states that whites can be adopted by Indians and "a white man would be like an Indian if he becomes a *Hunka*" (Afraid of Bear 1980: 201). Afraid of Bear extends the inclusivity of being a *Hunka* by pointing out that that particular person would be a brother of all other *Hunka* (Afraid of Bear 1980: 202). Ringing Shield, another of Walker's teachers, emphasizes that it was the spirits who taught the Oglala how to correctly perform the ceremony (Ringing Shield 1980: 206).

Afraid of Bear gives a list of requirements for the *Hunka* ceremony identical to Sword's: a religious leader (shaman), a person agreeing to be adopted and an adopter, guests, a feast, and presents. He goes on to give an intricate list of necessary items:

> two *Hunka* wands; two *Hunka* rattles; a mysterious ear of corn; a meat scaffold, dried meat, both fat and lean; dried willow bark; tobacco; a pipe; sweetgrass; an eagle feather; an eagle plume; mysterious paints, red, black, and white; invitation wands, a mysterious fire stick, a mysterious counting stick; a buffalo skull; presents for the shaman, presents for the Ate; presents for the guests; a dog for the feast; plenty of food for the feast; two tipis; a drum (Afraid of Bear 1980: 202).

He continues with a list of persons necessary to perform the ceremony:

> *Walowan* (the master of ceremonies), *pte pawa* (the marker, assistant to the master), *wowasi* (helper, assistant to the marker), *wahuwapi yuha kin he* (bearer of the mysterious corn), two *Hunka koza kin* (two bearers of the wands) (Afraid of Bear 1980: 202).

John Blunt Horn is particularly sensitive to the economic element of the *Hunka* relationship, although all Lakota commentators stress that the relationship of *Hunka* is more than ceremonial and requires the pair to help each other in all material needs, including provisioning and warfare. Blunt Horn points out that if someone is poor, then another might take a man as a father to help him. Anyone could engage in this practice. Blunt Horn also stresses that *Hunka* became a class of people who are mutually obligated to one another. He states: "It was like the Church among the white people" (Blunt Horn 1980: 204).

Blue Horse contends that the shamans who first learned how to perform the *Hunka* ceremony became Oglalas and that other Lakota bands received the ceremony from them (Blue Horse 1980: 207). In a bit of nationalistic pride he claims that no one can become a full *Hunka* like the

Oglalas. Black Elk also contends that the *Hunka* was begun, not by other tribes, but with the Lakota through a vision (Brown 1989: 101).

Takes the Gun explains that horse tails are waved over the *Hunka* because in the past there were not enough horses to give everyone and the symbolic waving indicated that the generous adopter would give horses away if he had them. His narrative explains the symbolic meaning of some of the ritual objects used during the ceremony and provides a glimpse at the heart of the meaning of the ceremony:

> The horses' tails and the eagle feathers on the wands are to wave over the one who is to be made *Hunka*, to wish that one prosperity, peace, happiness and to promise help to that one. And it is waved over all those present to show that they all join in this (Takes the Gun 1980: 213).

Takes the Gun also says that the making-someone-a-*Hunka* ceremony proclaims a male adoptee as brave or the wish that he be brave. In the case of a woman, the ceremony proclaims the wish that the female adoptee become industrious or that she have happiness in her life (Takes the Gun 1980: 212–13). The corn is a symbol of prosperity and plenty as is the buffalo meat. Both of these are blessed and prayed over by the medicine man (Takes the Gun 1980: 213–14). Feather on Head describes the symbolism of the *Hunka* wand and its ornamentation: "The horse's tail is to go far and fast, to go without fatigue. The eagle feathers are to be brave and chief of the air. The wand is to be strong. The ornaments are to have plenty" (Feather on Head 1980: 215).

Bad Wound, another of Walker's instructors, gives some reasons why an individual might adopt someone: "because he has been sick and gotten well or because of friendship to the person or his parent or because a medicine man told him to do so or as a reward for some reason" (Bad Wound 1980: 210). In friendship adoptions, one might adopt either the actual person or the child of that person. In most cases there are only two people involved in the actual adoption. Bad Wound also describes a preliminary arrangement in which the two individuals agree to the relationship and then pray with a pipe to the spirits of the four directions, earth and sky to give a bright, warm and generous day for the actual ceremony (Bad Wound 1980: 210).

Walker employs the accounts above, along with his own experience of witnessing the ceremony to write two detailed descriptions of the ritual (Walker 1917: 122–40; Walker 1980). He provides a model of an ideal ceremony in the fashion of his time. Both he and his informants agree that any actual ceremony would vary from this ideal. Densmore adds that the ceremony originally took several days but eventually became a single day. Like Walker, she describes the ceremony based on descriptions by her teachers and includes two songs with musical notations, photographs of a *Hunka* wand and ceremonial corn, a Native drawing of a *Hunka* ceremony, and an image of the Winter Count mnemonic picture depicting a *Hunka* ceremony (Densmore 1918: 69–77). Edward Curtis provides an extensive description of the *Hunka* ceremony including musical notations for the chants, prayers, and photographs of key moments in the ceremony itself (Curtis 1970: 71–81). He succinctly explains the purpose of the ceremony:

> The principal purpose of the *Hunka-lowanpi* is to implant in the initiate the virtues of kindness, generosity, hospitality, truthfulness, fairness, and honesty. At the same time it is a prayer for continues prosperity—for abundance of food, for health, strength, and moral well-being as a people (Curtis 1970: 71).

Black Elk's description of the origins of the *Hunka* also contains an elaborate description of the first *Hunka* ceremony. Ritual elements include the use of symbolic elements such as corn and a sacred pipe; verbal promises of support of the adoptees; the erection of a special ceremonial lodge; exchanges of gifts; prayers to the four directions, earth and heaven; and ritual feeding and feasting (Brown 1989: 101–15). Black Elk casts this ritual as a peace making ceremony between nations as much as a making of relatives. In this regard his description is unique. Walker's teachers consistently see the ritual as primarily intended for creating and strengthening relationships within groups and with specific outsiders such as individuals from other tribes or individual white people.

Disuse and Revival

Several of Walker's consultants discuss the demise of this ceremony among the Oglala. Blue Horse says: "The young people do not become *Hunka* now. It is of no use to them. The old people do not pay much attention to a *Hunka* now. The *Hunka* are not what they were in old times"

(Blue Horse 1980: 207–8). Sword corroborates this: "The *Hunka* ceremony is hardly ever performed now. The young people do not care for it now" (Sword 1980: 200). Densmore states that the *Hunka* had been in disuse by the Dakota for many years and thus it was difficult to gather information about it (Densmore 1918: 68). James Howard, an anthropologist who worked among the Canadian Dakota in the summer of 1972, provides this commentary from one of his teachers, John Goodwill (Standing Buffalo):

We used to have Adoption Feasts quite often, but they are rare now. I think the last one on this reserve was held five years ago (1967). My son was killed when his bed caught fire. I guess he was smoking in bed. We adopted Sam Corrigan (an anthropologist) to replace my son. We had a feast and dressed Sam in my boy's Indian costume. This was the last Adoption Feast held on this reserve, though there have been others in the past ten years (Howard 1984: 130).

Walker's informants bemoaned the passing of this ceremony at the turn of the twentieth century, but like much of Lakota and Dakota ceremonial life, the *Hunka* has had a remarkable revival, or, as some would say, a public resurfacing because of the opprobrium placed on Native religion and culture by government and missionaries. There are a significant number of accounts of the contemporary *Hunka* in the anthropological literature (M. Powers 1986: 64–65; 1991; W. Powers 1975: 100–101) as well as in other Lakota narratives (Catches, Catches, and Holden 1997: 125–34; McGaa 1990: 113–18; St. Pierre and Long Soldier 1995: 60–62, 71–74). The ceremony is once again performed frequently, yet another testimony to the resilience and vitality of Lakota culture.

The Contemporary *Hunka*

The *Hunka* ceremony today comprises two ritual and social acts, sometimes combined and sometimes separate: the making of a relative and the giving of a Lakota name. Both acts are in the context of honoring an individual to be adopted and creating a social and spiritual bond between individuals through public prayer, feasting, and gift giving. These acts may be done with varying degrees of ceremony, formally in a *Hunka* ceremony or informally in other contexts such as a sweat lodge ceremony.

A Lakota man or a woman may initiate an adoption, which may be brother/sister, father/son, mother/daughter, brother/brother, mother/son, father/daughter, or sister/sister. In all instances these are very close kinship relationships. Relatives who are distantly related can intensify their relationship by adoption into a closer kinship category. Non-Lakota and non-Indians may also be adopted into extended families in this way.

A 1937 Oglala Sioux tribal ordinance from Pine Ridge regulates adoption:

> Any Indian or Indians wishing to adopt an adult according to Indian custom (*waliyacinpi*) shall appear before the Superior Court of the Oglala Sioux Tribe with the party to be adopted and all other parties and declare their intention. The Court, if after examination, finds the person or persons requesting the adoption be made is of sound mind and that the request is free and voluntary, may authorize such adoption, and make a record thereof upon the payment of a fee of one dollar ($1.00), which is to be deposited to the Court Funds.
>
> All adoptions made heretofore by Tribal custom shall be null and void unless they are renewed in the manner as above described (cited in Powers and Powers 2001: 127).

Powers and Powers point out that this law is unknown outside of court circles. The fact that this law was made makes it clear, however, that ceremonial adoption remained an important institution in Lakota life.

Contemporary authors point out that the *Hunka* has become a rite of passage for young people (M. Powers 1991: 1 ; St. Pierre and Long Soldier 1995: 72). Important elements of the ceremony in this context include blessing the child and giving him or her a Lakota name. In fact, this ceremony is often called a naming ceremony and names are bestowed without creating a new familial relationship. In some cases, sponsors of the child are moved to a new kinship position or close kin may serve as sponsors thus strengthening the kinship bond through prayer, public recognition, and gift giving.

Personal Experience

There is an ironic twist to this investigation of ritual adoption. As we have seen, some of the Lakota at the beginning of the twentieth century lamented what they assumed was the demise of the *Hunka* ceremony. No Flesh is quite specific as to why this was happening: the missionaries said that the ceremony was wrong (No Flesh 1980: 195). I, however, a "missionary" and an "anthropologist," have attended many adoption ceremonies and, furthermore, have been adopted in a variety of ways by multiple Native families, Lakota and non-Lakota. I do not present this fact as a matter of pride or accomplishment but, as my Lakota relatives would say, with a sense of humility for honors bestowed on me and in recognition of close friendships that have grown over the years. This number does not reflect my popularity but rather the generosity and permeability of Native families and the affection and love of people whom I have encountered in my own life.

I am fond of explaining the phenomenon of fuzzy boundaries to my anthropology students when speaking of the human tendency to classify everything even though many things refuse to fit neatly into categories. In rituals we call this liminality, a point between two recognized positions. This essay is, perhaps, liminal in that it began with a traditional anthropological investigation of the literature and now continues with a personal narrative that I have never written about and whose field notes are in my heart, rather than on my computer. I feel something of the ambivalence my own Native teachers encounter when students attempt to record what they experience. They have taught me, however, that these recordings are important for future generations and allow other people to learn about and respect native rituals.

My first encounter with Native people came in the summer of 1975 when, as a Jesuit novice, I was assigned to the Fort Belknap reservation in northern Montana. Full of enthusiasm I went around the reservation meeting everyone I could and asking a lot of probably annoying questions. I was interested in learning the language and fortunate to meet a very good speaker of Assiniboine who soon took me under her wing. She had a brother-in-law with whom, according to Native custom, she had a joking relationship. She began teaching me Assiniboine phrases to convey to her in-law, mostly of a humorous and teasing nature. He would always return the favor. One day at the home of the brother-in-law, his wife casually told me that the family called me "Nakota Hoksina" and that that was my name in Indian. Her husband then chimed in that the name, Assiniboine Boy, was given because of my interest in the language and the culture. At this point in time I had no idea about naming or Indian names! While it was not a formal naming, it did represent a redefinition of who I was in that community.

That same summer I met a Gros Ventre Indian family who began extending kinship terms towards me and formed a kinship alliance which has lasted to the present. When one of the young sons, who met me after a long absence from the reservation, asked me who I was, I told him my name was Ray Bucko. He thought a bit, saying my name again and again. Then, with a look of recognition, he said, "You're my brother, aren't you?" I was very moved by this and said "Yes I am." He looked a bit puzzled and asked "Did you used to be Indian?" I told our mother this amusing story and she exclaimed, "You might know!"

In the summer of 1976 I worked at a summer camp on the Pine Ridge Reservation in South Dakota and became friends with another family. One of their sons was thrown from a horse and hospitalized for some time. I drove his parents and siblings to the hospital each day and joked with the family to help keep spirits up. The boy recovered and now is a man with a family of his own. At the end of the summer the boy's eldest brother stood behind me and gave me a pipe that his uncle had made. He told me that the family wanted me to have this so that I would never forget them. I returned to Pine Ridge from 1978 to 1980 to teach high school and became even closer to this family, which began using kinship terms towards me. In 1998 my Ina (mother), who had lost her husband the year before, put on a *Hunka* ceremony to give her sons, daughter, and grandson Lakota names and to adopt me formally as her son and give me a name also. I was very moved by this and realized that this would be a great sacrifice for her to put together a feast, give presents, and bring in a medicine man, but she said that it was time for her to do things the right way. So a ceremony took place and she adopted me as her son and gave me a Lakota name. Fall of 2001 I visited with my Ina; she gave me a bag that contained a wooden peg used for piercing in the Sun Dance. She explained that my youngest brother danced four days that summer in a Sun Dance; he dedicated one day of dancing and suffering to me, and wanted me to have this peg as a memento of this act. I accepted it gratefully.

Another family I got to know while teaching at the high school and working at their parish on Pine Ridge adopted me as their son. I was given the name of their deceased son and told that I resembled him quite a bit. They had a Mass and dinner to make the adoption public, and gave me a beautiful red star quilt. In that community, I am still known by the name they gave me.

While doing my doctoral dissertation fieldwork on Pine Ridge from

1988 to 1990, a woman took me as her brother in a very formal *Hunka* ceremony. We met in a most unusual way. I was attending the Good Friday prayer walk in one of the communities. I was in the front of the line talking with some friends as we walked, joking that I could be their Lakota translator if they went to Hollywood with their son who is a very skilled dancer, and I would translate everything for them wrong! I thought we were laughing quietly and discreetly. It was Good Friday, but even the most serious of Lakota ceremonies has laughter somewhere, so I figured this joking would be acceptable. But my own laugh is distinctive and rarely quiet for long. At the back of the line was a woman who asked who was laughing so loud up in front. Her friend told her it was Ray Bucko, and she told the friend that she wanted to meet me. We met at the feast after the prayer walk—a pot of meatless soup for the Catholics, a pot of meat soup for the Presbyterians, Episcopalians, and Traditionals. Of course, everyone had some from both pots. I accompanied the woman to her house where we continued talking long into the night. We talked about our experiences in life, our joys and sorrows, struggles and successes. It felt as though I had known this woman my whole life. To my surprise, she later told me that she felt the same way that night, and proposed that we were twins in a former life and had finally found each other! We became close friends over the time I was on the reservation doing my fieldwork, and this relationship was recognized when she adopted me formally and her father provided a name for me. This was the most elaborate and traditional of the adoptions I have undergone. It had many of the elements mentioned in the nineteenth century texts, including the ceremony conducted by a spiritual leader, prayers, prayer songs, a wand with eagle feathers suspended from it and corn on the end, rattles, feasting, gift-giving, and the feeding and dressing of the adoptees. As is frequently the case, there were multiple adoptions and honorings at this occasion.

I have been adopted formally and informally, by complex ceremony and by the simple extension of kinship terms. All of these adoptions have meant far more than research. It was not until I was invited to give a paper at a symposium on Religion and Family that I considered writing about this topic. I have worked with several different Indian groups and have found Ella Deloria's dicta on kinship to be true for all of these groups. Extending kinship to other Natives, to members of one's own group, and to non-Indians, represents a way of strengthening the family, literally extending it. It also sanctifies the relationships that already exist.

No culture's kinship system is timelessly perfect, but through adoption, marriage, and birth, kinship systems constantly renew, repair, and rebuild themselves. Being a relative and acting properly in one's kinship roles is a moral, religious, and social imperative in Lakota culture. One has to work at kinship relations and obligations; they are not given once and for all, not bestowed genetically. To be a kin through birth, marriage, or adoption is to act as a kin. Among the Lakota, kinship is not merely a biological fact, or simply a ritual honor, but a series of mutual obligations. Kinship is a sacred as well as a human matter that requires prayer, humility, and the leading of a moral life expressed through reciprocity with the divine and the human.

My encounters with Native families and my incorporation into these units have been an affair of the heart, and never until now a matter of scholarship. My dissertation work was on the sweat lodge, a ceremony that also brought me close to many people through an exchange of prayer, laughter, gifts, experiences, joys and sorrows. My current role as university professor is also rooted in kinship; I now teach and work with Lakota students, who are related to me through these adoptions, as well as with students, faculty, and staff who are from many other tribal groups.

Perhaps this essay has shifted from social science to socialization, from research to personal narrative, but I think as scholars we make a mistake if we always separate these things. An anthropologist not only learns from a community but also commits to its well being in terms of ethical behavior as well as mutual social and religious obligations. In the case of adoption, specific Lakota families took the initiative to make me a part of them. In accepting adoption, I promised, in turn, to be a good relative towards those people. This continues to be part of my prayer, social interaction, and commitment as a relative, a teacher, and a scholar.

To conduct research on the family we must first be family with all our flaws and strengths. The frequency of my adoption by Native peoples, and similar adoptions of both my Jesuit brothers and fellow anthropologists, speaks of the centrality and dynamism of Native kinship, a dynamism from which we can learn and become enriched—without becoming Indian or taking on another culture. The old joke that a typical Navajo family consists of five children, four grandparents, two parents and an anthropologist also speaks of the nature of extended interpersonal relations across cultures. The transcultural as well as intracultural nature of adoption speaks of peace and unity, familiarity and alliance, mutual aide and fidelity—enacted, recognized, and honored.

Three Stories

I conclude not with erudite theoretical musings or in a flurry of footnotes and theory but with three stories that speak of the continued connectedness in which adoption marks not distinction but incorporation into a dynamic system. Literally, while typing the first draft of this paper I received an e-mail from a Lakota Ciye (older brother) by adoption. I asked him for advice and he replied: "OK, this is your older brother talking and so you can completely ignore what I say, if you wish." He ends his letter with: "I love you, no matter how you are!"

In the fall of my second year of graduate school in Chicago I had reluctantly barricaded myself into my third floor room in the Jesuit House to write yet another paper, this time on the Gros Ventres sweat lodge. Our doorbell rang and I kept writing, hoping that someone else was home to get the door. The bell rang again and I headed down the stairs. At the door was a young man who shyly put out his hand, told me his name, and then said that he was from Fort Belknap (home of the Gros Ventre Indians). His aunt told him that I was his relative and that he should call on me. I brought him in, fed him lunch, and then walked the campus with him. During the semester I did my best to help him adjust to life in Chicago and at the university. Eventually, I even managed to finish my paper.

Over the last few years I have accumulated a large dollar amount of readers' fees. I wanted to do something significant with this to express my gratitude for being at Creighton University and being part of the Native Studies Program. Working with the Native American Association and their advisor, I arranged to honor the Native American Association with the money. They, in turn, used the money to buy books for the Creighton library. The students decided to have a commemorative bookplate placed in each book to honor an individual from among the faculty, staff, and students who have been supportive of the Native American Programs at Creighton. They included my name on their list. The book they chose for me: Strangers to Relatives: The Adoption and Naming of Anthropologists in Native North America.

Notes

1. I am grateful to Ronald A. Simkins and the Center for the Study of Religion and Society at Creighton University for the invitation to their symposium on Religion and Family. I also thank Christina Burke for reading versions of this paper and for help with the winter count material. Jim and Bernice Green also made helpful comments on versions of this paper, as did Violet Catches. Mary Russell generously made editorial suggestions.

References

Afraid of Bear. 1980. "*Hunka* and the White Man." Pp. 200–2 in *Lakota Belief and Ritual*. R. J. DeMallie and E. A. Jahner, eds. Lincoln: University of Nebraska Press.

Bad Wound. 1980. "Counseling the *Hunka*." Pp. 208–11 in *Lakota Belief and Ritual*. R. J. DeMallie and E. A. Jahner, eds. Lincoln: University of Nebraska Press.

Blue Horse. 1980. "The Spirits No Longer Come." Pp. 207–8 in *Lakota Belief and Ritual*. R. J. DeMallie and E. A. Jahner, eds. Lincoln: University of Nebraska Press.

Blunt Horn, John. 1980. "The Secret that the Spirits Told." Pp. 201–4 in *Lakota Belief and Ritual*. R. J. DeMallie and E. A. Jahner, eds. Lincoln: University of Nebraska Press.

Brown, Joseph E. 1953. *The Sacred Pipe: Black Elk's Account of the Seven Rites of the Oglala Sioux*. Norman: University of Oklahoma Press.

Buechel, S. J., Eugene. 1970. *Lakota-English Dictionary*. S. J. Paul Manhart, ed. Pine Ridge, SD: Holy Rosary Mission.

Catches, Peter, Sr., Peter V. Catches, and Robert I. Holden. 1997. *Oceti Wakan (Sacred Fireplace)*. Pine Ridge, SD: Oceti Wakan.

Curtis, Edward. 1970. *The North American Indian*. Vol. 3. New York: Johnson Reprint.

Deloria, Ella C. 1944. *Speaking of Indians*. New York: Friendship.

DeMallie, Raymond J. 2001. "Teton." Pp. 794–820 in *Handbook of North American Indians*. R. J. DeMallie, ed. Vol. 13; Part 2. Washington: Smithsonian Institution.

DeMallie, Raymond J, and Elaine A Jahner. 1980. "James R. Walker: His Life and Work." Pp. 3–61 in *Lakota Belief and Ritual*. R. J. DeMallie and E. A. Jahner, eds. Lincoln: University of Nebraska Press.

Densmore, Frances. 1918. Teton Sioux Music. Vol. 61. Bulletin of the Bureau of American Ethnology. Washington: Government Printing Office.

Feather on Head. 1980. "Preparing the *Hunka* Implements." Pp. 215–16 in *Lakota Belief and Ritual*. R. J. DeMallie and E. A. Jahner, eds. Lincoln: University of Nebraska Press.

Howard, James H. 1960. "Dakota Winter Counts as a Source of Plains History." Anthropological Papers No. 61, *Bureau of American Ethnology, Bulletin* 173: 335–416.

Howard, James H. 1984. *The Canadian Sioux*. Lincoln: University of Nebraska Press.

Lewis, Thomas. 1990. *The Medicine Men: Oglala Sioux Ceremony and Healing*. Lincoln: University of Nebraska Press.

McGaa, Ed. 1990. *Mother Earth Spirituality*. San Francisco: Harper and Row.

No Flesh. 1980. "Legend of the First *Hunka*." Pp. 193–95 in *Lakota Belief and Ritual*. R. J. DeMallie and E. A. Jahner, eds. Lincoln: University of Nebraska Press.

Powers, Marla N. 1986. *Oglala Women*. Chicago: University of Chicago Press.

Powers, Marla N. 1991. *Lakota Naming: A Modern-day* Hunka *Ceremony*. Kendall Park, NJ: Lakota Books.

Powers, William K. 1975. *Oglala Religion*. Lincoln: University of Nebraska Press.

Powers, William K., and Marla N. Powers. 2001. "All My Relations: The Significance of Adoption in Anthropological Research." Pp. 119–40 in *Strangers to Relatives: The Adoption and Naming of Anthropologists in Native North America*. S. Kan, ed. Lincoln: University of Nebraska Press.

Riggs, Stephen Return. 1890. *A Dakota-English Dictionary*. Vol. 7. Contributions to North American Ethnology. Washington, D.C.: Government Printing Office.

Ringing Shield. 1980. "The Spirits Taught the Oglala." Pp. 206–7 in *Lakota Belief and Ritual*. R. J. DeMallie and E. A. Jahner, eds. Lincoln: University of Nebraska Press.

St. Pierre, Mark, and Tilda Long Soldier. 1995. *Walking in the Sacred Manner: Healers, Dreamers, and Pipe Carriers—Medicine Women of the Plains Indians*. New York: Simon & Schuster.

Sword, George. 1980. "The *Hunka*." Pp. 198–200 in *Lakota Belief and Ritual*. R. J. DeMallie and E. A. Jahner, eds. Lincoln: University of Nebraska Press.

Takes the Gun. 1980. "Implements used in the *Hunka* Ceremony." Pp. 211–14 in Lakota Belief and Ritual. R. J. DeMallie and E. A. Jahner, eds. Lincoln: University of Nebraska.

Walker, James. 1917. "The Sun Dance and Other Ceremonies of the Oglala Division of the Teton Sioux." *Anthropological Papers of the American Museum of Natural History* 16, 2: 51–221.

Walker, James. 1980. "The *Hunka* Ceremony." Pp. 216–39 in *Lakota Belief and Ritual*. R. J. DeMallie and E. A. Jahner, eds. Lincoln: University of Nebraska Press.

Williamson, John P. 1992. *An English-Dakota Dictionary*. St. Paul: Minnesota Historical Society Press.

Competing Portraits of the Israelite Family[1]

RONALD A. SIMKINS

The significance of family in ancient Israel is reflected in the competing portraits of the family that are presented in the Bible's first story. In the Yahwist version of the story, God creates a helper for the man from his own bone and flesh. In the setting of the garden, the woman is created for the man, so that he will not be alone. They are identified as husband (*ish*) and wife (*ishsha*) and set forth as an exemplar or even as an archetype of marriage—"Therefore a man leaves his father and his mother and clings to his wife, and they become one flesh" (Gen 2:24)—but reference to their roles in procreation is absent. The human couple at best is only a nascent family. They are like children, sexually unaware and lacking the knowledge necessary for family life. Only after the human couple disobey God's prohibition and eat the fruit from the tree of the knowledge of good and evil do they become aware of their gendered family roles. They now know how to create "like God." Once they are expelled from the comfort and security of the garden, the husband and wife proceed to build the first family by having sexual relations and giving birth to Cain and Abel.

The Yahwist's presentation of the family is ambiguous at best. The role of children oddly plays no role in God's creation of man and woman in the garden. God appears to make no provision for children, and indeed, without the prohibited knowledge of good and evil the human couple seems to be incapable of procreation. The lack of concern for children is mirrored by the man's detachment from his own parents: He leaves his parents to join with his wife in marriage. Although leaving one's parents to get married seems wholly natural in our society, it is quite odd in the patrilineal and patrilocal society of ancient Israel. In marriage a son brings his wife into his "father's house" (*beth ab*), and they physically reside in or near his parent's house after marriage. However, in the garden the human couple stands alone with no connection to their parents or their children. The Yahwist has highlighted the significance of marriage at the expense of the family. Whereas marriage is clearly presented as a divine institution, instituted by God at creation, the family is presented as a *human* institution, created as a result of human disobedience to God.[2]

The date of the first creation story is debated and uncertain. Whereas scholars thirty years ago could assert with confidence that the garden narrative belonged to the Yahwist source of the Pentateuch and that it dated from the early period of the Judean monarchy, such a consensus no longer exists. Without taking a position on the several current competing compositional models, it is reasonable to argue that significant portions of the Yahwist (or non-Priestly) material in Genesis—most notably the primeval history and the Jacob narrative—have their origin in the monarchic period of ancient Israel.[3] During the post-exilic period, after the collapse of the Kingdom of Judah, the Priestly Writer revised the Yahwist's narrative to communicate a new message to the Judean community. Specifically, the Priestly Writer prefaced the Yahwist's story of the garden with a new account of creation, and thereby shaped how subsequent readers would read the original tale. In this new creation account, God creates humans male and female in God's own image, and commands the humans to be fruitful and multiply. That which the Yahwist attributes to human disobedience, the Priestly Writer attributes to God's acts and directives. In this presentation of creation, the human couple is created for family; procreation is the first of God's commands. The Priestly Writer's revision of the creation story thus redeems the role of the family in God's purpose for creation.

The two competing views of the family represented by the Yahwist and Priestly versions of creation express a tension in the political economy of ancient Israelite society regarding the loyalties and obligations of the man within the Israelite family. In the domestic mode of production of early (pre-monarchical) Israel, the social relations of production were fellow kin, and the few biblical texts reflecting this period (the so-called Covenant Code and parts of the books of Joshua and Judges) present the family within the context of an extended kinship network—the man's brothers, father, uncles, and cousins. Israel's transition from a tribal society to a monarchical state was accompanied by a similar shift from a domestic mode of production to a mode in which the social relations of production were structured by patronage. Because kinship relations tended to undermine patron-client relations, the biblical texts produced by the state, such as the Yahwist's narrative, emphasize the primacy of the marital unit and the resulting nuclear family at the expense of the extended family. Finally, with the collapse of the monarchy and the state, the domestic mode of production re-emerged along with an emphasis on extended family relations. Texts produced during this period, such as the revision by the Priestly Writer, again place the human couple within the context of an extended family. This paper will focus on the competing portraits of the Israelite family in the biblical literature and will argue that the loyalties and obligations of the family man was shaped by the political economy of the period.

The Political Economy in Ancient Israel

The Marxian concepts of mode of production and social formation provide an effective model to evaluate the role of the family in the political economy of ancient Israel. A mode of production is a historically determined combination of the forces and relations of production that make up the society's economic base. It is defined by the way in which the surplus is drawn-off, allocated, and utilized. A mode of production is also a dynamic concept; changes in the environment, technology, or new social relations result in the configuration of new modes of production.[4] As a result, complex societies are organized by social formations that are a combination of at least two modes of production, one of which is dominant. The secondary modes of production are either vestiges of an earlier period or newly emerging modes that serve a subsidiary function. In either case, the dominant mode of production subjects the functioning of the other modes to the requirements of its own reproduction.[5]

The value of the Marxian model is that it treats the economic base in connection with a political and ideological superstructure. However, the relationship between the economic base and the superstructure is configured differently in pre-capitalist societies than in the capitalist societies to which the Marxian model is usually applied. In capitalist societies, for example, conflict is inherent in the relations of production, and is expressed as conflict between social classes. The political and ideological superstructure functions within this conflict to justify and reproduce the relations of production. In many pre-capitalist societies, such as ancient Israel, the social conflict is "not between social groups that are denied access to the means of resources or socially segregated into classes and exploited, but rather in the activity of individuals who attempt to increase their political power at the expense of kin members."[6] This social conflict may thus be expressed as a tension between an existing economic base and a newly evolving superstructure. The new superstructure will eventually reproduce a new economic base and thus a new mode of production, but the existing mode of production will endure and remain in tension with the new mode.

In order to understand the political economy of monarchic Israel, we must begin with the dominant mode of production in early Israel, for this mode of production continued to function in a subordinate role throughout the monarchic period. The dominant mode of production in early Israel may be termed the domestic[7] or the household[8] mode of production. The primary productive unit in early Israel was the family unit known as the *beth ab*, consisting of several nuclear families covering as many as four generations, and linked in an extended kinship unit, the *mishpacha*.[9] The *beth ab* was a self-sustaining unit, which owned the means of production—primarily, the land (*nachala*), which was shared in common by the members of the kinship unit. Kinship relations served as the social relations of production and distribution, regulating access to the means of production and determining the distribution of the products of labor. However, within the domestic mode of production, the kinship system functioned simultaneously as the superstructure. The kinship system formed the condition for its own reproduction by regulating marriages. It provided the social framework for political and religious activity, and it functioned as an ideology expressing the relationship between kinsmen and between men and women.[10]

Early Israel has often been characterized as an egalitarian society, as have many other societies structured by kinship relations. The assumption often made is that these kinship relations functioned to regulate and diminish social and economic inequalities. However, this assumption is not supported by ethnographic studies. Although tribal societies maintain egalitarian principles through their ideology, social and economic differentiation is the common experience of the people. The rich maintain and increase their wealth, often at the expense of the poor, and the poor inherit the poverty of their parents. Moreover, it is not uncommon for a kinsman to exploit his own kin for his personal or patrimonial advantage.[11] Social and economic inequalities are common even within extended kinship units. The domestic mode of production in early Israel undoubtedly reproduced and generated social and economic inequalities. In fact, the rise of the monarchy presupposed significant inequalities across Israelite society. The Bible itself attests to such inequalities.

The increasing social and economic inequalities that resulted from the domestic mode of production in early Israel gave rise to a new mode of production. The social conditions for the existence of this mode of production were in fact these inequalities and the relative weakness of corporate kinship groups to neutralize the effects of these inequalities.[12] Some households produced surpluses beyond the needs of subsistence;[13] others tended toward underproduction. The inequalities were largely due to differential access to fertile land and material resources, size of the labor force, and ability, effort, and opportunity. Although the kinship system undoubtedly served to mitigate some of the inequalities between the nuclear families within the *beth ab* and the *mishpacha* through a generalized exchange based on familial loyalty and obligation, it was unable to prevent the growing social and economic disparity within the extended family and across the society. In order to compensate for this disparity, the formation of social and economic relations across kinship boundaries was necessary. These relations were also based on a generalized exchange, but the inequality between the two members in their access and control of resources resulted in the formation of patron-client relationships.[14]

Patronage is a system of social relations rooted in an unequal distribution of power and goods, and expressed socially through a generalized exchange of different types of resources. The structure of these relations is hierarchical. Patrons are those who have access to goods and the centers of power, whereas clients are in need of such access. In fact, patronage is most prominent in those societies that are characterized by "highly elaborated hierarchies of rank and position, often related to the differential access of various groups to the center."[15] In spite of the social and economic hierarchy, the exchange between patrons and clients is based on reciprocity, and the relationship between them is idealized as friendship and expressed in terms of kinship. The patron is a "father" to his clients, who honor him as "sons" and faithful "servants." Patron-client relations are foremost personal bonds to which one's identity and honor is committed.

The bonds are held together by mutual commitments of loyalty, though rarely ever formalized. The patron commits himself to protect and support his clients, and the client commits himself to serve his patron.[16] By means of these interpersonal obligations, exercised through a generalized exchange, patron-client relations function to regulate and mitigate the effects of economic inequalities. Based on generalized exchange as the mode of surplus appropriation,[17] the dominant mode of production in monarchic Israel can be characterized as a clientelistic mode of production.

Patron-client relations constituted the social relations of this new mode of production. The condition of their existence entailed an inequality of wealth and power between individuals who had social interaction and would mutually benefit from a generalized exchange.[18] The patron usually controlled access to the means of production, to the major markets, and to the administrative centers of the society, whereas the client was in need of such access. The generalized exchange that characterized these relations took place on two distinct levels. On one level, the patron and client exchanged different types of resources, goods, or services. For example, the patron might secure for the client a "fair" exchange for his agricultural surplus, or grant him access to land for grazing his flock, or provide him seed for planting. The client in turn might give to the patron a percentage of his surplus, or provide the patron with his labor. Although framed as a reciprocal exchange, the patron was in a position to receive the best possible benefit for himself through his monopolization of needed resources or access to centers of power. The material imbalance of the exchange was concealed by the patron's frequent displays of generosity, even though the product of his generosity had been appropriated from the client. On another level, however, the patron and client exchanged intangibles. The client offered loyalty, honor, and support to the patron in exchange for protection, loyalty, and the promise of reciprocity.

> The client "buys," as it were, protection, first, against the exigencies of markets or nature; second, against the arbitrariness or weakness of the centre, or against the demands of other strong people or groups. The price the client pays is not just the rendering of a specific service but his acceptance of the patron's control over his (the client's) access to markets and to public goods, as well as over his ability fully to convert some of his own resources.[19]

By simultaneously exchanging tangibles and intangibles, the patron-client relationship mitigated the effects of the inherent social and economic inequalities between the members of society, while at the same time reproducing those inequalities. Moreover, the addition of intangibles to the exchange reinforced the ideological framework of an equitable and balanced exchange (i.e. reciprocity), despite the fact that the patron generally benefited materially at the client's expense.

The formation of patron-client relationships and the subsequent rise of the clientelistic mode of production in monarchic Israel stood in conflict with the earlier domestic mode of production, which it eventually subsumed under its own functioning. Although the primary productive unit in monarchic Israel continued to be the family, its social configuration was different in relation to each mode of production. The political superstructure of patronage, expressed most clearly through the establishment of kingship in Israel, posed a challenge to the economic base and the ideological superstructure of early Israel by transforming the social relations of production and distribution.

As discussed above, the family under the domestic mode of production in early Israel was configured along extended kinship lines—the *beth ab* and the *mishpacha*. The relations of production and distribution were kinship relations, further strengthening familial bonds and one's loyalty and obligation toward family members. Although the male members of the family controlled the production and distribution of the social product, all members of the family benefited from the product. Competition for resources among kin was unnecessary, at least according to the ideology. The economic reality, however, was characterized by inequalities, even among kinsmen. With the formation of patron-client relationships, the relations of production and distribution cut across kinship boundaries. Patrons and clients were determined not by kinship relations but by control and access to needed material resources. Only those who entered into patron-client relationships were able to benefit directly from them. Kinsmen were no longer the primary recipients of one's loyalty and obligation. The structure of patronage placed kinsmen in competition with one another—for access to resources by those in the lower social strata, and for control of large client bases by those in the upper social strata. Although established to compensate for the inequalities inherent in the kinship system, patron-client relations functioned to weaken kinship bonds and thus to give rise to a new mode of production and social formation.

When the state and the monarchy of Judah collapsed in 586 B.C.E., the clientelistic mode of production lost the political and ideological superstructure necessary for its reproduction. Judah became a province of the Babylonian and then the Persian empire. The archaeological and textual evidence indicates that this period was characterized by a ruralization of the society and an increasingly crumbling economy. Most of the surplus seems to have been extracted for taxes to the Babylonian and Persian courts, and perhaps also to a few local elite who were loyal to and supported by the imperial courts. Most of the surplus seems to have been extracted for taxes to the Babylonian and Persian courts through a tributary mode of production. This mode functioned as a pariah on the local political economy. It functioned to benefit only the Babylonian and Persian administrations, and perhaps also a few local elite who were loyal to and supported by the imperial courts. Although we are unable in this context to reconstruct fully the social formation of Judah during this period, we can simply note that the society was organized by ancestral houses and the domestic mode of production, though now subsumed into the tributary mode, characterized the political economy of Judah. The political and ideological superstructure of this social formation was expressed through the biblical exilic and post-exilic literature, which places emphasis on the extended family within the context of an acceptance of Babylonian and Persian rule.[20]

The Israelite Family: Nuclear or Extended?

The inability of the kinship system to neutralize social and economic inequalities provided the social conditions for the existence of the patronage system and the clientelistic mode of production. In order to provide for its own reproduction, the patronage system exploited the weaknesses of the corporate kinship groups through its ideology. Moreover, because the patron benefited disproportionately from the exchange with his clients, the abatement of his clients' loyalty and obligation to their *beth ab* and *mishpacha* was in the patron's own best interest. By undermining the kinship bond, the ideology of patronage functioned to increase both the number of clients dependent upon the patron and the value of their dependence to him.

Yet, the patronage system could not just simply undermine the kinship system with impunity, for the clientelistic mode of production was also dependent on the production of the family unit. But unlike the domestic mode of production, which was dependent on extended kinship bonds, the clientelistic mode was dependent only on the production of the nuclear family. Indeed, extended family bonds posed an obstacle to the development of the patronage system. They provided the nuclear family with a network of relations and access to resources that minimized an individual's contact with other social strata and impeded the formation of patron-client relations. As a result, the inherent contradiction between the clientelistic and the domestic modes of production took the form of a conflict between the interests of the nuclear family and the interests of the extended family—the *beth ab* and especially the *mishpacha*. The successful functioning of the social formation of monarchic Israel was dependent on the resolution of this contradiction through the ideological superstructure.

At the core of the resolution of the contradiction between the clientelistic and the domestic modes of production was a redefinition of the family and the man's loyalties and obligations. The process by which the ideological superstructure resolved this contradiction was expressed through several biblical texts produced by the state. These texts suggest that the ideological superstructure functioned to resolve the contradiction and redefine the family in four ways. First, the ideological superstructure functioned to weaken extended kinship bonds, especially relations to one's *mishpacha*, by extending the structure of kinship relations to incorporate all Israel so that all Israelites—patrons and clients—were considered kin, descendants of the family of Jacob. The genealogy of Jacob (Gen 29:31–30:24), for example, functions to incorporate all the Israelites, irrespective of their clan and tribal loyalties, within a single kinship group. Segmented genealogies, which are usually fluid in their configuration, function to express social relations between persons and to rank the status of groups and individuals. Indeed, the earliest lists of Israelite tribes differ in number and order depending on the prominence of the individual tribes and regions.[21] At some point during the monarchy, presumably early in the monarchy, the genealogy of the traditional twelve Israelite tribes was frozen in form. Rather than functioning to rank one tribe over another, it functioned in the religious or ideological sphere as an expression of the ideal Israel.[22] All Israelites were presented as equal members of the family of Jacob. By giving precedence to the unity of Israel, the genealogy and narratives of Jacob function to diminish tribal and clan loyalties.

In the post-exilic period the extended family again became important in the political economy of Judah. The post-exilic Priestly Writer placed the family of Jacob, first, within the extended human family descending from Adam and Noah, and then within the extended family of Terah. He also included the lineages of Ishmael, Esau, Moses, and Aaron. The Priestly writer was concerned to define Israel as a distinct people among the peoples of the Persian Empire[23] and the priestly families within Israel. The Chronicler, on the other hand, similarly developed an extensive genealogy of Adam and the families of Israel, especially the Judahites and Levites, concluding with the prominent families of Jerusalem who were taken into exile (1 Chr 1–9). This genealogy bolstered the claims of the descendants of the exilic community who had returned to Judah over against the Samarian community. Only the families of Judah and Benjamin who had gone into exile were the true representatives of Israel in the post-exilic community. In both cases, the post-exilic writers define the family in terms of extended relationships.

Second, the political and ideological superstructure functioned to weaken the influence of the extended family on the nuclear family through a process of political and religious centralization. At the political level, the state replaced tribal and clan leaders with state appointed judges and officials (Deut 16:18). The extended family would no longer be the domain in which the issues of justice were decided. Individuals would thus take their cases directly to the state and its officials. At the religious level, the state prohibited sacrifice to Yahweh outside of Jerusalem. All tithes, sacrifices, donations, and votive offerings should be brought to the temple in Jerusalem (Deut 12:5–7). The traditional family festivals of unleavened bread (Passover), weeks, and booths should also be held in Jerusalem (Deut 16:1–17). The family's worship of Yahweh is now under the sponsorship or patronage of the state.[24]

The effects of centralization on the family can be illustrated by examining the laws regarding a man who has sexual relations with an unbetrothed virgin. In the Covenant Code, which reflects the customary practices of early Israel, the law is stated:

> When a man seduces a virgin who is not engaged to be married, and lies with her, he shall give the bride-price for her and make her his wife. But if her father refuses to give her to him, he shall pay an amount equal to the bride-price for virgins (Exod 22:16–18).

According to this law, the father should be compensated for the loss of his daughter's virginity—an economic commodity to the father.[25] The father is also in control of whether or not the daughter is given in marriage to her seducer. In the Deuteronomic Code, however, the law is revised in accordance with the ideological superstructure of the social formation of monarchic Israel. The new law states:

> If a man meets a virgin who is not engaged, and seizes her and lies with her, and they are caught in the act, the man who lay with her shall give fifty shekels of silver to the young woman's father, and she shall become his wife. Because he violated her he shall not be permitted to divorce her as long as he lives (Deut 22:28–29).

According to this formulation, the role of the father is taken out of the equation. He will still be compensated for his economic loss, but his compensation is fixed by the state and he appears to have no say in whether the seducer marries his daughter. Emphasis is placed instead on the requirement that the man marry the woman he seduced, and that he never divorce her.

Several other laws similarly reduce the power of the *paterfamilias* over his kin.[26] In Deut 21:15–17, a man who is married to two wives, each with sons, must designate his eldest son—whether or not he is born from his favorite wife—to be his firstborn. The law was promulgated to protect the rights of the eldest son to the double portion share of the inheritance, but the law also undermines the power of the father to determine his own heir. Deut 21:18–21 states that if a father and mother have a rebellious son, they must take their case before the elders of the town who will decide his fate. Likewise, if a wife is accused of not being a virgin at marriage, the father and mother of the wife take their evidence to the city elders who determine the merits of the charge (Deut 22:13–21). In both cases, issues of justice are taken out of the context of the family and assigned to state appointed officials.

A third way in which the ideological superstructure weakened extended family loyalties was by prohibiting the practice of consulting the dead. The dead in ancient Israel offered both benevolent and malevolent powers; they were deified and sources of knowledge. The deified ancestors of the family, if properly attended through feeding and cult, secured the future prosperity of the family. Moreover, the practice of the cult of the dead provided potent symbols of the solidarity of the extended family. The family's connection to their dead ancestors was integral to the future cohesion and success of the extended family, and thus a threat to the social formation of monarchic Israel. The archaeological evidence suggests that the state had little effect on a family's care and treatment of the dead.[27] The mortuary practices and beliefs were too embedded in the society to be significantly challenged. Instead, the state focused on the role of intermediaries.[28] Several laws in the Deuteronomic and Holiness Codes[29] prohibit necromancy and threaten its practitioners with death (Deut 18:10–11; Lev 19:26, 31; 20:6, 27). On the one hand, such a prohibition, along with the process of centralization, secured for the temple cult in Jerusalem a monopoly on divine intermediation. The prohibitions in the Holiness Code continued to serve this function for the post-exilic temple cult as they were incorporated in the Priestly composition. On the other hand, the prohibition against consulting the dead minimized the role that the deceased could play in the politics of the extended family. The extended family's connection to their ancestors was established through genealogy, not necromancy.

Fourth, the ideological superstructure functioned to strengthen the nuclear family at the expense of extended kinship relations by emphasizing the importance of the conjugal bond between a husband and his wife.[30] The ideology of the Yahwist creation myth discussed above, for example, emphasizes the affective ties between husband and wife and thereby undermines the husband's bond to his consanguineous kin. The husband and the wife are "one flesh." The message is clear: A man's loyalty and obligation to his parents, his siblings, and his extended kin—his *beth ab* and *mishpacha*—should be secondary to his devotion and responsibility to his wife. The man's independence from his parents that is highlighted in the Yahwist's myth is also expressed negatively in the Deuteronomic Code:

> Parents should not be put to death for their children, nor shall children be put to death for their parents; only for their own crimes may persons be put to death (Deut 24:16).

Like the emphasis on the conjugal bond, the importance placed on individual responsibility and guilt functions to weaken the ties of the extended family.[31]

The conjugal bond of the nuclear family was also strengthened at the expense of the extended family through laws regulating sexual relations and prohibiting adultery. The Deuteronomic Code carefully defines the different circumstances that result in adultery (Deut 22:22–27). At its root, adultery takes place when a man has sexual relations with another man's wife. Both the man and the woman should be executed. Adultery also occurs when a man has sexual relations with a woman betrothed to another man. Under these circumstances, if the sexual relations take place in the town, then both the man and the woman should be stoned to death. If the woman cries out for help, however, the assumption of the law is that only the man should be killed. She is a victim of rape rather than an adulteress. By a similar logic, if the sexual relations take place out in the open country, only the man should be executed. The woman receives no punishment, for no one would have heard the woman if she had cried out. Another law in the Deuteronomic Code prohibits the restoration of a marriage if a man's former wife has married and divorced another man (Deut 21:10–14). The logic of this law implies that such a remarriage would be comparable to adultery. In regulating sexual behavior, these laws remove the matter from the jurisdiction of the *paterfamilias* or the extended family, where it traditionally belonged, and place it in the hands of the central authority.

In Lev 18:6–18 and 20:10–21 the Holiness Code specifies those women with whom a man may not have sexual relations. Although the distinction is not always clear in the text, sexual relations with some of the women are prohibited because they would be adulterous (e.g., "You shall not uncover the nakedness of your brother's wife; it is your brother's nakedness" [Lev 18:16]), while others are prohibited because they would be incestuous (e.g., "You shall not uncover the nakedness of your father's wife's daughter, begotten by your father, since she is your sister" [Lev 18:11]). It is interesting that the Deuteronomic Code gives no attention to incest; its focus is on the integrity of the nuclear family and the prohibition of sexual relations with members of one's nuclear family could be assumed. In the Holiness Code the incest prohibitions are placed in the context of the extended family where it is more complicated with whom one may have sexual relations. Thus, a man may have sexual relations with his first cousin or with his niece, but not with his aunt, his wife's sister (while his wife is living), or his daughter-in-law. A man's sexual activity was restricted in order to preserve the integrity and relations of his extended family. The Priestly Writer's inclusion of these incest prohibitions in his composition thus functioned to redefine the family and the man's loyalty and obligation in terms of the extended family in the postexilic period.

The conjugal bond and the nuclear family are also strengthened through laws that regulated marriage and divorce. We have already noted above the law regarding a man who has sexual relations with an unbetrothed virgin (Deut 22:28–29). By requiring the man to marry the woman, the law creates a new conjugal bond outside the jurisdiction of the *paterfamilias*. Moreover, by prohibiting the man from divorcing her, the law protects the social and economic security of the woman who might not otherwise be able to marry. In a similar way, Deut 21:10–14 regulates how a man may treat a woman captured in war. He may marry her, but he must first allow her one month to mourn her father and mother. If he is not satisfied with her, he must let her go free; he cannot treat her as a slave or sell her for money. As with the previous law, this law protects the woman by preserving the integrity of the conjugal bond. A man's sexual relations with a woman belong in the context of marriage. By restricting divorce, the law stresses the importance of the conjugal relationship. Elsewhere, the importance of the conjugal bond is stated directly:

> When a man is newly married, he shall not go out with the army or be charged with any related duty. He shall be free at home one year, to be happy with the wife whom he has married (Deut 24:5; compare Deut 20:7).

This law distinguishes the conjugal relationship from the larger extended family on which the burden of war or some other obligation might fall. A man's loyalty and obligation belongs first and foremost to his wife, and the development of this relationship supersedes other commitments.

The relationship between the nuclear and the extended family is highlighted in the law of the Levirate marriage (Deut 25:5–10). The context of this law is the extended family, where "brothers reside together" and have not yet divided the family estate. Within this context, if one brother dies and leaves a childless widow, his wife should be given in marriage to another brother. The child that is born from that union will then represent the deceased brother (literally: "stand on the name of his dead brother") so that "his name may not be blotted out of Israel." At issue in this law is the deceased brother's inheritance of the family estate. His "name" refers essentially to the possession of his land.³² Without a descendant, a man cannot pass on his land in his name, and his share of the land would be divided among his brothers. Thus the law makes this provision for a man who dies prematurely without an heir: his brother will father an heir for him.

A brother might not want to act as a Levir under some circumstances. At the very least, he may not want the family estate divided up into one more parcel for his deceased brother. Indeed, it is in the interests of the family to have as few heirs as possible to reduce the division of the estate. Thus, the law provides a mechanism in case the brother refuses to act as a Levir. First, the widow, for whom the Levirate marriage custom also provides social and economic security, takes the case before the elders of the city. Then the elders confront the brother to persuade him to do his duty. Finally, if the brother still refuses, the widow of the deceased publicly shames the brother and his house. The law of the Levirate marriage functions to protect the deceased's brother's right to maintain his name with his land. Moreover, the deceased's right outweighs the interests of the extended family and receives the support of the state.

The law of the Levirate marriage supports the interests of the individual family member, and hence the nuclear family, over the interests of the extended family. This conflict also lies behind the stories of the daughters of Zelophehad (Num 27:1–11; 36:1–12). In the story in Numbers 27, the five daughters of Zelophehad bring their request to inherit their father's land before Moses and the leaders of the people:

> Our father died in the wilderness; he was not among the company of those who gathered themselves together against the LORD in the company of Korah, but died for his own sin; and he had no sons. Why should the name of our father be taken away from his clan because he had no son? Give us a possession among our father's brothers (Num 27:3–4).

As with the law of the Levirate marriage, the daughters' concern is the continuation of their father's name—or more precisely, the possession of his land. Without a male heir, Zelophehad's land would be given to his brothers, one of the *mishpachoth*, "clans," of Manasseh. If his daughters inherit the land, however, his name will continue for the land will be registered in the name of his nuclear family. In other words, Zelophehad's share of the land will be divided into five parcels and registered in the names of Mahlah, Noah, Hoglah, Milcah, and Tirzah, daughters of Zelophehad. It is interesting that Moses and the leaders of the people do not decide the case themselves. Rather, Moses takes the case to the LORD, who decides in favor of the daughters' petition. The ideological superstructure roots itself in divine sanction. A new law is thus instituted at the command of the LORD that if a man dies and has no son, his inheritance shall be given to his daughter. Only if he has no descendants should his inheritance be given to members of his extended family (Num 27:8–11).

Although the story of the daughters of Zelophehad is preserved by the Priestly Writer, the tradition dates much earlier to the period of the monarchy. The tradition is also preserved, for example, in the Deuteronomistic History (Josh 17:3–6), and might have its origin in explaining why the tribe of Manasseh possessed land on the west side of the Jordan in addition to the lands of Gilead and Bashan on the east side.[33] In any case, by the time of the compilation of the book of Numbers—perhaps by the time of Ezra and Nehemiah—the precedent set by the daughters of Zelophehad raised concerns for the extended family, now living under a new mode of production—the resurgence of the domestic mode. Therefore, a new story was added as an addendum to the book (Numbers 36) in order to mitigate the effects of the case law established in Numbers 27. In this story, the heads of the Manassite clans bring their case to Moses and the leaders of the people. In regard to the daughters of Zelophehad inheriting the land of their father, they complain:

> If they are married into another Israelite tribe, then their inheritance will be taken away from the allotted portion of our inheritance (Num 36:3).

If the daughters of Zelophehad marry outside of the tribe of Manasseh, then their father's land would be passed down to their heirs who would belong to another tribe, resulting in the reduction of the land apportioned to the tribe of Manasseh. As in the previous case of the daughters, this case is decided directly by God, who revises the original legislation. The daughters of Zelophehad will continue to inherit the land that would be apportioned to their father, but now they must marry into the clan of their father's tribe (Num 36:6–8). During the post-exilic period with the resurgence of the domestic mode of production, it was no longer possible to ignore the interests of the extended family. The revised form of the legislation thus ensured that no land would be transferred from one tribe to another. At the same time, the legislation balanced the interests of the individual family member and the nuclear family, which were inherited in the tradition, with the interests of the extended family.

Summary

The family was the most significant and enduring institution in ancient Israel. At the center of the nuclear family was the man—the Israelite family was both patrilineal and patrilocal, and the needs of the family largely corresponded to the needs of the man—but the relationship between the man's nuclear family and extended family was shaped largely by the political economy of the period. The pre-monarchical and post-exilic periods were dominated by a domestic mode of production in which the social relations of production were fellow kin. A man's loyalties and obligations were first and foremost to his *beth ab* and *mishpacha*—to his brothers, father, uncles, and cousins. The interests of his nuclear family were placed within the context of the interests of his extended family. During the period of the monarchy, however, the family man was subject to competing demands for allegiance. His extended kinship network continued to demand his loyalty and placed obligations upon him, but these demands were usurped by a new mode of production. The formation of patron-client relations placed new loyalties and obligations on the family man by providing him with access to resources, goods, and services that he was unable to obtain through his kin relations. However, these new loyalties and obligations were in conflict with the former social relations of production. Therefore, in order to ensure the reproduction of these new social relations, the political superstructure sought to weaken a man's ties to his extended family by incorporating all Israelites into a fictive kinship network, centralizing political and religious institutions, prohibiting necromancy, and strengthening the conjugal bond between the man and his wife.

Notes

1. This chapter was first published as an article, "Family in the Political Economy

of Monarchic Israel," in the journal *The Bible and Critical Theory* (2004, paper no. BC 040006), published by Monash University Press— www.epress.monash.edu.

2. Although commentators early this century commonly argued that this passage reflects memory of an earlier matriarchal society, recent commentators have rightly rejected this interpretation as untenable. Nevertheless, this passage seems to be in conflict with the recognition that ancient Israel was a patrilocal society. What does it mean for a man to "leave" his parents and "cling" to his wife? Because a son physically remained in or near his parent's house after marriage, scholars have interpreted the Hebrew verbs figuratively in terms of the man's loyalty and affection. Gerhard von Rad argues: "The alliance of one sex to another [in marriage] is seen as a divine ordinance of creation" (*Genesis: A Commentary* [revised edition; Philadelphia: Westminster, 1972], 85). Claus Westermann suggests that this verse "points to the basic power of love between man and woman" (*Genesis 1–11: A Commentary* [Minneapolis: Augsburg, 1984], 233). Gordon Wenham recognizes that this verse signals a shift in the man's obligations: "On marriage a man's priorities change. Beforehand his first obligations are to his parents: afterwards they are to his wife" (*Genesis 1–15* [Word Biblical Commentary 1; Waco, TX: Word, 1987], 71). Anthropologists have recognized that the strength of the conjugal bond is in inverse proportion to the strength of the bonds between extended kin. See Yehudi A. Cohen, "End and Means in Political Control: State Organization and Punishment of Adultery, Incest, and Violation of Celibacy," *American Anthropologist* 71 (1969), 665. By emphasizing the affective ties between husband and wife, the Yahwist myth undermines the husband's bond to his consanguineous kin.

3. John Van Seters argues that the non-P material of Genesis was composed by the Yahwist during the exile (*Prologue to History: The Yahwist as Historian in Genesis* [Louisville, KY: Westminster John Knox, 1992]), but his focus is primarily on the literary activity of the "Yahwist," who produced the final composition of the non-P material. He gives less attention to the origin of the Yahwist's source material. In contrast, David Carr has uncovered the multiple layers of the non-P material, and has argued sufficiently that the primeval history and the Jacob narrative were first composed during the monarchy (*Reading the Fractures of Genesis: Historical and Literary Approaches* [Louisville, KY: Westminster John Knox. 1996], 233–89).

4. See Maurice Godelier, *Perspectives in Marxist Anthropology* (Cambridge: Cambridge University Press, 1977), and Jonathan Friedman, "Marxism, Structuralism and Vulgar Materialism," *Man* n.s. 9 (1974), 444–69.

5. See the discussion in Emmanuel Terray, "Classes and Class Consciousness in the Abron Kingdom of Gyaman," *Marxist Analysis and Social Anthropology*, M. Block, ed. (London: Malaby, 1975), 91.

6. Arthur Tuden, "An Exploration of a Precapitalist Mode of Production," *New Directions in Political Economy: An Approach from Anthropology*, M. B. Léons and F. Rothstein, eds. (Westport, CT: Greenwood, 1979), 27.
7. Marshall Sahlins, *Stone Age Economic* (New York: Aldine de Gruyter, 1972).
8. Carol Meyers, *Discovering Eve: Ancient Israelite Women in Context* (New York: Oxford University Press, 1988), 142.
9. See Shunya Bendor, *The Social Structure of Ancient Israel* (Jerusalem: Simor, 1996), 121–204; Niels Peter Lemche, *Early Israel: Anthropological and Historical Studies on the Israelite Society Before the Monarchy* (Supplements to *Vetus Testamentum* 37; Leiden: E. J. Brill, 1985), 245–90; and Norman Gottwald, *The Tribes of Yahweh: A Sociology of the Religion of Liberated Israel, 1250–1050 B.C.E.* (Maryknoll, NY: Orbis, 1979), 237–341.
10. Compare the discussion in Maurice Godelier, "Modes of Production, Kinship, and Demographic Structures," *Marxist Analysis and Social Anthropology*, M. Black, ed. (London: Malaby, 1975), 3–27.
11. See Jacob Black, "Tyranny as a Strategy for Survival in an 'Egalitarian' Society: Luri Facts versus an Anthropological Mystique," *Man* n.s. 7 (1972), 614–34.
12. S. N. Eisenstadt and L. Roniger, *Patrons, Clients and Friends: Interpersonal Relations and the Structure of Trust in Society* (Cambridge: Cambridge University Press, 1984), 206.
13. The archaeological evidence is discussed by John S. Holladay, Jr., "The Kingdoms of Israel and Judah: Economic Centralization in Iron IIA-B (ca. 1000–750 BCE)," *The Archaeology of Society in the Holy Land*, T. E. Levy, ed. (New York: Facts on File, 1995), 376–79.
14. Compare the discussion by Eric R. Wolf, "Kinship, Friendship, and Patron-Client Relations in Complex Societies," *The Social Anthropology of Complex Societies*, M. Banton, ed. (London: Tavistock, 1966), 1–22.
15. Eisenstadt and Roniger, *Patrons, Clients and Friends*, 209–10.
16. Patronage provides an appropriate framework for interpreting the patterned social relations that are observable in the biblical literature. Saul, for example, uses his gifts of fields and vineyards and appointments to military rank to secure the loyalty of his troops in his conflict with David (1 Sam 22:7–8). David, for his part, claims to be a faithful client to Saul, acknowledging him as his "father" (1 Sam 24:11). After David spares his life (a second time), Saul also acknowledges this relationship, repeatedly addressing David as his "son" (1 Sam 26:17–25). Elisha addresses Elijah as his patron by calling him "father" (2 Kgs 2:12). The servants of Naaman similarly address their patron as "father" (2 Kgs 5:13). 2 Kings 16:5–9 describes the patron-client relationship between Ahaz and Tiglath-pileser. In or-

der to gain protection against the assault of Rezin and Pekah, Ahaz sought to become the client of Tiglath-pileser. He initiated the relationship by seeking military help from Tiglath-pileser as his "servant and son." Ahaz then demonstrated his loyalty and friendship by sending gifts of silver and gold. Tiglath-pileser reciprocated by rescuing Ahaz from his enemies (2 Kgs 16:5–9). This suzerain-vassal relationship was an expression of patronage.

17. As a mode of appropriation, generalized exchange encompasses many forms of surplus appropriation under a single ideological superstructure that places the exchange in the context of reciprocity. Each party in the exchange receives some benefit—tangible or intangible. Although the exchange usually involves a material imbalance in favor of the patron, the ideology corresponding to this mode conceals the exploitation of the client. See Sahlins, *Stone Age Economics*, 134. Even state taxation could be interpreted as simply an institutionalized form of this exchange, representing the people's obligation to their great patron, the king (compare the priestly justification for the tithe in Num 18:21–24). By framing the exchange in terms of reciprocity, the ideology provides the conditions for the continual reproduction of the generalized exchange.
18. Eisenstadt and Roniger, *Patrons, Clients and Friends*, 216–18.
19. Eisenstadt and Roniger, *Patrons, Clients and Friends*, 214.
20. See the summary discussion by Paula McNutt, *Reconstructing the Society of Ancient Israel* (Library of Ancient Israel; Louisville, KY: Westminster John Knox, 1999), 195–200, and Jeremiah Cataldo, "Persian Policy and the Yehud Community During Nehemiah" *Journal for the Study of the Old Testament* 28, 2 (2003), 240–52.
21. In the tribal list in the Song of Deborah (Jud 5), for example, only ten tribes are listed and Ephraim is listed first. Moreover, Judah and Simeon are not listed at all, though they could be included in Benjamin (which is listed second) as an inclusive reference to the southern regions of Israel. Gilead is named instead of Gad, and Machir is included instead of Manasseh. Because of the particular configuration of the tribes and the prominence given to Ephraim, Benjamin, and Machir (listed third), scholars have argued that this tribal list reflects the political situation of premonarchical Israel. Other early tribal lists, in Deuteronomy 33 and Genesis 49, similarly reflect the political situation of early monarchic Israel (see the thorough analysis of Baruch Halpern, *The Emergence of Israel in Canaan* [Chico, CA: Scholars, 1983], 109–64).
22. See Robert R. Wilson, *Genealogy and History in the Biblical World* (New Haven: Yale University Press, 1977), 193–95.
23. See Frank Crüsemann, "Human Solidarity and Ethnic Identity: Israel's Self-Defi-

nition in the Genealogical System of Genesis," in *Ethnicity and the Bible*, M. G. Brett, ed. (Leiden: E. J. Brill, 1996), 57–76.

24. See Bernard M. Levinson, *Deuteronomy and the Hermeneutics of Legal Innovation* (New York: Oxford University Press, 1997), 53–97.

25. See also Carolyn Pressler, "Sexual Violence and Deuteronomic Law," *A Feminist Companion to Exodus to Deuteronomy*, A. Brenner, ed. (Sheffield: Sheffield Academic Press, 1994), 102–112.

26. That the Deuteronomic laws reduce the power of the *paterfamilias* is also recognized by Louis Stulman, "Encroachment in Deuteronomy: An Analysis of the Social World of the D Code," *Journal of Biblical Literature* 109 (1990), 613–32, and "Sex and Familial Crimes in the D Code: A Witness to Mores in Transition," *Journal for the Study of the Old Testament* 53 (1992), 47–63.

27. Halpern argues that a shift in the construction of the widely attested bench tombs can be detected. Although multi-chambered tombs were still used in the seventh century, Halpern notes an increase in the use of single-chambered bench tombs, especially in the countryside. In Jerusalem these smaller tombs were being constructed in the eighth century or earlier. For Halpern, the single-chambered bench tombs placed the focus of the funerary cult on the individual, married couple, or the nuclear family in contrast to the extended family or clan, which was the focus of the traditional multi-chambered tombs ("Jerusalem and the Lineages in the Seventh Century BCE: Kinship and the Rise of Individual Moral Liability" in *Law and Ideology in Monarchic Israel*, B. Halpern and D. W. Hobson, eds. [Sheffield: JSOT, 1991], 71–73).

28. See Elizabeth Bloch-Smith, *Judahite Burial Practices and Beliefs about the Dead* (Sheffield: Sheffield Academic Press, 1992), 109–32.

29. Scholars disagree on whether the Holiness Code (Lev 17–26) was composed before the Priestly Writer incorporated this material into his composition. Although the composition of the text probably dates to the exilic period at the earliest, much of the material has its origin in the period of the monarchy.

30. See also Naomi Steinberg, "The Deuteronomic Law Code and the Politics of State Centralization," *The Bible and the Politics of Exegesis: Essays in Honor of Norman Gottwald on His Sixty-Fifth Birthday*, D. Jobling, P. L. Day, and G. T. Sheppard, eds. (Cleveland: Pilgrim, 1991), 161–70.

31. Joel S. Kaminsky cautions that the individualism of Deuteronomy should not be interpreted as the similarly to the radical individualism that characterizes contemporary Western culture. The individualism of Deuteronomy remains embedded in the collective responsibility of the nation (*Corporate Responsibility in the Hebrew Bible* [Sheffield: Sheffield Academic Press, 1995], 119–23; see Deut 26:16–19). A

similar individualism has been attributed to Jeremiah 31:29–30 and Ezekiel 18. In the context of the destruction of Jerusalem by the Babylonians and the subsequent exile, both texts seek to refute the commonly embraced parable: "The fathers have eaten sour grapes, and the children's teeth are set on edge." The exilic generation of Judeans were placing the blame for the national catastrophe on the sins of the previous generation. Both Jeremiah and Ezekiel use the language of individualism to challenge the people to recognize their own guilt in the catastrophe. They reject the notion of trans-generational retribution, not corporate responsibility per se (Kaminsky, *Corporate Responsibility*, 139–78).

32. See the discussion in Carolyn Pressler, *The View of Women Found in the Deuteronomic Family Laws* (Berlin: Walter de Gruyter, 1993), 66–69.
33. See N. H. Snaith, "The Daughters of Zelophehad," *Vetus Testamentum* 16 (1966), 124–27.

Reshaping Family in Egypt:
The Islamist Discourse

JOHN C. M. CALVERT

Family life has always held an important place in the cultural traditions of Islam. This importance is reflected in the centrality of family law in the Shari'a, the code of conduct for Muslims based on the Qur'an, Islam's holy scripture, and the canonical collections of the hadith, which together provide Muslims with the guidance required to live purposeful lives in accordance with the divine mandate "Thus, the traditional family social structure as well as the roles and responsibilities of its members and family values, may be identified in the law."[1]

For much of Islam's history, the legal basis by which Muslim family life was articulated remained more or less constant. However, in the course of the twentieth century new discourses emerged in Muslim countries that questioned traditional Islamic understandings of family life, particularly in the realms of marriage, divorce, and succession. This divergence of social practice from tradition resulted from developments associated with secular modernity. In response to economic forces and cultural influences stemming from Europe, many Muslims, especially among the socioeconomic elite, began to question the system of conjugality and reproduction sanctioned by the Shari'a and to adopt, in various ways and to various degrees, Western-inspired patterns of family organization. In many cases the state took the lead in this development but individual reformers were also important. In the Arabic-speaking world, figures such as Huda Sha'rawi, Nazira Zayn al-Din, Malak Hifni Nasif, and Fatima Mernissi stand out.[2]

This article examines the conceptions of family that have been put forward by Islamist critics in response to these transformations in Muslim family life. Focusing on the case of Egypt, it argues that the dissipation of the traditional family in the face of increasing urban pressures, coupled with the felt need to distance the national culture from the colonizing Western "other," has prompted the Islamist opposition to provide Islamic direction to the contemporary family structure. In so far as it is possible, the Islamists aim to recreate in the modern environment the ethos associated with the "cosy, enclosed courtyard life of the extended family in the rural village and the traditional country town."[3] However, the entrenched nature of the socioeconomic change requires that they address the issue of family life within the new contexts of female employment and the withering of patriarchal authority within the household. The response of the Islamists to these financial and social pressures has been to "give the modern, nuclear middle-class family Islamic content in the definition of the private roles of men and women."[4] In so doing, they explicitly conceive the family as the moral center of Egyptian-Muslim collective life. In their view, the family is the most significant manifestation of Islamic exceptionalism.

These purposes and strategies are illustrated by drawing upon the writings of two prominent Islamists who have sought to instill a new Islamic consciousness within the institution of the Muslim family. One of these, Zaynab al-Ghazali, was a pioneer in the articulation of an Islamist vision for women and was close to Hasan al-Banna and the Muslim Brotherhood. The other, the Egyptian born, Qatar-based, Yusuf al-Qaradawi, represents a conservative, Shari'a minded version of Islamism that is increasingly influential within the matrices of the Egyptian state and society. Although these writer-activists differ on particulars, both are dedicated to the revival and propagation of what they consider to be authentic Islamic family values.

The Islamist Discourse on the Family

Islamism confounds easy description. In its most basic sense it may be defined as Islam interpreted as ideology to support political and social activism. Against the western hegemony of secularism, Islamists represent Islam not as a privatized religion, but as a comprehensive way of life concerned with all aspects of spiritual, social, and political existence. Although some Islamists call for the revival of the Caliphate, abolished in 1924 by Mustafa Kemal Ataturk, the founder of the Turkish Republic, others insist that a true Islamic system does not require "any particular political order—the historical Caliphate included. What matters is the purpose of the state and the principles it rests upon."⁵

Islamists decry Muslims who focus on the devotional practices of individual and community-oriented piety at the expense of seeking significant social and political change. In the Islamist view, Muslims are obliged to challenge the governments of the various postcolonial states in which they live on account of their having imposed on Muslim populations secular polices and western-cultural values, all at the expense of the Shari'a. Feeling their Islamic identity to be at risk, the Islamists seek to fortify it by selectively retrieving doctrines, beliefs, and practices taken from Islam's sacred past. Like their Christian and Jewish fundamentalist counterparts, "they may well consider that they are adopting the whole of the pure past, but their energies go into employing those features which will best reinforce their identity, keep their movements together, build defenses around its boundaries, and keep others at some distance."⁶ According to Islamists, once the Qur'anic principles have been fully implemented in the form of a reborn Shari'a, Muslim societies will find their God-given potential and slough off the defeatism, malaise and underdevelopment that has plagued their countries for over a century. Strengthened thus, the Islamic countries of the world will take their place among the developed nations and be shining examples of modernity imbued with spiritual values.

Since the middle decades of the twentieth century, Islamists have employed two basic strategies to bring about their moral revolution. One strategy, which is relatively small in terms of adherents, adopts the model of direct action. The aim of the radicals representative of this trend is to knock out the agencies of government, violently if needs be, and impose an Islamic state from above. In their reading, *Jihad*, which refers to the "endeavor" to construct a perfect Islamic polity, is a *fard 'ayn*, an obligation incumbent upon individual Muslims. Drawing upon the theories of the Egyptian Islamist ideologue Sayyid Qutb (1906–1966), some go so far as to regard those who do not actively participate in the quest for power, either directly or through financial contributions, as "disbelievers" (*kuffar*). This brand of Islamism, with its emphasis on self-sacrifice and its resort to assassination and terror, is familiar to Americans through the myopic eye of their news networks. Yet, with the notable exception of the 1979 Iranian Revolution, which unfolded in a distinctive Shi'ite setting, radical Islamism has scored few successes. The effective defeat of the

Jama'a al-Islamiyya and Islamic Jihad in Egypt and the withering of the Armed Islamic Group in Algeria, coupled with the intellectual poverty their ideologies, have prompted the diplomat-scholar Olivier Roy to speak of the "failure of political Islam." Within this context, Osama bin Laden's bid to generate an "Islamist International" would appear to be the last desperate gasp of the phenomenon, at least judging from the lukewarm response to his front against "Crusaders" and Jews of the overwhelming majority of Muslims in the Middle East and elsewhere.[7]

Far more important for our purposes is the other major strand of Islamism, which is far more widespread than the radical variety, encompassing significant numbers of middle class Muslim throughout the world. In contrast to the top-down model of the radicals, the goal of this orientation is to build an Islamic society from the ground up through processes of political advocacy and social mobilization. By winning the hearts and minds of the majority population, these "moderate" Islamists aim to pressure governments to accede to their demands. In countries such as Egypt, Pakistan, and Indonesia large Islamist organizations have developed networks of Islamic institutions, including schools, hospitals and charities. These exist, more or less, independently of the State and make available to the general population services that the government is either unable or unwilling to provide. In some countries, Islamists have been allowed to contest elections, though it is doubtful whether any government in the Muslim World would fully and without hesitation recognize an Islamist electoral victory. When, for example, the Islamist Salvation Front in Algeria appeared set to win that country's national elections in 1991, the government called a halt to the proceedings, triggering a grassroots rebellion that is still in progress. The Islamists representative of this approach may be compared in terms of their ethical demeanor and tactical orientation to elements within the Christian evangelical tradition, which have organized politically in the United States. Both are interested in cleansing state and society of political corruption and individual selfishness through the provision of scriptural principles. Both view with alarm "modern modes of sovereignty . . . and the rationalist cosmology that underlies and justifies them."[8]

In common with Islamist movements in other predominately Muslim countries, the moderate trend within Egyptian Islamism is by no means homogeneous. Among the several currents that compete for primacy among the population, pride of place belongs to the Muslim Brotherhood, the Middle East's most influential Islamist organization. Founded in 1928 by a primary school teacher named Hasan al-Banna (1906–1949), the purpose of the Brotherhood remains today what it was at its foundation, namely, "to give [the nation] light by means of the Qur'an [and] to destroy the darkness of materialism through knowing God."[9] In practice this has involved sophisticated and effective methods of propaganda employing all manner of media and the infiltration of Muslim Brothers into positions of influence within the institutions of civil society, most notably the professional syndicates.

Originally, the Brothers favored a rigid interpretation of the Shari'a, one that took into serious account the teachings of the *salaf*, the exemplary first generation of Muslims. However, more recently they have insisted that Islamic law be adapted in a more liberal manner to the needs of contemporary society. According to the Brothers, such a body of law will guarantee fair economic practice, integrity in public affairs, and a foreign policy for Egypt that prioritizes the interests of the worldwide community of Muslims. Further, the general population will be granted a voice in government through the instrument of *shura*, the Qur'anically sanctioned consultation of rulers with ruled. Indeed, in the view of many, "The existing parliamentary democracy in Egypt, however imperfect under [President] Mubarak and his predecessors, could be made to coexist comfortably with Islamic principles."[10] Always existing on the fringes of legality, the Muslim Brotherhood has experienced periods of tolerance interspersed with episodic persecutions at the hand of the state. In the late 1940s and again in the 1950s and early 1980s, the organization was subjected to massive arrests. The most recent of these state-enforced roundups occurred in 1995 in response to the threat that Brotherhood candidates posed to government party incumbents in the parliamentary elections. Despite these pressures, the Brotherhood and spin-off organizations such as the Hizb al-Wasat continue to exert a powerful influence among the disaffected, modern educated middle class.

The other major strand of moderate Islamism is more recent and draws quietly upon the support of the more traditional sectors of society, including the religious establishment of *'ulama* (religious scholars), the old style merchants of the bazaars, and religiously observant professionals and civil servants. It is closely tied to the ethical and moral teaching of al-Azhar, the venerable mosque-university in Cairo, but is also influenced by the more austere Wahhabi Islam brought by Egyptians returning from work in Saudi Arabia. More so than the Muslim Brotherhood, this version of Islamism works within the officially sanctioned order of the state and upholds the values of property, hierarchy, and authority with reference to established religious texts. In contrast to other more vociferous manifestations of Islamism, its activism is confined primarily to public preaching, publishing and in-house debate among *ulama*. For these reasons, it has sometimes been termed "conservative Islamism."[11]

The bases of Azhari-oriented Islamism predate the emergence of the Islamist current in the 1970s and were originally independent of it. During the presidencies of Gamal Abd al-Nasser (1954–1970) and Anwar Sadat (1970–1981), the state controlled significant aspects of the Azhar's bureaucracy and enjoyed the support of its Grand Shaykhs. The collusion between the state and the Azhar is illustrated in the fact that when a radical Islamist group chose to strike at the state in 1977, an Azhari shaykh appeared the natural target.[12] However, beginning in the late 1980s, many Azharis began to distance themselves from the government, especially on issues in which the state was perceived to deviate from Islamic norms. Throughout his tenure, Gad al-Haq 'Ali Gad al-Haq, Grand Shaykh of the Azhar from 1982–1996, consistently criticized the secular state on the basis of conservative interpretations of the Qur'an and the hadith. Today, rebels within the Azhar continue to censor cultural production and dictate standards of public morality, often in direct defiance of state policy. In so doing, they aim to put the Azhar forward as a player in the contemporary Islamic revival in Egypt, thus enabling it to escape social and political irrelevancy amid an increasingly religious population eager for moral reform.[13]

Despite differences relating to educational background and exegetical practice, the Muslim Brotherhood and the conservative shaykhs of the Azhar are united in their concern for the health of the Muslim family, which they consider to be at risk. The danger to family organization is considered to be two-pronged and relates in the first instance to the entry of women into the workplace, a trend that became especially strong in the decades following World War II. Historically, women who were compelled to work outside of the home for reasons of need were regarded as objects of pity and scorn. However, economic circumstances have made the practice common in recent decades—in the 1990s about 25 percent of Egyptian women undertook salaried employment.[14] Although many of these employed women take pride in the fact that they now perform jobs and are entering professions once reserved for men, for most Islamists it is a dangerous trend that leads to the dissolution of traditional gender roles associated with the extended family. In the Islamist view, women who work in factories, business, government and professional offices bring shame not only upon themselves but also upon their husbands and fathers for exposing them to this indignity. Muhammad Qutb, brother of Sayyid, summarizes this sentiment in the following paraphrase of one his writings: "The Industrial Revolution, in order to inhabit and exploit the earth has followed a damaging path. One source of damage is caused by the forcing of women to forsake the home and go to work. The family system has been destroyed, leading to unhappiness for both men and women."[15]

The economic participation of women in the workforce correlates with the state's support for the legal emancipation of women, the second major grievance of the Islamists. In the early years of the 1952 Egyptian revolution, Egyptian feminist organizations pressured the Nasser regime to address the issue of women's rights. The regime responded by granting women the rights to vote and hold public office. "In 1959, Labor Law 91 upheld women's right to work by providing them with fifty days maternity leave, providing daycare services where there were more than one hundred workers, and protecting women from unfair termination of work following the birth of a child."[16] At the same time, secular reformers pressured the government to make major amendments in the realm of Islamic family law. Minor changes to the Shari'a laws of personal status had already been made in 1920 and 1929, which allowed women to initiate divorce on the basis of non-maintenance and placed restrictions on the husband's right of divorce by pronouncement of *Talaq* (repudiation), "making sure that it must be a clear, sober, and deliberate decision."[17] In the 1960s, the attempt was made to go further in the reformist direction by abolishing the *bayt al-ta'a*, the right of a husband to retrieve a wife who has fled the conjugal household. However, the effort sputtered and it was not until the presidencies of Anwar Sadat and Husni Mubarak that serious attempts were made to implement the secular reforms mooted in the Nasser period. The most serious effort was Law 44 put forward by Sadat in 1979. Widely referred to as "Jihan's Law" on account of the influence on it exerted by Sadat's wife, its principle provision severely curtailed the institution of polygamy by stipulating that a second marriage constituted an injury to the first wife and was therefore grounds for divorce. Another important provision of the law favored the mother over the father as the custodial parent by granting her the right to the home during the period of custody.

Law 44 was hailed by secularists and human rights groups within Egypt but harshly condemned by a coalition of Muslim Brothers and Azhari shaykhs who regarded it as a serious challenge to the sanctity of the Islamic family unit. Bowing to the sustained pressure of the Islamists, the National Assembly struck down the law as unconstitutional in 1985. Shortly thereafter, a watered down version of Law 44 was passed that upheld polygamy by stating that a second marriage does not necessarily cause harm to the first wife unless she can prove otherwise and granted the divorced husband the exclusive right to his dwelling, although during the period of custody he was obligated to provide his wife with rental accommodation.[18]

The Islamists see the defense of the Shari'a's family code as the essential feature in their struggle against the secular state, which is seen to subordinate the identity and virtue of Egyptians to imported Western models of development. The struggle is intense, especially in that family law is the only feature of Shari'a law that survives in anything like full measure. In the course of the middle and late nineteenth century, the modernizing Muhammad 'Ali dynasty diminished the purview of the Shari'a by covering the realms of commercial, criminal, and civil law with legal codes adopted from Europe. From the mid-twentieth century onwards, these laws were modified and expanded by Egypt's republican regimes, which sought to limit religion to the private realm. In the view of state officials, the replacement of the Shari'a with secular law was in accord with the universal political and economic project of modernity. For the moderate Islamists of today, the protection of the laws of personal status is regarded as the necessary first stage in reclaiming the public sphere for Islam.

In these circumstances, it is perhaps natural that the Islamists should provide detailed instructions of the ethical precepts that the members of the Muslim family are to observe. Following the methodology of classical Islamic jurisprudence, Islamists propagate a system of classification that pronounces on all forms of behavioral and cultural activity as either *haram* (disallowed) or *halal* (allowed). These directives tend overwhelmingly to focus on issues related to the body, sexuality, reproduction, and legitimate authority within the household.[19] Some of the most controversial judgments came from the pen of the late Shaykh al-Azhar Gad al-Haq, who in 1994 issued a *fatwa* (juridical opinion) forbidding the practice of family planning. At the same time, he ruled against the state's attempt to eradicate the ancient practice of female circumcision, arguing that it is a religious duty for women as well as men.[20] Islamists who speak for the Muslim Brotherhood tend to be more didactic in their writings, eschewing the complex enterprise of jurisprudence in favor of broad moral principles. Nevertheless, the teachings of all moderate Islamists, whether Azharis or syndicate leaders, tend to resonate among the ranks of the pious middle class, many of whom are only one generation away from the old Muslim traditions of the countryside. The harsh and uncompromising nature of many of their pronouncements suggests that they function as boundary mechanisms, marking off "true" Muslim believers from the Westernized culture shared by the political elite. In their appeal to the Qur'an and Prophetic Sunna, Islamists are able to provide their quest for empowerment with a "cultural affect" grounded in the validating sentiment of Islamic identity. As Partha Chatterjee, a historian of colonial and postcolonial culture in Bengal writes, "The most powerful as well as the most creative results of the nationalist imagination in Asian and Africa are posited not on identity but rather on difference with the modular forms of national society propagated by the modern West."[21]

A Muslim Sister, Azhar Shaykh

Two examples will illustrate in more depth the Islamist discourse on the family. The first is the long career of Zaynab al-Ghazali (born 1918), whose reputation as an advocate of the Islamist cause remains strong and intact. The second example derives from several of the published writings of Shaykh Yusuf al-Qaradawi, an eminent jurist of the Azhar whose opinions carry weight among Sunni Muslims throughout the Arab World, not least in his home country of Egypt. Both thinkers address the pressures attendant on the contemporary Muslim family life and argue for the Muslim woman's return to domesticity.

Zaynab al-Ghazali's life has unfolded against the backdrop of Egypt's fractious national politics.[22] She began her career as a teenage disciple of Huda Sharawi, founder of the European-inspired Egyptian Feminist Union in the 1920s. However, in 1935, one year after joining Sharawi's organization, al-Ghazali took a different path and dedicated her life to

Islam. As Miriam Cooke writes, "It was not so much that she was embracing patriarchal values, but rather that . . . she was resisting what she considered to be the Western bias of the Egyptian Feminist Union, which had 'wanted to establish the civilization of the Western woman in Egypt and the rest of the Arab and Islamic worlds.'"[23] In 1936 al-Ghazali founded her own group, the Muslim Woman's Association whose purpose was to help women study Islam and to engage in welfare activities. Hasan al-Banna, Supreme Guide of the Muslim Brotherhood, tried to persuade al-Ghazali to incorporate her group into his own movement but she resisted, offering instead to foster a relationship between the two Islamist organizations based on close cooperation and mutual respect.

Al-Ghazali survived the Egyptian government's clampdown on Islamists in the late 1940s. However, she did not manage to elude the more severe proscriptions of the Nasser era. In 1965 al-Ghazali was caught in the police dragnet that followed revelations of an alleged Islamist conspiracy to overthrow the regime. She spent six years in prison, first at Liman Tura, where Sayyid Qutb was also interned, and then at Qanatir, the woman's prison in Cairo. Her year at Liman Tura is recounted in gripping detail in her autobiography, *Days from My Life* (translated as *Return of the Pharaoh*).[24] In it, she describes the whippings, mauling by attack dogs, and weighted suspensions and immersions in water that she endured at the hands of her jailors who, she tells us, invoked the name of Nasser "before speaking just as Muslims invoke God's name before performing any action."[25] Yet, through all of this torment, she was apparently able to protect her virtue. Her will remained unbroken and in the manner of the Muslim saints she was able to transcend the horror. After her release by President Anwar Sadat in 1971 she returned to the world to minister to others. Today she is aged and frail and resides at her apartment in Heliopolis, a well-heeled suburb of Cairo, where she sometimes entertains visitors.

Throughout her writings, al-Ghazali's starting point is the same. Although men and women are equal before God and have the same devotional and creedal obligations, they have unique functions within the family and society. The husband is the patriarch whose prime duty is to maintain the family financially and make decisions relevant to its overall welfare. The role of the woman, conversely, is that of wife and mother who defers to the authority of her husband. In al-Ghazali's view, these roles are complementary in the sense that one fulfills the other to form a complete whole. To step beyond these divinely ordained gender roles is to invite discord and disharmony, a circumstance to be avoided at all costs. In family life, as in other aspects of Islamic social existence, balance, or equilibrium, is the ideal.

The functional differentiation of labor of which al-Ghazali writes was, of course, a social condition articulated by Muslim jurists of the pre-modern era. However, unlike the medieval jurists, al-Ghazali regards this organizational principle not as the historical product of numerous juridical decisions but as an ideal type against which the irregularities of the current situation are to be measured. In other words, her discourse on the Muslim family emerges from within a context of cultural contestation that determines the content of its argument. The ideological thrust of her discourse is implicit in her judgment that all the ills that have befallen Muslim society can be traced to a "Western conspiracy" that has influenced women to leave the home "in order to obtain her food and drink from the fruits of her own labor."[26] It is evident also in the picture she paints of the happy Muslim home, which directly challenges notions of the "good life" put forward by Westerners. According to al-Ghazali, a woman must earn her husband's love and respect by fulfilling joyfully her domestic duties of childrearing, cooking, and cleaning. Moreover, she should protect her Islamic conscience by carefully choosing her friends who "should be respectable, virtuous, and well behaved. Their visits should be planned and used to discuss the Qur'anic views on the family and other issues of importance to women."[27] The significant aspects of a woman's life are to unfold within the family house or apartment. When outside this protected enclosure she must carry her seclusion with her in the form of modest dress, though the precise mode of a woman's dress is up to the husband, provided it is "within boundaries set by God."[28]

These and other stipulations suggest to the contemporary Westerner a condition of abject subservience to a domineering patriarchal authority. Yet al-Ghazali deflects such criticism by detailing how important the Muslim woman's role was to the construction of a modern, Islamic-based society and nation. In following the directives of the Qur'an and the example of the Prophet, a mother creates the conditions of a strong and pious household. Because a mother is the central figure in the lives of her children, she is in a unique position to instill in them a love of Islam and a deep appreciation of its social practice. Such an influence, according to al-Ghazali, will result in the raising of God-fearing men who will strive to establish and sustain a true Islamic polity. The responsibility of mothers to guide the development of their children requires that they be properly educated in the foundations of the faith, and this should be the prime goal of girls' education in the Muslim world. Indeed, according to al-Ghazali, so important is the role of women that the ultimate fortunes of the *umma*, the worldwide Muslim community, rest upon their shoulders. If much of the Muslim world today is weak and politically and economically dominated by the West, it is because Muslim women have failed in their primary task of building God fearing Muslim homes. It is a strong indictment, but one that is meant to challenge Muslim women to do better.

It is important to emphasize that the importance granted to women, whether Muslim or otherwise, in nation-building projects is of relatively recent provenance in world history. In this respect it is worth comparing al-Ghazali's injunctions with those of Qasim Amin (1865–1908), widely considered to be the progenitor of Egyptian feminism, who likewise identified the family as the source of national "moral strength," albeit in a secular setting. "The work of women in society is to form the morals of the nation," he wrote. "In our present society, and in Muslim countries in general, neither men nor women are properly educated and will therefore fail to create together a nurturing climate in the family."[29] In approaching the discourse of Zaynab al-Ghazali, we are on the distinctly modern terrain of the nation-state.

It remains to address the obvious contradiction between al-Ghazali's call for domesticity and her strident activism in the public sphere. One possible explanation is that she regarded herself as exceptional and thus exempt from the requirement she preached to others. In this reading of her behavior, al-Ghazali selflessly set herself the task of creating the space in which her Muslim sisters could realize their Islamic identity in an authentic fashion.[30] The seriousness with which she approached this responsibility is reflected in the way she approached her own marriages. Having divorced her first husband on account of his unwillingness to sanction her activism, she wrote in the contract of her second marriage the stipulation that she be allowed to carry on with her mission work, a condition her second husband evidently accepted. However, there may be another explanation. Miriam Cooke suggests that al-Ghazali prioritized women's responsibilities. During times of mission and struggle women who had fulfilled their domestic duties could, if they chose, devote their extra time and energy to the cause. As Cooke writes, her "argument strongly suggests that public action represents the culmination of private activities. These are not separate realms but rather behaviors ranging across a continuous spectrum. To be a wife and a mother in Islam entails a religious, political activism that cannot be confined to the home, even if that is where it starts."[31]

Zaynab al-Ghazali's principled activism contrasts to the deliberate and methodical practice of jurisprudence employed by Shaykh Yusuf al-Qaradawi (born 1928). Much more so than al-Ghazali, this shaykh of the Azhar peppers his writings with passages drawn from the Qur'an and the hadith, extrapolating from these rules of guidance for life. Al-Qaradawi was born in the Delta Province of Gharbiyya at a time when Egypt was still attempting to gain its full independence from Great Britain.[32] A combination of talent and ambition led him early on in his life to the Azhar in Cairo, where he studied the time-honored disciplines of *usul al-fiqh*, the fundaments of doctrine. His studies at the Azhar were periodically interrupted by his involvements with the Muslim Brotherhood. It was unusual for a scholar in training to be involved with what was essentially a lay movement. He distinguished himself by supporting his fellow Muslim Brothers in the anti-British Canal Zone insurgency of 1952 and by weathering arrests and a prison sentence. His Islamist stance did not endear him to the Nasser regime, which banned him from preaching in 1959. A break came in 1962 when the Azhar sent him to the Gulf emirate of Qatar to aid the ruling Al Thani family in establishing an institute of religious studies.

The support he gained from the Al Thani family provided al-Qaradawi with a comfort level he had not known in Egypt. His practical approach to the scripture established him as an Islamic thinker who was able to couch the learned discourse of the *rijal al-din*, the "men of religion," in terms that were accessible to a global audience of Muslims. More recently, his broadcasts on the Qatar-based al-Jazira TV, in addition to his much visited website,[33] have put him in the forefront of contemporary Muslim scholars who are attempting to craft an "enlightened *fiqh*" relevant to the requirements of modernity. In crafting his opinions he does not confine himself to the methodologies of any one of the four recognized schools (*madhahab*) of jurisprudence but rather makes his own independent judgments in ways that to him seem prudent.

On matters of family law, al-Qaradawi begins with the familiar premise of the family's fundamental importance to Islamic social life. As he writes in *The Lawful and Prohibited in Islam*, a book commissioned by the Azhar's Institute of Islamic Culture,

> It is only in the shade of a stable family that mercy, love, affection, and the capacity to sacrifice for others, develop in a human being, emotions without which a cohesive society cannot come into being. Thus, if there had been no family system, there would have been no society through which mankind would be able to progress towards perfection.[34]

He tells his readers how marriage and family is "the way of Islam," to such an extent that God's Book and the teachings of His Prophet decry the practice of celibacy, which is common, for instance, to the Christian and Hindu traditions. Yet, according to al-Qaradawi, the Muslim family is today under siege. The increasing numbers of Muslims living in the hedonistic societies of Europe and North America are especially at risk of absorbing behaviors at odds with God's plan for humankind. Al-Qaradawi makes the strong point that Muslims must be aware of the limits God has set for men and women in their family life and in other aspects of social existence. These boundaries, he writes, are in their best interests and are "part of the great trust [which] requires man to carry out the duties placed on him by Allah as his viceregent on earth and to assume accountability concerning them."[35]

According to al-Qaradawi, Islam is a practical religion that provides people with precautionary safeguards to protect them from their base inclinations, thus ensuring a healthy social environment. "When Islam prohibits something, it closes the avenues of approach to it. This is achieved by prohibiting every step and every means leading to the *haram* [forbidden]."[36] Matters relating to sexuality, he says, are especially dangerous. Echoing generations of scholars, he explains how the sexual urge is a potentially destabilizing force in society that is able to provoke even the most disciplined men to commit acts of fornication (*zina*), resulting in the confusion of lineages, bitterness in relationships, the spread of venereal disease, and the breakup of families.[37] Although the Qur'an and the hadith regard sexual activity as one of the desirable pleasures of life, it must, he says, be regulated if the negative consequences of this tempestuous urge are to be kept at bay.

The legitimate outlet provided by marriage is the most obvious solution to this quandary but al-Qaradawi prescribes other, complementary forms of external moral enforcement. With an eye on the youth of Islam's crowded and modernizing cities, al-Qaradawi underlines Islam's prohibition of men and women not married to one another meeting alone, unless they are relatives, for according to a well-documented hadith "Satan will be the third party with them."[38] Similarly, he emphasizes the Qur'anic injunction (Qur'an 24:30–31) that "believing men and women" should lower their gazes when addressing individuals of the opposite sex, since the eyes are capable of committing *zina* (fornication).[39] As regards women's dress, he follows the standard Islamist injunction of modesty but is more explicit than Zaynab al-Ghazali in the parts of a woman's body that should be covered, namely, all but the face and the hands. They should not wear cosmetics; the men, too, must dress modestly and must certainly cover the areas extending from their navels to their knees. These covered areas constitute the *'awra*, the areas of the body that Islam requires to be covered in front of others whether of the same or the opposite sex. Again, al-Qaradawi justifies his stipulations with reference to Qur'anic texts and hadith.[40] It is telling of al-Qaradawi's support of patriarchy that he lays much of the blame for the alleged loose morals of many contemporary Muslim women on the weakness of their husbands who are either unable or unwilling to control them. In another of his writings, "he issues an impassioned appeal for men to regain their masculinity and impose their will over women—if not for the sake of religion, then for the sake of their manhood."[41]

Al-Qaradawi's defense of patriarchy, which, in his view, has been unjustly compromised by the trend to women's emancipation, extends to his explanation of polygamy. Putting himself forward as its champion he points to the well-known Qur'anic condition that marriage to more than one woman is permissible only if the husband is able financially to maintain each wife at the same level and is able also to show them equal affection. According to al-Qaradawi, if a man is able to fulfill this condition he is helping to preserve the fabric of society. In taking a second, third, or even fourth wife he may end up taking care of a woman who might otherwise be denied family life. Even more importantly, he is directing his lust in legitimate channels. Striking a cynical tone, he stated,

Westerners who reject polygamy are doing it themselves. The difference between their polygamy and our polygamy is that theirs is immoral and inhuman. The man [in the West] . . . sleeps with more than one woman, and if [the second woman] gets pregnant, he denies responsibility for the child and supports the woman financially. It is nothing more than lust.[42]

In *The Lawful and the Prohibited in Islam*, al-Qaradawi states boldly that he did not adopt the apologetic stance common among some Muslims, whereby elements of Islam are emphasized that bear close resemblance to the liberal ethos of Europe while those that do not are either ignored or explained away. As he states, "I cannot compromise my religion by taking the West as my god after accepting Allah as the Lord, Islam as the religion, and Muhammad (peace be on him) as the Messenger."[43]

Conclusion

In much the same way as other moderate and conservative Islamists, Zaynab al-Ghazali and Shaykh Yusuf al-Qaradawi react in their writings to the social, economic, and cultural transformations that have marked Egypt in recent decades. In their view, these changes have had a negative effect on the structure and function of the family unit, which they consider to be the backbone of a viable Islamic society. Of particular concern to them are the entry of women into the workforce and the concomitant decline of male authority in the home. These developments in social life have weakened the interdependence of family members without replacing them with alternative relationships that command the same kind of moral force. In response to this confusion, the Islamists have sought to redirect men and women to a model defined by women's domesticity. In so doing, they explicitly articulate a position between modernity and indigenous culture. For while the Islamists are willing to recognize the utility of Western organizational and technical expertise, which they tend to view as value neutral, they are insistent that the inner domain of culture, especially as it relates to the intimate realm of home and family, remain wed to what they perceive to be Islamic norms. As indicated, much of the inspiration of this counter discourse comes from the juridical texts of medieval Islam. The Islamists selectively adopt these texts in order to refashion personal relations in ways congruent with the purposes of the Islamic revival.

Notes

1. John L. Esposito, *Women in Muslim Family Law* (Syracuse: Syracuse University Press, 1982), 13.
2. For studies of feminist reformers in the Arab World see Part 3 of Leila Ahmed's, *Women and Gender in Islam* (New Haven and London: Yale University Press, 1992) and Margot Badran, *Feminists, Islam, and Nation: Gender and the Making of Modern Egypt* (Princeton: Princeton University Press, 1995).
3. Nazih Ayubi, *Political Islam: Religion and Politics in the Arab World* (London: Routledge, 1991), 39.
4. Mervat F. Hatem, "Secularist and Islamist Discourses on Modernity in Egypt and the Evolution of the Postcolonial Nation-State," in *Islam, Gender and Social Change*, Yvonne Haddad and John Esposito, eds. (Baltimore: Oxford University Press, 1998), 92–3.
5. Gudrun Kramer, "Islamist Notions of Democracy," *Middle East Report* (July–August 1993), 4.
6. Martin E. Marty and R. Scott Appleby, "The Fundamentalisms Project: A User's Guide," in *Fundamentalisms Observed*, vol. 1, M. Marty and R. S. Appleby, eds. (Chicago and London: University of Chicago Press, 1991), ix.
7. Olivier Roy, *The Failure of Political Islam* (Cambridge, MA: Harvard University Press, 1994). See also the commentary of Salwa Ismail, "The Paradox of Islamist Politics," *Middle East Report* (Winter 2001), 34–39.
8. Roxanne L. Euben, *Enemy in the Mirror: Islamic Fundamentalism and the Limits of Modern Rationalism* (Princeton: Princeton University Press, 1999), 157.
9. Richard Mitchell, *The Society of the Muslim Brothers* (London: Oxford University Press, 1969), 29.
10. Geneive Abdo, *No God but God: Egypt and the Triumph of Islam* (Oxford: Oxford University Press, 2000), 75.
11. See Salwa Ismail, "Confronting the Other: Identity, Culture, Politics, and Conservative Islamism in Egypt," *International Journal of Middle East Studies* 30 (1998), 199–225, and Sami Zubaida, "Islam and the politics of Community and Citizenship," *Middle East Report* (Winter 2001), 20–27.
12. Gilles Kepel, *Muslim Extremism in Egypt: The Prophet and Pharaoh* (Berkeley: University of California Press, 1993), 96–101.
13. Abdo, *No God but God*, 66.
14. Carolyn Fluehr-Lobban, *Islamic Society in Practice* (Gainesville: University Press of Florida, 1994), 137.
15. Muhamad Qutb, "Community Life in Islam," http://www.zawaj.com/articles/community_qutb.html.

16. Hatem, "Secularist and Islamist Discourses," 87.
17. Fluerhr-Lobban, *Islamic Society in Practice*, 125.
18. Ibid., 126–30.
19. Ismail, "The Paradox of Islamist Politics," 36.
20. Abdo, *No God but God*, 55–57. Also see "Debate over Female Circumcision in Egypt," *Memri Special Dispatch Series*, no. 42, August 3, 1999 at http://www.memri.org.
21. Partha Chatterjee, *The Nation and its Fragments: Colonial and Postcolonial Histories* (Princeton: Princeton University Press, 1993), 5.
22. The following discussion on Zaynab al-Ghazali draws upon Ahmad, *Women and Gender in Islam*, 197–207; Miriam Cooke, *Women Claim Islam: Creating Islamic Feminism through Literature* (New York and London: Routledge, 2001), 83–106; Azza M. Karam, *Women, Islamisms and the State: Contemporary feminisms in Egypt* (London: MacMillan, 1998), 207–15; Hatem, "Secularist and Islamist Discourses," 95–97; Zainab al-Ghazali, *Return of the Pharaoh: Memoir in Nasir's Prision*, trans. Mokrane Guezzou (Leicester: The Islamic Foundation, 1994), and Valerie Hoffman, "An Islamic Activist: Zaynab al-Ghazali," in *Women and the Family in the Middle East: New Voices of Change*, Elizabeth W. Fernea, ed. (Austin: University of Texas Press, 1985).
23. Miriam Cooke, *Women Claim Islam*, 86.
24. See above note 22 for full reference.
25. Quoted in Cooke, *Women Claim Islam*, 93.
26. Quoted in Karam, *Women, Islamisms and the State*, 210.
27. Hatem, "Secularist and Islamist Discourses," 95.
28. Ibid., 97.
29. Quoted in Fayza Hassan, "A Spirit of Enchantment, " *Al-Ahram Weekly* (11–17 November 1999), at http://www.ahram.org.eg/weekly/1999/455/bk1_455.html. See also Albert Hourani, *Arabic Thought in the Liberal Age, 1798–1939* (Cambridge: Cambridge University Press, 1983), 164–70.
30. Karam, *Women, Islamism and the State*, 213–15.
31. Cooke, *Women Claim Islam*, 91.
32. Biographical details at http://www.Islamfortoday.com/qaradawi.htm#profile. For a brief summary of his thought, see Karam, *Women, Islamism and the State*, 192–97.
33. http://www.qaradawi.net.
34. Yusuf Al-Qaradawi, *The Lawful and the Prohibited in Islam (Al-Halal wal Haram fil Islam)*, trans. reviewed by Ahmad Zaki Hammad (Plainfield, IN: American Trust Publications, 1994), 149.

35. Ibid., 5.
36. Ibid., 149.
37. Ibid.
38. Ibid., 150.
39. Ibid., 153.
40. Ibid., 154–61.
41. Karam, *Women, Islamisms and the State*, 195.
42. "Islamic Clerics Explain the Rationale," *Memri: Inquiry and Analysis Series*, no. 42 (February 7, 2002) at http://www.memri.org.
43. al-Qaradawi, *The Lawful and the Prohibited in Islam*, 2–3.

The Sacramental Texture of Family Life: *A Contemporary Roman Catholic Perspective*

WENDY M. WRIGHT

Can family life be considered a spiritual milieu? Can mortgages, car pools, diapers, college tuition, and Thanksgiving at the in-laws qualify as formative environments for cultivating spiritual awareness? For centuries, the Christian spiritual tradition assumed that the authentic Spirit-filled life was to be discovered on the margins of society, in the hoary solitude of desert landscapes, the undisturbed silence of monastic cloister, or amid the exotic foreignness of the mission field. The spiritual life was set apart from the mundane, "worldly" cares of ordinary life and family.

Ambivalence of the Tradition

Marriage and child-rearing were for centuries seen as hindrances to discipleship. A prime example is the passion narrative of second-century martyrs Perpetua, a young Roman matron with infant at breast, and Felicitas, a pregnant slave girl. This story, widely circulated in the early church, demonstrated that both women chose Christian baptism although it meant leaving their children, disgracing their families, and certain death.[1] Perpetua and Felicitas were not alone during their era in thinking that family life and Christian commitment were not easily reconciled. The essays by Calef and Hunter in this volume also discuss the ambivalence of our Christian forbearers toward family life. None of those venerated by the nascent community as "saints" saw the biological family as the preferred place of spiritual formation. Indeed, the "true" family was the one in which members were all brothers and sisters with one heavenly father who replaced the "natural" family kinship unit.

It was not until the middle ages that individuals who lived as spouses and parents appeared on lists of those held up in the Christian liturgy as holy ones. Even then, their holiness had little to do with their families but with their heroic exploits on behalf of the faith, their visionary genius or their founding of religious institutions.[2] An example of this is discovered in the fourteenth century *Vitae* of Birgitta (Bridget) of Sweden. Renowned for her prophetic visions as well as for founding the Brigittine order and disposed toward an ascetic life, the Swedish queen, given her state responsibilities, was nevertheless obliged to honor the marital bed to produce heirs. Her *vita* depicts Birgitta's parental love as directed primarily toward the salvation of her children's souls, and insists that it should not detract from her love of God. Seeing a vision of the Virgin Mary and her own deceased mother, Ingeborg, Birgitta reported that her mother, like all the souls in heaven, might love her own child only if that child loved God.[3] The "spiritual motherhood" of holy women was a far more significant category in medieval spiritual literature than physical motherhood.[4] Even as lay spirituality flourished in the thirteenth and fourteenth centuries in such forms as the Northern European Beguines, the Italian mendicant Third Orders and the Spanish Beatas, the ideals of the authentic Christian life still were informed by the spirit that renounced "the world."[5] Much of the classical language of Christian spirituality was forged out of the experience of martyrdom, the desert, the monastery and the celibate life.

The rhetoric of Christian holiness changed during the period of sixteenth century reform. Protestants embraced marriage and family as the prescribed Christian vocation as they abandoned the set-apart life of the cloister. Thus Protestantism gave the Christian community a sense of family life as a calling. Indeed, among the Puritans we discover a rich language of the spirituality of the household with the father conceived as spiritual guide, the affirmation of spousal love as spiritually fruitful and the practice of daily family prayer.[6] Generally, Protestant traditions over the centuries either rejected or gradually abandoned the traditional language of the spiritual life.

Early modern Catholicism did encourage married persons to think of their Christian vocation in terms of commitment to those they had been given to love. Francis de Sales' popular seventeenth century spiritual manual for laity, *Introduction to the Devout Life,* counseled married couples to invite God's "well beloved Son" to their marriage, "as He was to that of Cana. Then the wine of His consolation and blessing would never be wanting."[7] In fact, I will be drawing upon the Christian humanist perspective from which de Sales hails in the following. Yet for centuries the Catholic Church continued to uphold the superiority of the vowed, celibate life as more "perfect" than the ordinary life of family ties. Echoes of this are still heard in the twentieth century documents of Vatican II that, while proclaiming the "universal call to holiness," assert that the evangelical counsels that frame traditional vowed religious life outline the spiritually superior path.[8]

Family Spirituality Today

At the dawn of the new millennium, clearly things have changed; family and spirituality are topics that are *au courant*. The rhetoric of family values thunders from American pulpits across denominations, and serious scientific studies of family life and family ministry, motivated by Christian concern for marital and familial stability, have emerged.[9] Creighton University's own Center for Marriage and Family, for example, is dedicated to the proactive promotion of healthy Christian marriages and families in a contemporary culture of divorce and family dissolution. Pope John Paul II, more than any of his papal predecessors, has emphasized the centrality of the family in Christian life.[10] The ecumenical professional journal *Family Ministry: Empowering Through Faith* draws upon theological and social scientific perspectives to help those who tend Christian households do their jobs well. The Center for Congregations and Family Ministries at Louisville Presbyterian Seminary seeks to strengthen the church's ability to support families and their capacity to nurture the life of faith. And James Dobson's institute, *Focus on the Family*, represents a theologically conservative, Evangelical approach to the many issues facing American families today. Considerable resources across the denominational spectrum are allocated for ministry to families. In Christian circles family is big.

So is spirituality big. A cursory visit to any American bookstore will usher the browser into a virtual library of new books on "spirituality," a category until recently unknown.[11] The spirituality section can include self-help books, "wellness" literature, popular psychology, inspirational titles that draw eclectically from varied religious traditions, nature writing, gender studies, and any number of categories. Many of these books treat of the "sacred in the ordinary" or the awakening of perception to the holy in the natural, familiar world of everyday. Still, it remains difficult for many persons to equate the spiritual journey with the adventure of family life. The term spirituality often tends to suggest the cultivation of inner calm and the creation of peaceful environments while family means chaos, busyness and conflict, hardly a place to focus on the spiritual. Or if family and spirituality are linked, often the dominant model of family ministry, which is oriented to crisis intervention or problem solving, informs the approach. Or the focus is pedagogical and moral, concerned primarily with raising children in the faith.[12] While this is clearly a portion of the spirituality of family life, I would assert that the spiritual life in all its fullness is no stranger to the home.

Catholic Sacramentality

The assumption that underlies all schools of Christian spirituality, one that is drawn from the book of Genesis, is that human beings are *imago dei,* created in the divine image and likeness. However, the Genesis account also suggests that the divine image with which we are imprinted does not retain its original vitality. Depending upon the denominational perspective and the resultant theological anthropology held, that image is wounded, tarnished, marred, or even effaced.[13] Denominations that hold that the *imago dei* is not beyond repair emphasize spiritual formation, the gradual reshaping and reclaiming of the entire person by the Spirit of God so that he or she might become what God intended. Spiritual practices of all sorts—prayer, fasting, worship, spiritual reading, the works of mercy, spiritual guidance, disciplines of all kinds—are designed to assist this process of formation. The denomination within which I find myself, the Roman Catholic, has a long and varied history of spiritual practice and a long history of affirming that, while all human effort is prompted and sustained by grace, what human beings do in the way of practice matters. Men and women grow, become holy, and gain spiritual wisdom through practice. Roman Catholicism also has been described as having a sacramental sensibility. The imaginative world of Catholics tends to be sacramental in the sense that created reality is perceived as revelatory of the presence of God. The entire fabric of this visible world is potentially a window upon the invisible world. Catholic perceptions tend to be analogical, that is, they start with the premise that one can deduce something about the creator from the creation. Metaphors abound in the Catholic imagination; the ultimate mystery that is God can be intuited as "like" this or that sensible thing. For example, something of divine Love might be known in the experience of human love.[14] It is this sacramental, analogical sensitivity that allows a glimpse of the spiritual in the midst of family life.

A Salesian Perspective

I locate myself more specifically within the Salesian tradition, a school of Catholic spirituality born in the seventeenth century that takes its name and vision from its founders, Francis de Sales and Jane de Chantal. Both Salesian spirituality and its cousin, the more familiar Ignatian spirituality, which is based on the teachings of the sixteenth century Basque Ignatius of Loyola, are spiritual traditions born in an historical era when Humanism was a prevalent Christian philosophy.[15] The Christian Humanism implied in Salesian and Ignatian spirituality gives rise to a particularly positive view of the created world and of human nature. The created world is perceived as revelatory of divine life and as God-directed. Moreover, what is deepest and truest in human beings is not their sinfulness, their propensity to turn away from God, but their goodness, their innate longing to orient to the divine source. That deep and essential goodness, that longing for God, is an expression of the *imago dei*. Created by the Trinitarian God of Love, human beings are created to know and love God in return. The spiritual journey is about that return. It is about the loving union of divine and human hearts. But the journey is not only concerned with an ultimate destination—union—but with the process of journeying as well. One travels with others. The traveling itself is revelatory: God is glimpsed along the way in relationships of love and care. One expects to see God in what is most human. One expects to glimpse the holy within the created fabric of human life. The mystery of the incarnation, in which the human and divine meet and, as it were, kiss, is central to Salesian spirituality. This mystery reveals itself whenever and wherever the human and divine intersect, whether that be in worship, in intentional spiritual discipline or in the ordinary fabric of everyday life: in work, in community, in family. Salesian spirituality affirms that the encounter with the infinite does not occur in by-passing the finite—by leaping over or transcending it—but precisely in going through the finite. The *particular* place is the privileged place of encounter with the universal.[16]

With these more theoretical considerations in place, I offer now an example of what I hope will illustrate the truth that the spiritual life in all its fullness is no stranger to the home. As suggested, my primary resource is the Christian spiritual tradition itself, elaborated, enriched and sometimes modified or corrected by the lived experience of family life. The particular example that follows was written a number of years ago.[17] In the piece, the experience of parenting a teenaged daughter is brought together with wisdom from the spiritual heritage. This is not a matter of superimposing that heritage upon family life (as if one could consult a spiritual master to claim here is what so and so says to do in *this* case) but a matter of letting varied fragments of knowing culled from the tradition to emerge in the process of parenting. The specific resources in this case are scripture, the ancient practice of spiritual discernment, and the devotional tradition.[18]

The Sacramental Texture of Family Life

A summer afternoon, Santa Barbara, 1977.

From the porch, my view is azure and green, mottled with red and gold. At the horizon, the thin blue of the sky fades imperceptibly into the richer blue of the sea. The gradual descent of the land between myself and the distant shore is marked by descending tiers of trees: palms, jacaranda, and olives with their muted greens of every shade. They canopy the patchwork of adobe tile roofs. Gold bursts of sunlight caught by glass, metal, and water glitter and disappear.

Suddenly, I become aware of it: a flick, a brush. So swift and subtle I catch my breath and bring the swing to a full stop, hoping to feel it again. Yes, there it is again, like the touch of an angel's wing or feather passing in the breeze. For months now I have known. All the tests came back positive. The predictable physiological symptoms followed suit: the cessation of bleeding, the fatigue, nausea, tenderness, weight loss then gain. But somehow it still did not feel real—more like a lingering illness than an impending birth. But here, on this wooden porch swing on a summer's azure afternoon, I experience it and I do know. The momentary quickening—an angel's touch—from an aliveness at the root of my being speaks the volumes all the other assurances cannot.

Christians for centuries have not only listened to scripture but they have gazed on scripture as well in the stained glass, statuary, paintings, mosaics, and carvings that have adorned their places of worship. Thus they have experienced the Word of God not only as a narrative but also as a series of visual moments—snapshots, so to speak—with which they prayed. They gazed at and into the images about them not only to be informed of the story of faith but also to be formed, to be changed by and into the image they beheld. Among the images especially favored in the tradition is the annunciation, the image described in Luke of the young girl, Mary, usually shown seated alone in a quiet room or open space, receiving an unexpected message from her angelic visitor. She is frequently depicted as bemused, startled, or humbled, yet always open to receive him. Her visitor is generally a majestic presence, unfurling his wide wings, never intrusive, always respectful of her reticence. The salutation is simple: Hail! The import of the greeting staggering: You shall bear a child, God's child. For generations of believers, Mary has been not only the chosen mother of the child Jesus but the model of the human soul in its most profound relationship with God. In her humble yet welcoming reception of the angel, she exemplifies the spiritual attitude that each person must adopt in order that God might become incarnate, might be implanted in human hearts and minds, gestate, be born, and made manifest in the world. Her free and chosen assent—her yes—mirrors the yes each one must give to become a Mother of God, to become someone who bears divine life into the world. Mary was a woman visited, a woman made aware of the aliveness at the root of her being, the quickening within known through the touch of a passing angel's wing.

For centuries Christians have sought the brush of wings, the assurance that God's life quickens in us. We ask, where do we look? What does it feel like? How do we listen? Will we know? And we have named this inner art of paying attention. We have called it "the discernment of spirits." Through time we have honed the practice of this art, for it is at the core of the spiritual life. Although there are various methods or schools of thought on discernment—Ignatian, Quaker, San Juanist—in general it might be said that discernment is about two things: attentiveness and discrimination.[19]

We have claimed that the spiritual life consists in paying attention to the Spirit of God moving in and among us and distinguishing that Spirit from the vast array of other spirits vying for our attention. These other spirits have been characterized as having a variety of origins: they may be spirits of "the world" (the purposes of normative culture that do not align with the purposes of God), spirits of the "flesh" (variously conceived as the addictive demands of bodily need or the ego-centric demands of the self-absorbed life), or the spirit of the "evil one" (active forces working against good or the disordered meanderings of the human heart and mind that destroy and enslave rather than enliven and free). However the spirits are conceived, the Spirit of God is one touch, one inner brush among many, and much of the spiritual life consists in knowing which touch is which.

If it is to the annunciation of the angel Gabriel to the virgin in Nazareth that the church has looked to enact the dynamic of the human soul welcoming the Spirit of God, it has looked to another scriptural image to enact the drama of discernment. That image is of Jesus and his temptation in the wilderness. The three synoptic gospels (Matthew, Mark, and Luke) all contain accounts of this event. In each case, it is recorded as occurring immediately after Jesus' baptism by John the Baptist. Above the waters of the river Jordan, the Spirit descends and a voice declares that Jesus is God's beloved son. God's favor rests on him. The Spirit then prompts the favored one to venture into the wilderness for forty days. There he encounters Satan and his wiles. The temptations to change stones into bread in his hunger, to throw himself off a parapet so that angels will rescue him, and to worship Satan in exchange for all the kingdoms he surveys, have represented, in the minds of generations of interpreters, the temptations of power, pride, and possession.

To the prayerful viewer, the scene of the wilderness temptation is not only a narrative segment from Jesus' life but a paradigmatic image on which to gaze to learn something of the nature of the human soul. It is an image of discernment. Jesus recognizes the nature of the attractive, alluring, invitations to be able to procure what one hungers for, to be admired, even worshipped, and to own all imaginable goods. They are suggestions from a spirit different from the one that compelled him into the desert in the first place. That first Spirit prompted him to refuse and to embrace powerlessness, humility, and poverty. When he had embraced these, scripture relays, he was ministered to by angels.

The wilderness scene gives us a vivid, if not too subtle, image of the discrimination involved in discernment. It says that there are desert places into which God invites us where we will be asked to pay attention, to look deep into our lives, and to sort out the various motivations for our thoughts and actions. Of the many inner and outer voices that prompt us, which will we heed?

In traditional iconography, the baptism in the Jordan and the temptation in the wilderness are distinct. Stained-glass windows and altarpieces do not visually connect the two events. Yet, as narrative, scripture makes it clear that the two are inseparable. Jesus is baptized, the Spirit descends, the voice declares, "This is my beloved Son." Then that Spirit leads him out into the desert. Some years ago, while on retreat, I heard a reflection on this series of actions. It was significant, the preacher claimed, not only that the Spirit sent Jesus forth but that the Spirit sent him forth having heard that he was "child" and, perhaps even more important, that he was "beloved." It was this deep-rooted knowledge of this beloved-ness that made the desert discernment possible. It was his identity as cherished child that enabled the carpenter from Nazareth to define himself as other than one who wields power, commands prestige, or holds wealth.

This insight arrests my attention. It says discernment is not simply about resisting what is evil, self-absorbed, or destructive. It is about foundational identity. It is about who we know ourselves ultimately to be. It is about paying attention to the ways in which the limited power we wield, the modest respect we command, the taken-for-granted resources we hold provide us with our primary sense of meaning. To what extent do we "experience" ourselves primarily as civic and church leaders or as respectable citizens or conscientious parents or homeowners or degree holders or job-holders and, only later or not at all, as beloved daughters and sons of God?

We are beloved not because of what *we* do. *We* are beloved because we are.

≈≈≈

Discernment requires that we pay attention. We must attend to both what goes on around us and within us. An attentive pregnant woman pays attention on many levels. She is aware of the need for proper food, rest, and exercise for her body, which now must operate at peak capacity. She is aware, especially if she is a first-time mother, of the advice, stories, encouragement, and admonitions of doctors, relatives, and friends. She is aware of the changing configuration of her form, the new ways of moving and being required of her. She notes new thoughts and feelings, the dreams coming to be, the emerging fears, the changing relationships with her partner, parents, or siblings. She realizes she is changing. Her sense of who she is is changing. She feels the dynamism of the strong other growing within her—its habits and cycles, its enlarging demands.

Perhaps she is attentive to the mystery of life itself that impinges more and more on her ordinary consciousness: the God questions, the life-and-death questions, the deep-joy and deep-grieving questions.

Discernment asks us to attend to what goes on around us and within us. Ideally, this attentiveness goes on much of the time, a sort of low-level, constant, spiritual sifting of the data of our experience. But there are times when discernment becomes much more focused, when a crossroad is reached or a choice called for. At times like these, the cumulative wisdom of tradition tells us to pay attention on many levels, to consult scripture, to seek the advice of trusted advisers, to heed the *sensus fidelium* (the collective sense of the faithful), to read widely and deeply the best ancient and contemporary thinking, to pray, to attend to the prick of conscience and to the yearnings and dreamings of our hearts, to watch, to wait, to listen.

Discernment is about discriminating, sifting through and evaluating the evidence of our focused attention. It is not, however, identical to problem solving. It is not simply a question of lining up the pros and cons concerning a particular decision we must make and then judging which choice is feasible or determining which gains the most support or which will benefit us, or others, in the long run. Discernment is more like the turning of the sunflower to the sun, or the intuitive hunch of the scientist seeking new and creative solutions for unexplainable, contradictory observations, or the restless seeking of a heart longing to find its way home to an estranged lover, or the artistry of the musician, sculptor, or choreographer delineating in sound, stone, or the human body the emergent, self-propellant, rightful line that says yes.

Discernment is about feeling texture, assessing weight, watching the plumb line, listening for overtones, searching for shards, feeling the quickening, surrendering to love. It is being grasped in the Spirit's arms and led in the rhythms of an unknown dance.

Winter, the middle of the night, Omaha, Nebraska, 1995.
I lie awake in the darkened bedroom, my husband's somnambulant breathing accompanied on and off by the onrush of sound from the forced-air heating ducts. I press my ear to the air space between these two respirations, where I hear the click of the key in the downstairs lock that signals my teenage daughter's arrival home, just before her 1 a.m. curfew. I try to read her step—cautious or self-assured, fatigued or ener-

gized? I note the tone of her response to my verbal welcome—hearty, irritated, ringing with contentment? Or tense and preoccupied?

It has been a roller-coaster year—not atypical, others assure me, but painful nonetheless, pressing all the buttons and boundaries that have been in place for some time. Her bedroom door snaps smartly shut behind her—an audible symbol of the unique, emergent psychic space she is structuring for herself. I stare into the dark void above the bed, aware now of my own breath, a light cadence like a descant above my sleeping spouse's airway melody and the furnace's punctuating bass.

In the last year, there have been many decisions to make about how to respond to the vigorous stretching of adolescent wings. We have received advice about tough love, and about unconditional acceptance, admonitions to stand firm and to make space. We've muddled through on the level of "how to" and "what's best" and problem solving. But the level on which it has been perhaps the most challenging has been the level of spiritual discernment. By this I do not mean, What would God want the perfect family to look like? or What are the proper roles that daughter, father, mother, and son are supposed to play? No, the spiritual discernment has been more akin to the sort of groping, confused reorientation I experienced as a first-time mother when the call was to recast myself as a parent, to learn painfully, by trial and error, not only the new psychological identity but the new spiritual challenges to which that identity called me.

The plumb-line question that has emerged in this recent process is, Where does love lie? I have learned a lot about myself, which, the spiritual masters say, is the beginning of knowing God. Now, having thought all along that I was cultivating a certain simplicity of person, I discover myself to be in fact a person preoccupied with unfavorable appearances. My heretofore-always-commendable daughter has been brashly unconcerned about what anyone else thinks. And I have had to struggle to avoid seeing this primarily as a projection of my own inadequate parenting skills; I've struggled to let go of embarrassment about what others might think and keep faith with her in her uniqueness. "Can't you make this awkward transition a little less public?," I find myself thinking to her. But the question rips away my own precarious spiritualized mask. If it looks good, it must be good. Win God's and others' love by looking good. Cover up the deep wounds. Keep them private. Maybe they'll just go away. And I am forced back to the question, Where does love lie? The depth to which the question falls—the level of the Spirit's dancing—says, "Looking good is not the point. The point is, you don't earn beloved-ness. You receive it. It descends like a dove, unbidden, and you open your ears and heart and life and receive."

I have learned too that my cowardice, my fear of not being loved in return, can masquerade as maternal solicitude, that my inability to love the real wounds, the real out-of-boundness in myself because they seem unlovable is, in fact, a kind of spiritual pride, a closing in on myself away from the radical freedom and joy to which we are invited. I have groped about asking, Where does love lie, and for whom and when and how? The hundreds of half-answers to the questions emerge only in the groping, only in the process of feeling texture, assessing weight, listening for overtones, feeling the quickening, surrendering to love.

≈≈≈

When Jesus faced the temptations in the wilderness, he had just heard himself named as beloved child. What did he have to face in his own heart that kept him from knowing, from really embracing that truth? What groping did he do in the desert to find the level at which the Spirit moves free? What attentiveness, what discrimination was called for? Scripture says that when he was done, angels came and ministered to him. They must have done more than touch him as they passed; they must have unfurled their wings and beat the air and sung out for sheer Joy.

Notes

1. The *Passion of Perpetua and Felicitas* is found in *The Acts of Christian Martyrs*, Henry Chadwick, ed., Herbert Mursillo, trans. (Oxford: Clarendon, 1972).
2. On the development models of sanctity in Christian tradition, see Kenneth L. Woodward, *Making Saints: How the Catholic Church Determines Who Becomes a Saint, Who Doesn't and Why.* (New York: Simon and Schuster, 1990). Woodward makes a point of the fact that throughout the medieval era, monastic, celibate forms of sanctity predominated. Even when laypersons were recognized as holy, their spirituality often mimicked the older models. This continues to be the case in the present. There is no one on the official sanctoral calendar of the Catholic Church canonized because of their exemplary lives as parents or spouses.

3. Clarissa W. Atkinson, *The Oldest Vocation: Christian Motherhood in the Middle Ages* (Ithaca: Cornell University Press, 1991), 175. See also Julia Bolton Holloway, *Saint Bride and Her Book: Birgitta of Sweden's Revelations* (Newburyport, MA: Focus Texts, 1992).
4. Atkinson, 64ff.
5. Cf. *Lay Sanctity, Medieval and Modern: a Search for Models*, Ann W. Astell, ed. (Notre Dame: Notre Dame University Press, 2002).
6. See Belden Lane, "Two Schools of Desire: Nature and Marriage in Seventeenth Century Puritanism," *Church History* 69, 2 (2000), 372–402.
7. Francis de Sales, *Introduction the Devout Life*, John K. Ryan, trans. (Garden City: Doubleday Image Books, 1955), 214.
8. See *Lumen Gentium, Dogmatic Constitution on the Church* especially chapters 5, 6 and 7 on the Universal Call to Holiness, Religious Life, and the Eschatological Nature of the Pilgrim Church.
9. See the series of books produced by the Religion, Culture, and Family project, directed by Don Browning. The series, published by Westminster, John Knox Press in Louisville, KY, includes: *From Culture Wars to Common Ground: Religion and the American Family Debate,* Don S. Browning, Bonnie J. Miller-McLemore, Pamela D. Couture, K. Brynolf Lyon and Robert M. Franklin, eds. (1997), John Witte, Jr., *From Sacrament to Contract: Marriage, Religion and Law in Western Tradition* (1997), Max L. Stackhouse, *Covenant and Commitments: Faith, Family and Economic Life* (1997), Ted Peters, *For the Love of Children: Genetic Technology and the Future of the Family* (1996), *Faith Traditions and the Family,* Phyllis D. Airhart and Margaret Lamberts Bendroth, eds. (1996), *Religion, Feminism and the Family,* Anne Carr and Mary Stewart Van Leeuwen, eds. (1996), Leo Perdue, Joseph Blenkinsopp, John J. Collins, and Carol Meyers, *Families in Ancient Israel* (1997), Carolyn Osiek and David Balch, *Families in the New Testament World: Households and House Churches* (1997).
10. See Joseph F. Chorpenning, OSFS, "Icon of Family and Religious Life: the Historical Development of the Holy Family Devotion," in *The Holy Family as Prototype of the Civilization of Love: Images from the Viceregal Americas*, Joseph F. Chorpenning, OSFS, ed. (Philadelphia: St. Joseph's University Press, 1996), 3–40, and Chorpenning's *The Holy Family Devotion: a Brief History* (Montréal: Centre de recherche et de documentation Oratoire Saint-Joseph, 1997).
11. The bookstore category "religion" still exists but designates books identified with a specific faith tradition.
12. The best of this genre is John H. Westerhoff's classic book that originally ap-

peared in the 1970s. It has been revised and updated as *Will Our Children Have Faith?* (Morehouse Publishing, 2000).

13. Theologies, such as classic Lutheranism, that claim that the *imago dei* is effaced usually do not have much tolerance for notions of spiritual growth or intentional practices directed toward sanctification.

14. An accessible presentation of this imaginative world is found in Andrew Greeley, *The Catholic Imagination* (Berkeley/Los Angeles/London: University of California Press, 2000).

15. On Salesian spirituality see *Francis de Sales and Jane de Chantal: Letters of Spiritual Direction*, Péronne Marie Thibert, VHM, trans. (Mahwah, NJ: Paulist, 1988). See also Wendy M. Wright, "The Salesian-Ignatian Imagination and Familied Life," in *The Holy Family in Art and Devotion*, Joseph F. Chorpenning, OSFS, ed. (Philadelphia: Saint Joseph's University Press, 1998), 104–8.

16. For an extended discussion of the this idea of the finite and the infinite and the Catholic imagination see Gerald J. Bednar, *Faith As Imagination: the Contribution of William F. Lynch, SJ* (Kansas City: Sheed and Ward, 1996). It is Lynch who has written extensively on this topic and Bednar pulls together his varied insights.

17. This piece, with the title "Passing Angels: the Arts of Spiritual Discernment," originally appeared in an extended form in *Weavings* 10, 6 (1995): 6-15. It is incorporated in chapter 2 in my *Seasons of a Family's Life: Cultivating a Contemplative Spirit at Home* (San Francisco: Jossey-Bass, 2003).

18. Some of the books on family spirituality that have sustained me over the years and that take seriously the sacramental approach are Dolores Leckey, *The Ordinary Way: A Family Spirituality* (New York: Crossroad, 1982), Ernest Boyer, Jr., *Finding God at Home: Family Life as Spiritual Discipline*, originally published as *A Way in the World*, (San Francisco: Harper and Row, 1988), Gertrude Mueller Nelson, *To Dance With God: Family Ritual and Community Celebration* (New York: Paulist, 1986), David M. Thomas, *Christian Marriage: A Journey Together* (Wilmington, Delaware: Michael Glazier, 1990), Anne Broyles, *Growing Together in Love: God Known Through Family Life* (Nashville: Upper Room, 1993), Edward Hays, *Prayers for the Domestic Church: A Handbook for Worship in the Home* (Easton, KS: Forest of Peace Books, 1979). A more recent contribution is Denise Roy, *My Monastery is a Minivan: Where the Daily is Divine and the Routine becomes Prayer* (Chicago: Loyola, 2001).

19. Ignatian discernment (originated by the sixteenth century Spaniard, Ignatius of Loyola, founder of the Jesuits) stresses the discrimination of one's affectivity—how one feels. Put simply (although Ignatian discernment both in theory and practice is not simple), one is asked to pay attention to the "consolations" or "des-

olations" that result as one considers possibilities or undertakes actions. In general, and in the long term, for persons already embarked on a journey of faith, the Spirit of God presents itself as consoling, as peace and goodness. Spirits of other origins tend ultimately to give rise to experiences of confusion, disharmony, and anxiety. In the seventeenth and eighteenth centuries, The Society of Friends, or Quakers, developed a mode of communal discernment, a listening in shared silence, to the "weight" or grounded-ness of various alternatives proposed for consideration. The silence of the Quaker meeting itself, in its gravity or depth, was discriminated and the hearing of such depth validated by the intuitive acknowledgment of those gathered. The writings of a sixteenth century Carmelite mystic, John of the Cross, provide us with another alternative or complementary interpretation of discernment. A poet and spiritual theologian, John wrote of the desire of the human soul for its beloved, God. He described the process of this intense desiring as a gradual, ecstatic, painful process of stripping away all objects of desire and coming to know that it is only God, in God's unfathomable, unknowable mystery, where desire's end can be found. Desire propels one into intimacy with a love whose truest dynamics are death and resurrection. John often interprets the experience of inner suffering and pain that result from responding to divine desire as a sign that the spiritual purgation or emptying necessary for divine union is taking place.

Kids Caught in the Crossfire:
Reflections on the School Wars

BETTE NOVIT EVANS

Public schools have always been battlefields in the wars over the place of religion in public life in the United States. Indeed, controversies over religion in the public schools are almost a staple of the evening news. Commentators are still debating the Ninth Circuit decision that the words "under God" in the Pledge of Allegiance recited by school children violate the Establishment Clause,[1] and the US Supreme Court ruling that the Establishment Clause is not violated by state-funded vouchers used to pay tuition at private religious schools.[2] These controversies came at the heels of continuing controversies over prayers at public school functions, the content of teaching materials, assignments, and books in school libraries, as well as extra curricular activities. I refer to these conflicts in the aggregate as the "school wars." Since the beginning of public education in the United States, a variety of critics have found fault with the content of public education. During the past two decades the most consistent critics of public school policy have been conservative Christians, whose rhetoric tends to frame the issues as confrontation between the rights of families and the oppressive power of the state. But the school wars are really multi-faceted battles among parents, a variety of religious interest groups, a variety of secular interest groups, teachers, school administrators, educational scholars, elected school board members, legislators, and courts—and, lest we forget, students.

The term "school wars" has become commonplace, but I suggest there may be less war than meets the ear, in spite of some genuinely bellicose rhetoric. Wars or not, the school conflicts genuinely are *religious* ones. Many of the partisans and their beliefs are religious in the conventional sense. Many religious parents think public school teachings threaten the faith of their children, undermine their moral values, and undercut the rights of parents to transmit their religious heritage to their children. School wars are also religious in the broader sense of the word; they are about ultimate values, comprehensive explanations of the universe, human life, and its purposes.[3] The school with its curriculum, almost as much as any church with its doctrine, fits Clifford Geertz's classic definition of a religion:

> [Religion is] (1) a system of symbols which acts to (2) establish powerful, pervasive and long-lasting moods and motivations in men by formulating conceptions of a general order of existence and (4) clothing these conceptions with such an aura of factuality that (5) the moods and motivations seem uniquely realistic.[4]

Public schools are a primary venue of shared socialization in the United States; they are charged with the responsibility for conveying a body of information and values, motivations, and habits necessary to prepare students for adult responsibilities and the preservation of civil and democratic society. The importance of schools' influence on individual students and on the culture at large can hardly be overstated,[5] but our heterogeneous society demands an almost impossible balance. Public schools must convey society's fundamental knowledge and values without assuming a monopoly of that function. When the U.S. Supreme Court struck down an Oregon law prohibiting private education in 1925, it recognized the overwhelming value of educational pluralism.[6] There remain, however, enormous disagreements over what are shared values and what are alternative values, and the role of each in the public school curriculum.

All sides in the school wars advocate principles that are important, deeply held, and possibly incompatible. Here are some of them:

1. The rights of parents to rear their own children.
2. The duty of the state to protect and educate children and to perpetuate the requisites of democracy.
3. The constitutional prescriptions that the state not establish a religion.
4. The constitutional guarantee of free exercise of religion.
5. The constitutional rights of children as individuals.

6. The democratic values of majority rule in establishing the educational policies for a community.
7. The professional competence and expertise of teachers and professional educators.
8. The rights of interest groups to be represented in decision-making.
9. Commitments to the academic excellence in disciplines of science and mathematics, literature and history.
10. Commitments to a multi-cultural and democratic America.
11. Commitments to student mental and physical health and development.
12. Commitments to religious visions of the universe and to perceived divine commandments.

These principles are not trivial and may not be reconcilable. I make no pretence of offering solutions. Nor do I attempt here to add to the already copious analysis of the legal, pedagogical and political issues.[7] My purpose here is simply to survey the battlefield, and offer some reflections from a safe distance. Why have schools been the focus of so much religious conflict in the Untied States? With so many substantive issues facing Americans, why do these largely symbolic ones generate so much emotion? How do the language and history of the First Amendment shape the way different groups frame their concerns and grievances? What do the school wars tell us about American pluralism, and what prospects does pluralism suggest for solutions? In the end, without offering a resolution, I consider the school wars in the context of American pluralism and suggest that these nasty disputes may not be such a bad thing after all.

Why Schools?

Why have schools been the major battlefields in the "culture wars" between religious conservatives and liberals?[8] Why not the mass media or the venues of mass consumption, whose hedonistic and materialist messages are so antithetical to traditional religious values? Even electoral campaigns seem to generate less passion than public school controversies. Nothing seems to have elicited such deep and pervasive challenge as public schools.

Schools serve a religious function in many senses of the word. Like traditional religion, they offer what passes for comprehensive explanations of the world and our place in it. Indeed, one of the most important functions of schools is to provide a common body of knowledge and norms. It may be thin—it may often seem to be at the lowest common denominator—but schools have always served as the common source of socialization for Americans. Moreover, they are compulsory. To the extent that schools are perceived to have a kind of monopoly on the transmission of knowledge and values, they are a lightning rod for conflict over those values. Thus, the battle over school curricula is really a battle over what shall be the public values of the United States.

Schools and their teachings are deeply symbolic to Americans. The leaders of the civil rights movement recognized the symbolic importance of schools when they selected public education, rather than housing, employment, public accommodation, or even voting as the primary battlefield in the struggle against segregation and discrimination. Desegregated schools stood for a desegregated America—or at least the aspiration and the public commitment to a desegregated America. Consider two candidates for the most controversial Supreme Court decisions of the twentieth Century—*Brown v. Board of Education*[9] desegregating public schools, and *Engle v. Vitale*[10] prohibiting state-mandated school prayers. Even though the effect of the former was negligible for a generation, and the topic of the latter affected less than a minute of the school day, they were understood as sea changes in public values. Critics have claimed that the prayer and Bible reading decisions represent the Court's effort to banish God from the public schools. These symbolic decisions were not *merely symbolic* or in anyway unimportant. We live by symbols, particularly in our religious lives.

I do not believe that the conflict over prayer in the school is really about whether children may or must listen to a few seconds worth of muttered words at the beginning of the school day. I cannot imagine that those muttered words would either bring children closer to God or do them any serious harm. I do not believe that ninth grade biology is likely to undermine anyone's religious faith. Neither do I believe that the well being of school children will be much affected by whether or not religious clubs meet in school buildings or whether invocations are said at football games and graduations. But I do believe that these issues are of deeply symbolic value to religious advocates and their opponents because they express in an almost sacred venue their commitments.

Schools also symbolize communities. In many small towns and urban neighborhoods, schools are the real community centers—the places where people meet, the place where people have histories, the locus of community rivalries through athletic events, and the institution that gives an identity to a town or a neighborhood. When schools are perceived to teach things that no longer reflect community values, community life itself seems threatened.

Moreover, schools represent "government" to most people; they are the places where government touches us concretely and personally—through our children. The school is, perhaps, the most concrete instantiation of government most of us encounter in our daily lives. We seldom need to visit other government buildings—even trips to the post office are becoming obsolete, while school buildings remain tangible symbols of government. It is easy to project our feelings of frustrations with government as an abstraction onto schools as a concrete instantiation. Schools become the focus of a sense of disempowerment at the hands of what is perceived to be an overwhelming bureaucracy. Given the longstanding and pervasive anti-governmental ideology in the United States, it is not a stretch to sense that a somewhat sinister "government," is alienating children from their parents.

In fact, for conservative critics, schools seem to be the instantiation of "big government," the local representatives of an oppressive federal presence. This resentment began with the decades long conflict over school desegregation. It intensified after the adoption of federal aid to education in 1965, which began a gradual shift of school decision making from local to national authorities and professional educators in the Department of Education, the National Science Foundation, the National Endowment for the Humanities, and the like. The fact that schools remain predominately agents of individual states and are run by local school boards is lost in the rhetoric that equates public schools with big, distant and oppressive "government."

Conservative Protestants, especially those with a long historical memory, may feel a sense of loss, a sense that the schools have been taken away from them. There is some truth to this perception. From the earliest years of the common school movement through the early years of this century, the years of the famous McGuffey Readers, public schools overtly incorporated Protestant doctrines and materials aimed at creating a common Protestant culture.[11] Desegregation, the banning of school prayers and Bible readings, feminism and the impact of the sexual revolution progressively abandoned those roots. For some critics, schools represent all that is wrong with contemporary society and all their fears of racial pluralism, multiculturalism, New Age mysticism, and confused gender roles, and are vehicles for creating a demonic future. In the most extremist rhetoric, public schools are the means Satan uses to assure the dominance of the Antichrist.

For ethnic minorities, especially newer immigrant groups, the fears are similar but slightly different. Given the historic role of schools in Americanizing children, they sense, too, a loss of their cultures. Schools educate their children in a language many cannot understand and seem to force a choice between "fitting in" and maintaining cultural continuity. To them, schools and their personnel may seem like an overwhelming and threatening presence.

Participants

Different religious groups have different resources for influencing policies, and thus have adopted different strategies for pursuing their interests. Mainstream groups, including the largest Protestant denominations, seldom need to resort to litigation, because their understandings are shared by major decision makers. Groups representing majority values can rely on the electoral process to protect their interests. Minority groups who lack electoral strength may protect their interests through forming strategic alliances and acquiring access to decision makers. Since the mid-twentieth century, Jewish groups only occasionally have had to resort to the courts because they have nurtured the art of negotiation and access to decision makers in order to forestall problems before they require litigation.[12] Muslim, Hindu, and other non-Western religious groups are only beginning to exert a presence in either the electoral process or in litigation. Thus far, Catholics have not been major players in the current school wars. During the nineteenth century Catholics were at the forefront of the movement to disentangle public education from Protestant theology. The public schools combined Protestantism with Americanism in their attempt to "Americanize" generations of immigrants. Their insensitivity to the interests of Catholics led to the creation of the Catholic school system in the United States. By the second half of the twentieth century the anti-Catholic agenda of the public school system had mostly passed, and Catholics had become part of the mainstream. Individual Catholics have joined both conservative and liberal criticisms of school curricula, but I am not aware of any specifically Catholic organizations dedicated to this end.[13]

For the past quarter century, the most vigorous and well-organized opposition to school curricula and programs has come from Conservative Protestant groups. These groups have often been the *generators* of parental concerns as much as *responses* to them. In fact, some groups have worked to generate issues and manage the subsequent local conflicts in order to foster a national agenda and utilize a number of strategies to influence public school policies. Access to school policy-makers requires minimal resources and is often successful for "behind the scenes" influence. During the 1980s, flush with political victories, financial support, and organizational skills, conservative Christian groups adopted a strategy of attempting to gain control of school boards through the electoral process. They experienced a number of victories, but success fell short of their expectations. Like all groups, when electoral strategies fail, these groups turned to litigation, and specifically to the U.S. Constitution. Following religious minorities before them, conservative Christians developed impressive legal advocacy organizations, such as the Rutherford Foundation and the American Society for Law and Justice, with skills not only to win cases, but also to shape the course of constitutional interpretation. Some of the most active conservative organizations involved in the school wars have been the Christian Coalition, led throughout the 1990s by Rev. Pat Robertson, the Eagle Forum, founded by Phyllis Schafley in 1972, the now-defunct Moral Majority, founded by Rev. Jerry Falwell, Educational Research Analysts founded by Mel and Norma Gabler, Robert Simmonds' Citizens for Excellence in Education, and the Heritage Foundation. Among the most influential authors of school criticism books are Timothy LeHaye,[14] Barbara M. Morris,[15] and Rousas Rushdooney.[16]

These groups do not always agree among themselves, and at times appear to have adopted diametrically contradictory positions. Their first triumphal stance called for total victory for the Christian majority, official recognition that America is a Christian nation, and public policy in conformity with their understanding of biblical principles. Some demand a Christian character to the public schools; others aspire to the destruction of government education, and its replacement by a system of private religious education.[17] These groups depict themselves, however, as persecuted minorities, oppressed by secular powers, and seeking only the same recognition, respect, and sensitivity accorded to other American minorities.[18]

While conservative groups have been the primary critics of public schools in recent decades, professional educators and liberal groups have organized in response, and have also become major actors in school related issues. Among the most important interest groups opposing religious conservative agenda in education are People for the American Way, Americans United for Separation of Church and State, the Anti-Defamation League, the American Civil Liberties Union and various organizations of professional educators such as the National Council of English Teachers.

How the Religion Clauses Shape the Conflict

All parties in school wars controversies appeal to rights granted by the U.S. Constitution, and the most frequent arguments concern the First Amendment guarantee that "Congress shall make no law respecting an establishment of religion or abridging the free exercise thereof." These two religion clauses, commonly known as the Establishment Clause (grammarians note that they are not clauses at all), have tended to polarize constitutional arguments and their partisans.

The Establishment Clause is invoked by persons objecting to governmental support or endorsement of religion, violating the "wall of separation" between church and state. Usually secular or liberal groups bring Establishment Clause cases; conservative Christian groups seldom use this clause and usually defend the kinds of practices that are challenged under its *aegis*. Occasionally, these challenges have concerned religious teachings in the school curriculum itself, such as creationism as an alternative to evolution, but more often, the objectionable practices have concerned non-curricular practices such as prayers, Bible reading, and meditation before classes, religious clubs on school property, Christmas celebrations, and the like. Establishment Clause jurisprudence has both shaped the nature of their arguments and been shaped by it. The U.S. Supreme Court has adopted a number of doctrines for interpreting the Establishment Clause, so legal challenges to school policies are articulated in terms of these doctrines. The following are some of the most important Establishment Clause arguments used to challenge public school polices.

The Establishment Clause requires religious neutrality. The underlying value of the Establishment Clause demands that government be neutral among religions, and avoid at all costs actions that prefer one religion over another. Most commentators also believe that the Clause demands neutrality between religion and non-religion, and, therefore, government may not prefer religion in general over other alternatives. Almost every challenge brought under the Establishment Clause in some way invokes the requirement of neutrality.

The expenditure of public monies for religious ends violates the Establishment Clause. This argument plays a central role in the long series of arguments concerning public aid to religious schools,[19] and remains at the heart of the most recent decision regarding school vouchers.[20]

Religious activities in the schools violate the Establishment Clause by coercing children. The possibility of coercion has been a frequent theme in judicial thinking about Establishment Clause violations. In 1948, the Supreme Court ruled that the practice of reserving part of the school day for religious instruction in the public schools was coercive because school attendance was compulsory.[21] In 1992, Justice Kennedy argued that graduation ceremony prayers might coerce students to profess things they did not believe,[22] and the Ninth Circuit Court used this reasoning in its decision regarding the Pledge of Allegiance.[23]

Programs that serve religious rather than secular purposes violate the Establishment Clause. The influential but controversial *Lemon* test held that to avoid Establishment Clause violations, programs must (1) have a valid secular purpose, (2) have a primary effect which neither advances nor inhibits religion, and (3) not create excessive entanglement between governmental and religious institutions.[24] The first "prong" of the *Lemon* test thus invalidates programs whose primary purpose advances a particular religion or religion in general. A Kentucky law requiring that the Ten Commandments be posted in public school classrooms was invalidated on these grounds in 1980.[25] Similarly, Louisiana's law requiring that teaching of evolution be accompanied by equal time for creationist science was invalidated as lacking a valid secular purpose.[26] Alabama's law mandating a moment of silence at the beginning of the school day for prayer and meditation was also ruled unconstitutional on these grounds.[27]

Programs that advance religion violate the Establishment Clause. The second prong of the *Lemon* test requires that practices challenged under the

Establishment Clause must have primary effects that neither advances nor inhibits religion. State aid to private religious schools is vulnerable on this account, although court rulings on this point have been inconsistent. This doctrine requires school administrators to walk a very delicate line: they must neither discriminate against religion nor favor religious interests over other kinds of interests. School prayers and religious celebrations have been challenged as having the primary effect of advancing religion. On the other hand, the absence of religion in public schools has been challenged as inhibiting religion by conveying the message that religion is irrelevant.

Programs that entangle church and state violate the Establishment Clause. The third prong of the *Lemon* test holds unconstitutional any programs that create institutional links between governmental and religious institutions. The doctrine has been used primarily in the context of state aid to parochial schools[28] and to challenge government oversight of church school employment policies.[29]

Endorsement of religion violates the Establishment Clause. The *Lemon* test has always been controversial; critics find it too stringent, and thus hostile to religion. While it has never been officially rejected, in recent years, justices have turned instead to a doctrine proposed by Justice Sandra Day O'Connor. Her test asks whether the State has impermissibly *endorsed* religion or made religion relevant to one's standing in the political community. "Government endorsement of religion sends a message to nonadherents that they are outsiders, not full members of the political community, and an accompanying message to adherents that they are insiders, favored members of the political community."[30] Recent attempts to re-introduce school prayers have been constitutionally vulnerable as state endorsements of religion.[31]

It is worth reiterating that the Establishment Clause is usually invoked by people committed to a strict separation between church and state. With few exceptions,[32] religious conservatives reject strict separation, and thus oppose most of these arguments. Instead, they emphasize Free Exercise arguments, which single out religion for special constitutional protection.

Free Exercise Arguments

As the Establishment Clause protects people from state-imposed religious obligations, the Free Exercise Clause protects their rights to engage in religious beliefs or practices without undue governmental burdens. The Free Exercise Clause offers crucial protection for religious minorities against both intentional discrimination and inadvertent insensitivity by public decision makers. The Free Exercise Clause has often been interpreted to mandate a right to exemption from governmental policies which burden a person's religious beliefs or practices, even when the burdens are inadvertent.[33] That right must be balanced against state interests in the challenged policies, so requests for exemptions are by no means automatic. Often school authorities voluntarily grant exemptions without controversy. For example, a number of states provide exemptions from dress codes to allow Native Americans boys to wear long hair and Muslim girls and Jewish boys to wear head coverings. When accommodations are not made voluntarily, these requests have resulted in legal challenges with mixed results.[34] One of the more interesting accommodation issues concerns a conflict between school policies of no tolerance for weapons and the Sikh religious requirement that young men wear a *kirpan* or ceremonial knife.[35]

Using similar arguments, conservative Christians have sought to have their children excused from religiously offensive curricular materials and lessons,[36] and occasionally to remove offending materials entirely.[37] They have argued that curricular materials undermine the right of parents to direct the religious education of their children, disparage their beliefs, and coerce them to believe or act contrary to their faith. In addition, they have made Free Exercise arguments concerning the right to meet and pray on school property, and to engage in other religious activities without discrimination. Because the conservative challenges to public school curricula are less understood than the more well-publicized Establishment Clause issues, we will explore in some detail.

The Christian Conservative Challenge to Public School Curricula

The religious split over public school curricula takes its point of departure from John Dewey's progressivism. Dewey's influence included the cultivation of individuality, expression, and freedom, rather than external discipline. Dewey advocated experiential learning and practical application as opposed to authoritative texts and teachers, and emphasized life's present opportunities rather than disciplined preparation for a remote future. He sought to prepare students for a changing world, as opposed to a static one. These ideas amount to a comprehensive understanding of knowledge, the world, and the individual, and they spurred a comprehensive change in education: It was, in fact, a religious revolution in education. Religious conservatives, in various degrees, reject almost all of these founding principles of progressive education.[38]

At the heart of nearly all the specific criticisms is the belief that traditional Christian beliefs and values have been replaced by an ideology loosely called secular humanism. Critics use that term in a very generic sense to characterize an almost absurd variety of curricular ideas. Some groups have attempted to define secular humanism as a religion itself, and thus argue that humanist school curricula violate the constitutional prohibition against religious establishments.[39] Secular humanism has been used to characterize almost every aspect of the modern school curriculum, but especially evolution for undermining biblical creation, values clarification, and multicultural studies in literature and history, which suggest plural answers to life's big questions. Humanism rejects explanations that appeal to supernatural beings, authorities or commands. Both physical and natural science explanations are by definition humanistic. Conservative critics argue that by providing only these kinds of explanations, the curriculum marginalizes traditional religion, making its explanations and precepts appear to be irrelevant to an understanding of the world. These explanations seem to deny divine authority for values in general, and for American life in particular, thus undermining patriotism as well as faith. In addition, critics accuse the schools of instilling "New Age" values, an imprecise term which seems to refer especially to non-Western ideas, as well as introspection, concern with emotions, relationships, and creative exercises.

Many of the arguments surveyed below are phrased in the most alarmist, even apocryphal terms. But it is important to keep in mind that they are the products of the most ideologically committed spokespersons for their movement. Thus, these critiques may greatly overstate the views of rank and file parents.

Evolution. Ever since Darwin published *The Origin of the Species* in 1859, the theory of evolution has been the target of religious conservatives; in fact, it has become a symbol for the secularization of science and of education in general. Evolution is threatening not only because it is perceived as conflicting with the biblical account of creation in Genesis, but also because the notion of constant change disparages the notion of eternal, unalterable truths. If life forms can evolve, and develop from "lower" to "higher" forms, then truths, too, might evolve, and even progress. Such a belief would undercut the notion that biblical truths are valid for all time, and cannot be improved upon by subsequent thinkers.

The stories of battles over evolution are etched deep into American history, and continue to be the subject of legislative battles and the evening news. The famous Scopes trial over the right of a teacher to teach a non-biblical account of creation gained national attention in 1923.[40] The teaching of evolution generally disappeared from public school curricula, either by state law or by the discretion of textbook publishers, until the 1960s. The Soviet launch of Sputnik in 1958 generated an intense American effort to enhance science education, and among its products were modern textbooks, which included evolutionary biology. Ultimately, one of these books collided with a Scopes-era law in Arkansas, which produced the landmark Supreme Court decision *Epperson v. Arkansas*, striking down the law as an unconstitutional establishment of religion.[41] As evolution began to be the dominant model for teaching life sciences, opponents turned to new strategies, including laws requiring a "balanced treatment" of evolution and creationism.[42] In 1987, the Supreme Court decision in *Edwards v. Aguilard*[43] overturned one such law as violation of the Establishment Clause because it appeared to have no secular purpose, but a purely religious one. Public opinion polls show that the country is about equally divided between those who believe in evolution and those who reject it, and the issue has only grown in controversy.[44] Various states have developed a variety of strategies to counter the teaching of evolution: Kansas adopted, but later repealed, a policy removing evolutionary teachings from state proficiency examinations; Oklahoma and Alabama textbooks include a disclaimer that evolution is a theory, not a fact.[45] Recently, opponents of evolution have developed a much more scientifically sophisticated attack on evolutionary theory, arguing that evolution cannot explain certain patterns of irreducible complexity in life forms, and thus concluding that creation must be the result of an "intelligent design."[46] While other curricular issues have cooled in recent years, the evolution issue remains as contentious as ever.

New Math. Modern techniques for teaching mathematics are a more surprising subject for religious challenges. The earlier math drills had emphasized memorizing right answers; "new math" was concerned with conceptual education and process. It has both its defenders and its critics as a way of teaching mathematical ability, but some religious activists saw a moral issue. The method of "new math" undermines the sense of finite answers and concreteness. "On a moral basis there is fear that such abstract teachings to young minds will tend to destroy the student's belief in absolutes—to believe that nothing is concrete. This could be instrumental in helping erode their faith in other absolutes such as Christian faith."[47]

Reading. Mid-twentieth reforms replaced traditional phonetics with a reading method called "whole language," and decreased emphasis on traditional grammar rules. These changes, surprisingly, took on both political and religious significance. Much of the concern stems from a genuine distress about a perceived decrease in reading abilities in the last generation. The Gabler Foundation even claims that the whole language method is a conspiracy by elites to retain power by keeping the masses illiterate.[48] Christian coalition leader Pat Robertson claimed that reading by syllables is reading the way God intended.[49] Reading methods even became a political issue during the 1990s, and conservative demand for a return to the phonics method became part of a national political agenda. Behind the pedagogical issue is an ideological one. Conservative critics argue that whole language reading encourages children to create their own meaning from literature—again, undermining the notion of objective knowledge.

History. Teaching history is a constant source of controversy because the telling of a people's history is inseparable from its identity. Who is a part of that history and what roles they play are deeply contentious issues. As professional historians turned from the study of heroes, wars and statesmen to social history, these changes began to influence secondary textbooks. Newer books replaced the emphasis on traditional heroes with accounts of the lives of ordinary persons, including women and minorities, inevitably bringing to light some of the darker chapters of the American experience. Traditionalists claim by emphasizing the faults of traditional heroes and the failings of America, these books disparage patriotism. For many religious conservatives, the preeminence of America is a doctrine of religious faith because the United States is seen as "the new Israel," established and nurtured under God's special protection.

One of the most persistent complaints from religious critics concerns the exclusion of religion from the teaching of American history. Critics argue that books ignoring or minimizing the role of religion in American history convey a message that religion is not important. This challenge places school authorities in an untenable dilemma. Including religion in American history almost guarantees a challenge. Given the sensitivity of religion in America, almost any account would offend some group. On the other hand, the seemingly "safe" strategy of minimizing that risk can lead to challenges to the minimization.

Global and Multi-Cultural Education. Since about the 1970s, educators have recognized the importance of preparing students for life in an internationally interdependent world. Education for "globalism" includes teaching about foreign languages, non-Western history and literature, and perhaps some insights from anthropology. Critics of global education and multiculturalism see in it a relativism, which deprives Christian and American values of their preeminence. When multicultural lessons include study of non-Western religious beliefs and traditions, some conservative Christians accuse schools of teaching paganism and counter-religions.[50] Ultra-fundamentalists interpret global education as indoctrination for world government, a Satanic plot.

Literature. A constant source of controversy is the literature included in school reading assignments. Books that deal with contemporary problems are seen as too negative or morbid or too critical of contemporary society (i.e. discussions of poverty or race discrimination). Conservatives object to feminist themes that disparage traditional gender roles, or readings with vulgar language or explicit discussions of sex. Other sources of criticism are materials that disparage traditional religion, or portray non-Western stories, themes, cultures, or beliefs, or stories involving magic, sorcery, or fantasy.[51]

Sex Education. Nothing in the contemporary curriculum enrages conservative critics more than sex education programs, especially those including AIDS awareness and prevention and anything about homosexuality. Critics believe that teachings about "safe sex" and other issues undermine traditional sexual morality. In their view, these programs promote promiscuity, encourage homosexuality, and contribute to the rise in teenage pregnancy and sexually transmitted diseases. Many of these materials are sexually explicit in a way critics find pornographic.

Beyond the sexual content, conservative parents see them as the state usurpation of parental roles and authority. They assert strong parental rights and obligations to educate their children in sexual values consistent with their religion. More often than not, these assertions have not fared well in courts. Typically, courts determine that the strong parental interests are nevertheless outweighed by the public health importance of AIDS education and preventing teenage pregnancy.[52] In at least one instance, however, parents have successfully argued that mere exposure to the content of a sex education class would undermine the foundation of the children's faith.[53]

Subjective Materials. Conservative critics object to assignments that elicit subjective reactions, particularly emotional disclosure, from students. These might include assignments to create diaries or journals or the discussion of feelings. In addition to stressing non-objective truths, these are perceived as possible invasions of both individual and family privacy. Programs such as *Facilitative Teaching* drew deep hostility on these grounds.[54] Conservative critics also object to self-esteem programs, cognitive exercises such as thinking skills, and outcomes based education, characterizing these as mind control, and as New Age attempts to produce altered consciousness.

School Counseling. Self-esteem programs, psychological testing, and programs for at-risk children are often attacked as invading the privacy of students and their families, and attempting to usurp the role of parents. In response to this criticism, Congress in 1978 enacted the Protection Student Rights Act (known as the Hatch Amendment) that protects students from psychiatric or psychological testing or treatment, or from being asked to reveal things as political affiliation, sexual behavior and attitudes, economic status, or critical appraisal of family members.[55]

Values Clarification. Programs designed to identify values are particular targets of conservative criticism because they appear to introduce moral relativism in place of the objective morality of traditional religion. Religious conservatives oppose any programs resting on Lawrence Kohlberg's theory of moral development because of stage six emphasis on self-chosen values.

One good summary of the curriculum issues as understood by fundamentalist groups is found in the *Student's Bill of Rights*, published by the Eagle Forum, a conservative interest group. The following is an abbreviated statement of that document:

1. The right to be taught to read the English language in the first grade . . .

2. The right to privacy: Schoolpersons may not force me to discuss, or play Magic Circle, or answer questions, write assignments, or keep journals about my religion, moral values, family, attitudes and feeling, sex behavior and private parts of the body, political attitudes, or what I and my family do at home.
3. The right to my religious faith and beliefs. School persons may not force me to do assignments or engage in classroom activities that criticize or downgrade my religion. Examples of such practices are: teaching that any religion or non-religion is as good as another, that there are many gods, or that God did not create the world; teaching witchcraft, the occult, or astrology, conducting Eastern mystics, yoga, Transcendental Meditation, Quieting Reflex, guided fantasy or imagery, or "stress" courses using hypnotic practices.
4. The right to share information with parents by taking home my textbook, materials, lessons, and assignments . . .
5. The right to have and to hold my moral values and standards, my political opinions, and my cultural attitudes. School persons may not impose on me the value system that ethics are situational or that moral dilemmas have no right or wrong answers, . . . may not . . . require role-play open-ended psychological problems, may not put me in a school environment of premarital promiscuity . . .
6. The right to alternate assignments when I or my parents believe that school persons are violating my rights or imposing upon me lessons, films, or materials inappropriate for my grade level . . .
7. The right to have my family treated with respect . . .
8. The right to be inspired and encouraged by classroom lessons, not depressed or disturbed. I have a right to be taught the greatness of America and our Constitution and that ours is a land of freedom and opportunity for those who learn, work hard and persevere. Schoolpersons may not depress me with lessons, discussions or films about death, dying, violence, surgery, suicide or dire predictions about the end of the world.
9. The right to the sanctity of my body and to safety on the school premises . . .
10. The right to full compliance with federal and state laws . . .[56]

Religious Wars, School Wars, and Pluralism

If the battle over schools is as intense as advocates on both sides proclaim, why does school life appear so ordinary? If conservative parents truly believe that the public schools represent a Satanic plot to introduce the rule of the Antichrist, why have they not taken up arms? Conversely, if America were truly in danger of becoming a reactionary theocracy, as liberal leaders admonish, why do classes seem to be pursuing business as usual? There have indeed been, and continue to be, many ugly skirmishes in the school wars, but there appears to have been only one serious incident of curriculum generated violence, and that was a quarter century ago.[57]

Perhaps the intensity of the school wars has waned with the fortunes of its most prominent organizations, such as the now-defunct Moral Majority and the declining Christian Coalition. The most virulent criticisms of public education, at least that which has reached the attention of observers outside the movement, seems to date from the 1980s. More likely, the movement that began as a radical outsider has evolved to a position of insider, making radical criticism a victim of its own success. Clearly, battles over public schools continue in every state and involve every branch of the federal government, but the issues seem to be more prosaic, at least for the time being. While interest group leaders on both sides earn their living, in part, by stoking the fires of conflict, their followers seem to have lukewarm commitments. That situation reflects a general disparity between interest group leaders and their followers. It is simply the nature of public opinion to be more centrist while opinion leaders are more polarized.

Part of the credit for avoiding more serious school wars must be given to interest group leaders themselves, and to the extraordinary effort on all sides to find a common ground. Beginning in 1994, representatives from across the ideological and religious spectrum held a series of meetings to work out a statement of shared principles. Participants included, among others, the National Education Association, National School Board Association, American Association of School Administrators, the Christian Legal Society, the American Society for Law and Justice, Citizens for Excellence in Education, the Anti-Defamation League, the Union of American Hebrew Congregations, the Council on Islamic Education, the Christian Educators Association, the Christian Coalition and the People for the American Way. After a great deal of work, these leaders reached agreement on a *Statement of Principles*.[58] At the heart of these principles is a commitment to genuine state neutrality, both among religions and between religion and non-religion, in the public schools. Significantly, the signatories recognized that genuine neutrality is not achieved by ignoring religion. In a society in which the vast majority profess religious beliefs and activities, and in which religion is so entwined with history and culture, to ignore religion would be to convey a misguided account of American history and culture. Thus, the principles call for the objective teaching about religion wherever it is appropriate in the curriculum. In short, because Americans take religion seriously, the document called for educators to take religion seriously, but objectively. Of course, a world of disagreement is hidden behind the word "objectively," since participants have yet to agree on what would constitute an objective account of American religious history, or of human origins, or of the cultural issues that implicate religious values. Moreover, teachers are not yet educated in these subjects, nor trained to be able to deal with such sensitive subjects. The aspiration for objective teaching about religion remains mostly an aspiration, and schools, for the most part, prefer silence on such potentially confrontational topics.[59]

The signatories also reached agreement on the meaning of the constitution's religion clauses in public education, and published it as *Religion in the Public Schools: A Joint Statement of Current Law*,[60] widely disseminated to educators and parents. This document recognizes student rights to voluntary, student-initiated prayer in schools, as long as it is not disruptive and does not infringe on the rights of others. Students have a right to express personal religious views in class or in written assignments, and to distribute religious literature subject to reasonable administrative restrictions. Schools are obligated to accommodate students' religious needs by excusing them from classroom activities for religious reasons.

This consensus underscores the importance of the constitution's religion clauses in avoiding genuine school wars over religion. The agreement is bounded by and based upon the constitution's religion clauses, which all sides recognize as authoritative. It means that disagreements are at the margins rather than at the core. While they take strikingly different interpretations of many key judicial doctrines, constitutional authority exercises an immense gravitational pull on all of the significant actors and makes possible a consensus on principles.

A third explanation for the diminished intensity of the school wars is the fact that American pluralism offers a number of less-than-apocalyptic strategies for participants in the school wars. Over time, there have evolved mechanisms for dissenters to demand religious accommodation *within* the public school system. The First Amendment Free Exercise Clause has been interpreted to require the accommodation of religious needs in many circumstances, and many specific laws reinforce this requirement in the context of schools. For example, many states provide rights for parents to review curricular materials and demand alternate assignments for those that are religiously offensive.[61] Nationally, the Hatch Amendment guarantees rights of parents to review and consent to "experimental curricular materials."[62]

Conservative Christians have made use of religious accommodation to demand excusal from religiously offensive portions of the public school curriculum. Drawing their lessons from the civil rights movement, and taking the position of marginalized religious minorities, they appeal to the values of inclusion and respect, and somewhat ironically, to the values of pluralism and multiculturalism in insisting on the recognition of their beliefs. In particular, religious conservatives have demanded and often won the right to opt-out of religiously offensive school assignments, readings, and activities.

This strategy reached national attention during the mid 1980s, but it has a much longer history.[63] The most famous of these attempts were those brought by Jehovah's Witness children to be excused on religious grounds from being compelled to recite the Pledge of Allegiance, which they believed to be an act of idolatry. Their appeals were rejected in 1940,[64] but in a landmark decision, were upheld by the Supreme Court majority in *West Virginia Board of Education v. Barnette* in 1943.[65]

The case of *Mozert v. Hawkins County Public Schools*[66] argued in the mid 1980s brought this strategy to national attention. In this case, fundamentalist children and their parents raised numerous objections to the Holt Reinhart reading series used in the public schools. Parents sought to have their children excused from reading classes using the Holt series and from classroom discussions of the offending material, and demanded the right to instruction in an alternative textbook. They argued the books exposed their children to religiously objectionable materials, thereby undermining the tenets of their religious faith, and that their children were coerced to disbelieve and that the legitimacy of their religious beliefs are disparaged by textbooks. The heart of the Free Exercise challenges were that the state-required textbooks offended their religious beliefs and encouraged children to profess beliefs their religious doctrine found objectionable. Moreover, by diminishing the importance of traditional religion, parents argued, the textbooks disparaged the children's religious beliefs and implicitly substituted another belief system.

The complaints in *Mozert* mostly centered on the series' presentation of contemporary pluralism (including readings on different cultures, religions, and value systems) as conflicting with their belief in a singular religious truth and system of values. Hence, *Mozert* raises very directly the conflict between parents' religious right to perpetuate beliefs, and the state's interest in preparing children for a heterogeneous world in which tolerance of diversity seems necessary for survival. These arguments create a dilemma both for conservative parents and for school administrators. The parents often use the very language and values of multiculturalism in their own calls for inclusion and respect within the public school system. They argue that, in their search for inclusiveness, schools have excluded conservative views and diminished respect for traditional values and lifestyles. Multicultural education marginalizes traditional values; yet they demand inclusion of their own values in the name of multiculturalism.

Legal theorists, Mark Tushnet, comments on this dilemma:

> *Mozert* involved parents who objected to the content of some aspects of the public school curriculum on the grounds that certain reading lessons the school gave their child communicated messages inconsistent with the parents' religious beliefs. The school's response, and the court's, was basically this: we are in fact sensitive to questions of multiculturalism, but the day is short and curricula are hard to design. We have done a reasonably good job of expanding our curriculum to be sensitive to multiculturalist concerns, but there are limits on what we can do. In particular, we cannot be faulted for developing a curriculum that is sensitive to multiculturalist concerns, but that is not sensitive to the concerns of those, like the parents here, have objections to multiculturalism itself. These parents must understand that they are just one group within our multiculturalist society, and there is no way that we can privilege one such group over others without violating our commitment to multiculturalism.[67]

Tushnet continues with the best argument for permitting students to opt-out of offending assignments:

> We might say to the schools, "Consider the messages about multiculturalism that you are sending. By denying the child the right to opt out of the required reading program and to substitute other readings, as the parents are willing to do, you are visibly expressing the limits of your commitment to multiculturalism. If you gave the child that right, everyone in the school would see how deep the commitment to multiculturalism goes." The suggestion is that schools should consider their implicit curricula as well as their explicit ones in describing their commitment to multiculturalism.[68]

After a tortured series of lower court decisions, the Sixth Circuit ruled that the compulsory use of the offensive textbooks did not unconstitutionally burden the Free Exercise of religion.[69] Nevertheless, the opt-out strategy caught on, and the legal arguments have become more subtle. Parents who, like petitioners in *Mozert*, want to avoid an entire subject or body of assignments have usually not been successful, but those who make specific objections to well-defined materials can usually be accommodated with alternate assignments.[70]

In addition to the opt-out strategy, some school districts have adopted an opt-in strategy, requiring parental consent for participation in programs that may be controversial. Thus, if educators recommend an R-Rated film or reading assignment with potentially objectionable language, they may attempt to avoid conflict by making the assignments optional and requiring parental permission.

Neither the opt-out or opt-in strategy attempts to change the dominant curriculum, but seeks only the rights of a religious minority to accommodation. A more aggressive strategy attempts to influence the curriculum itself, by demanding the removal of offending textbooks, library materials, or other teaching materials.[71] The most well known national organization for exerting conservative influence on the curriculum is Educational Research Analysts, Incorporated, organized by Mel and Norma Gabler of Longview, Texas. Since the early 1960s, the Gablers have led the movement to purge school classrooms and libraries of objectionable material. Beginning in their own home, they grew into a powerful clearinghouse for conservative oversight of textbooks, and have exerted enormous influence over textbook adoptions. The influence they gained over textbook adoptions in Texas quickly developed national significance. Because Texas is such a large market for textbooks, publications that were unacceptable in Texas were simply not profitable for book publishers. Hence, many say that the Gablers have parlayed their local influence into a national power over textbook materials.[72] They also offer strategic advice to local groups for organizing opposition to curriculum materials.

When efforts to change the curriculum through the political or bureaucratic process are unsuccessful, critics have resorted to legal challenges. Two well-publicized but ultimately unsuccessful efforts of this sort occurred during the 1980s. The case of *Grove v. Mead School District No. 354* was brought by students who objected on religious grounds to reading *The Learning Tree*. The school district offered alternative assignments and permitted the children to leave the classroom during discussion of the offending book. The children and their parents, however, insisted on its removal from the curriculum, contending that exposure to children who had read the book was itself a danger to their religious values. Both the district and the appeals court denied the request, finding the voluntary accommodation adequate in light of the state's interest in both educational policy and academic freedom.

Parents in *Smith v. Board of Education of Mobile County* made the novel claim that the public schools were inculcating the "religion" of secular humanism in violation of the Establishment Clause, both by inculcating secular values and by failing to give adequate attention to religious values.[73] A rather eccentric district court ruling ultimately upheld this reasoning, but was overruled. Legal challenges demanding the removal of specific materials continue to be a possible strategy for religious critics, but they do not have a high rate of success, because judges are reluctant to second-guess school authorities.

The preceding strategies rely on challenging the curriculum piecemeal. A far more systematic strategy for religious critics of public education is to try to capture the public school system through elections to school boards. The Christian Coalition, initiated in 1989 by the combined forces of evangelist Pat Robertson and political organizer Ralph Reed, made the conquest of local elective offices one of its most important strategies.[74] This strategy clearly replaces the defensive tactic of challenging the curriculum, with the offensive tactic of creating it in the first place. The local strategy was accompanied by a major campaign to elect religious conservatives and their allies to national office, and thus attain Congressional and presidential support for a school prayer constitutional amendment, vouchers to support private education, public funds for religious social service agencies, and a number of other non-educational agenda items. Many observers have commented upon the strong influence of religious conservatives within the Republican Party, and their resulting success in achieving a number of these goals. In local elections, conservative interest groups experienced considerable initial success throughout the late 1980s and 1990s, but both their electoral success and their impact on school systems were less than they had hoped or their adversaries had feared.

I venture here an explanation for their disappointed hopes of transforming American schools. It seems that these critics underestimated the inertia of the American system of government, a system designed to minimize the success of what James Madison called "factions." Even in the smallest school district, power is fragmented among local elected officials, hired superintendents and other professionals, federal officials with specific mandates, state and local bureaucracies, and of course, the principles and teachers who actually implement policies. Madison recognized that a faction might well capture any particular institution—such as a local school board—but foresaw that its power was limited by the countervailing power of all the other actors, who may oppose them on ideological or professional grounds, for self-interest, or by sheer inertia. Changes in educational policy, like all others in this system, thus require coalition building and negotiation, and are likely to be only incremental. For this reason, conservative educational reform, like its predecessors, disappoints the hopes of its supporters and the fears of its opponents.

A final, and increasingly important strategy for religious opponents of the public schools is withdrawal, as Catholics withdrew from Protestant-dominated public schools in the nineteenth century. For almost two generations, conservative Protestants have been increasingly withdrawing into their own schools and into home schooling. Jewish schools, too, are on the increase, but they seem to stem from concerns other than religious objections to the content of pubic school curricula. Public support in the form of vouchers has been a crucial part of the campaign to encourage private education as an alternative to public schools.

The retreat to private education could be a relatively simple solution to the school wars, but like most simple solutions, it is a bad one. Encouraging the combatants to go their own separate ways with their own schools has a certain appeal. Privatization would probably take the pressure off public schools and diminish the intensity of the school wars. The Supreme Court decision upholding the constitutionality of Cleveland's voucher program has dominated the news regarding church/state issues in recent months.[75] Advocates of school vouchers believe that they would enhance the pluralism of educational offerings. I conclude just the opposite. The prospect of separate schools for every ideological, religious or pedagogical shade strikes me as a recipe for a *segmented* society, not a pluralistic one. I believe it would be disastrous for our children to separate off into schools for Christian fundamentalists and schools for liberal Jews and ambitious secularists, schools for Black consciousness, schools for aspiring football players, and schools for social activist Catholics. The public school wars might well be diminished, but only because public schools could end up on the sidelines. Rather than facing conflict over values within a common institution, our children could grow up in homogeneous institutions organized for institutional conflict with each other. In the end, I reach the odd conclusion that the school wars may be a very healthy phenomenon because conflict over values is really the heart of pluralism. In spite of the rhetoric of interest groups on all sides, and in spite of some genuinely serious problems, public schools still continue to be our most important shared institution. As our society has retreated from shared institutions (private malls instead of downtowns; private clubs instead of public parks, walled neighborhoods with privately contracted public services) our serious danger is not conflict, but segmented homogeneity. In the end, as a parent and as a social scientist, I conclude that the school wars are a healthy contribution to the education of our children. My hope is that the school wars continue to be played out in public school board meetings, classrooms, and courtrooms, and that our children learn that conflict over publicly shared values is better than retreat from the conflict into entrenched private spaces.

Notes

1. Newdow v. US Congress No. 00–16423 DC No. CV 00–00495 (9th Cir) decided June 26, 2002.
2. *Zelman et. al. v. Simmons-Harris*. Nos. 00–1171, 00–1177, and 00–1179 (2002).
3. See Franklin Gamwell, *The Meaning of Religions Freedom* (Albany: SUNY Press, 1995).

4. Clifford Geertz, "Religion as a Cultural System," in *Interpretation of Cultures: Selected Essays* (New York: Basic Books, 1973), 90.
5. Among the myriad of thinkers who have made this point, two of my favorite are Robert Cover, "Supreme Court 1982 Term: Forward: Nomos and Narrative," *Harvard Law Review* 97(1983), 60, and Amy Gutman, *Democratic Education* (Princeton: Princeton University Press, 1988).
6. *Pierce v. Society of Sisters* 268 US 510 (1925). The contemporary significance of this decision is made elegantly by Martha Minow in "Keynote: Before and After *Pierce*: A Colloquium on Parents, Children, Religion and Schools," *University of Detroit Mercy Law Review* 78 (2001), 407–23.
7. Literature on religion and the public schools is so enormous that it is impossible to sample it without omitting important works. Some of the most often cited studies are: Warren Nord, *Religion in American Education* (Chapel Hill: University of North Carolina Press, 1995); Charles Haynes and Oliver Thomas, *Finding Common Ground: A First Amendment Guide to Religion and Public Education* (Nashville: First Amendment Center, 1996); James Sears and James Casper, *Curriculum, Religion, and Public Education" Conversations for an Enlarging Public Square* (New York: Teachers College, 1998); James Fraser, *Between Church and State: Religion and Public Education in a Multicultural America* (New York: St. Martin's, 1999); Thomas C. Hunt and James C. Carper, *Religion and Schooling in Contemporary America: Confronting our Cultural Pluralism* (New York: Garland, 1997).
8. See James D. Hunter, *Culture Wars: The Struggle to Define America* (New York: Basic Books, 1991). Hunter's culture war thesis and the controversy surrounding it is discussed in Sue Crawford's essay in this volume.
9. 347 US 483 (1954).
10. 370 US 421 (1961). Two years later in *School District of Avington Township v. Schempp* 374 US 203 (1963) and in *Murray v. Curlett* 374 US 203 (1963) the Court ruled unconstitutional the practices of starting the school day with Bible readings and recitation of the Lord's Prayer.
11. See, for example, James Frasier, *Between Church and State: Religion and Public Education in a Multicultural America* (New York: St. Martin's, 1999).
12. This point is made in Robert B. Fowler, Allen Hertzke, and Laura Olson, *Religion and Politics in America*, second edition (Bolder: Westview, 1999), 75–79.
13. Pat Buchanan, a conservative Roman Catholic commentator, frequently echoes the criticisms of conservative Protestants.
14. Tim LeHaye, *The Battle for the Public Schools* (Old Tappan, NJ: Fleming H. Revell, 1980) and *The Battle for the Mind* (Old Tappan, NJ: Fleming H. Revell, 1980).

15. Barbara Morris, *Change Agents in the Schools* (Upland, CA: The Barbara Morris Report, 1979).
16. Rousas Rushdoney, *The Messianic Character of American Education: Studies in the History and Philosophy of Education* (Nutley, NJ: Craig, 1972) and *Intellectual Schizophrenia: Culture, Crisis and Education* (Philadelphia: Presbyterian Reformed Publishing Company, 1973).
17. This aspiration was stated by Rev. Jerry Falwell, *American Can be Saved* (Murfreesboro, TN: Sword of the Lord Publishers, 1979) and by Rev. Pat Robertson in his 700 Club Broadcast, October 2, 1981, quoted by Eugene Provenzo, Jr., *Religions Fundamentalism and American Education* (Albany: SUNY Press, 1990), xvii.
18. This apparent contradiction is noticed by Justin Watson, *The Christian Coalition: Dreams of Restoration, Demands for Recognition* (New York: St. Martin's, 1997).
19. In *Everson v. Board of Education* 330 US 1 (1947), the majority held that the use of tax money to pay transportation costs for parochial as well as public school children did not violate the Establishment Clause, because the aid was to the children, not to the church. Subsequent challenges to state aid for private religious schools have resulted in a constantly changing and fundamentally inconsistent body of precedents.
20. *Zelman et. al v. Simmons-Harris.* Nos. 00–1171, 00–1177, and 00–1179 (2002).
21. *McCollum v. Board of Education.*333 US 203 (1948). In *Zorach v. Clauson* 343 US 306 (1952) the Court ruled that released time for religious instruction off campus did not violate the Establishment Clause.
22. *Lee v. Weisman* 505 US 577 (1992). The Court followed this reasoning by prohibiting pre-football game prayers led by a student elected by the student body in *Santa Fe Independent School District v.* Doe 530 US 290 (2000). Litigation regarding student led prayers continues to filter through the lower courts.
23. *Newdown v. US. Congress* (9th Cir), decided June 26, 2002.
24. *Lemon v. Kurtzman* 403 US 602 (1971).
25. *Stone v. Graham* 449 US 39 (1980).
26. *Edwards v. Aguilard* 482 US 587 (1987).
27. *Wallace v. Jaffre* 472 US 38 (1985). In 2002, a circuit court upheld a moment of silence law in *Brown v. Gilmore* (4th Cir.), decided July 24, 2001.
28. The Supreme Court used this reasoning in three of the 1970s era decisions regarding aid to parochial schools. See *Lemon v. Kurtzman* 403 US 602 (1971), *Meek v. Pittinger* 421 US 349 (1975), and *Wolman v. Walters* 433 US 229 (1977). This kind of reasoning appeared less often in later cases.
29. *Catholic Bishop of Chicago v.* NLRB 440 US 490 1979. See also, for example, EEOC

v. *Mississippi College* 626 F. 2d 477 (5th Cir. 1980) and EEOC v. *Southwestern Baptist Theological Seminary* 651 F. 2d 277 (5th Cir. 1981).

30. *Lynch v. Donnelly* 465 US 668 (1984) Justice Sandra Day O'Connor, concurring.
31. For example, *Santa Fe Independent School District v. Doe* 530 US 290 (2000).
32. See *Smith v. Board of Education of Mobile County* 827 F. 2d 684 (11th Cir. 1987).
33. Prior to the controversial 1990 decision of *Employment Division of Oregon v. Smith*, 494 US 872 (1990), most First Amendment experts believed that the Free Exercise Clause required exemptions unless there was a compelling state interest in denying it. The *Smith* decision reversed that understanding. Congress attempted to reinstate the "compelling state interest test by adopting the Religious Freedom Restoration Act in 1993 but the Court struck down that act in the case of *City of Boerne v. Flores* 501 US 507 (1997).
34. For example, a Jewish high school student unsuccessfully sought exemption from a policy banning basketball players from wearing headgear on the basketball court. See *Menorah v. Illinois High School Athletic Association*, 683 F. 2d 1030 (7th Cir. Ill. 1982).
35. *Cheema v. Thompson*, 67 F. 3d 883 (9th Cir 1995). A compromise allowed the student to wear the kirpan riveted into its sheath underneath his clothes.
36. *Mozert v. Hawkins County Public Schools* 647 F. Supp. 1194 (E. Ten 1986); 827 F. 2d 1058 (7th Cir. 1987).
37. *Grove v. Mead School District #354*,753 F. 2d 1528 (9th Cir. 1985).
38. For a particularly good account of the philosophical differences between progressive education and the conservative educational agenda, see David Berliner, "Educational Psychology Meets the Christian Right: Different Views of Children, Schooling, Teaching, and Learning," *Teachers College Record* 98, 3 (1997), 381–416. Probably the most systematic account of American school history from the conservative Christian perspective is Rousas Rushdooney, *The Messianic Character of American Education*.
39. The possibility of defining secular humanism as a religion stems from an unfortunate footnote in the 1963 Supreme Court decision of *Torcaso v. Williams* 367 US 488 (1961), in which the Court said that a state requirement that candidates profess a belief in a Supreme Being excluded non-theistic religions such as Buddhism and secular humanism. In the mid-1980s, this argument became the basis for a challenge to curricula in the case of *Smith v. Board of Education of Mobile County*, 827 F. 2d 684 (11th Cir. 1987). Among the conservative literature asserting that public schools teach the "religion" of secular humanism, see Homer Duncan, *Secular Humanism: The Most Dangerous Religion in America* (Lubbock, TX: Missionary Crusade, 1980); Timothy LeHaye, *The Battle for the Mind*; Mel

and Norma Gabler, *Humanism/Moral Relativism in Textbooks* (Self-Published Pamphlet, 1992).

40. *Scopes v. Tennessee*, 154 Tenn. 105, 289 S.W. 363 (1927). See Edward J. Larson, *Summer for the Gods: The Scopes Trial and America's continuing Debate over Science and Religion* (New York: Basic Books, 1997). Also Edward J. Larson, *Trial and Error: The American Controversy over Creation and Evolution* (New York: Oxford University Press, 1985).

41. *Epperson v. Arkansas* 393 US 97 (1968).

42. This strategy was suggested by Wendell R. Bird in "Freedom from Establishment and Unneutrality in Public School Instruction and Religious School Regulation," *Harvard Journal of Law and Public Policy* 2 (1979), 197. See also Wendell R. Bird, "Freedom of Religion and Science Instruction in Public Schools, *The Yale Law Journal* 87 (1978), 515–70.

43. 482 US 578 (1987).

44. For two thoughtful alternative views, see Warren A. Nord, *Religion and American Education: Rethinking a National Dilemma* (Chapel Hill: University of North Carolina Press, 1995) and The National Academy of Science, *Teaching About Evolution and the Nature of Science* (Washington, DC, 1998).

45. See Nicholas P. Miller, "Life the Universe, and Everything Constitutional: Origins in the Public Schools," 43 *Journal of Church and State* (2001) 483. For another perspective, see Francis Beckwith, "Intelligent Design and First Amendment Jurisprudence: A Critical Analysis," paper delivered at American Political Science Association National Convention, Boston, MA, August 29, 2002.

46. The literature on this issue is immense. For a good survey, see Miller, "Life, the Universe, and Everything Constitutional," 483–510. For an alternate argument, see Francis Beckwith, *Law, Darwinism and Public Education: The Establishment Clause and the Challenge of Intelligent Design* (New York: Rowman and Littlefield, 2003).

47. Quoted in James C. Hefley, *Are Textbooks Harming Your Children: Norma and Mel Gabler Take Action and Show You How!* (Milford, MI: Mott Media, 1979).

48. Gabler and Gabler, *What Are They Teaching Our Children?* 108–12.

49. Robertson, *The New Millennium*, 171.

50. One dramatic example of this controversy that over the program entitled "Man: A Course of Study," a fifth and sixth grade program in comparative anthropology funded by the NSF. See Provenzo, 43–46.

51. The publication of Americans United for Separation of Church and State reports that the Harry Potter books were the most censored books in America. Religious conservatives argue that these books promote witchcraft and sorcery, and have attempted to expunge them not only from classrooms but also from school librar-

ies. See "Witch Hunt: The Religious Right Crusade Against Harry Potter," *Church and State*, 55, 3, (2002), 8–12.
52. See *Brown v. Hot, Sexy, and Safer Productions, Inc.*, 68 F. 3d 525, 533 (1st Cir. 1995).
53. *Ware v. Valley Stream High School District*, 550 NE 2d 420 (NY 1989) 406 US at 235. And in *Alfonso v. Fernandez*, 606 NYS 2d 251 (Ct. App. Div 1993) parental permission was required before a high school could distribute condoms to students.
54. See Witmer and Myrick, *Facilitative Teaching: Theory and Practice*, second edition (Minneapolis: Educational Media, 1980).
55. 20 USC 1232h (b).
56. *Student's Bill of Rights*, Eagle Forum, printed in "Fundamentalist Christians, The Public Schools and the Religion Clauses," *Denver University Law Review* 66: 305–6.
57. School conflict broke out into community violence in Kanawha County, West Virginia in 1974. The newly consolidated school district combined both rural and urban districts, including Charlestown, the state's largest city, thus setting the stage for a conflict between cosmopolitan and traditional values. Early in 1974 a committee recommended, and the school board adopted a list of language arts textbooks for use in the district. A school board member, and wife of local fundamentalist minister, asked to review proposed textbooks and found them to be full of disrespect for authority and religion, unpatriotic, obscene, and full negative references to Christianity and God, profanity, anti-American and anti-white materials. Critics of the books brought to town Mel and Norma Gabler, the Texas textbook critics who were rapidly becoming a dominant power in textbook adoptions. In the fall of 1974, 8,000 students boycotted the school in protest over the books, and then student supporters of the materials led their own walkout. Soon the community broke out in violence, including firebombs, gunshots, and vandalism to the public schools, and a coal miners strike. One minister even publicly prayed for the death of three school board members who had supported the books. See Provenzo, 20–25.
58. *Religious Liberty, Public Education, and the Future of American Democracy: A Statement of Principles*. Copies are available from the First Amendment Center, 1207 18th Ave. S., Nashville, TN 37212.
59. The best description of this "new consensus," and proposal for its implementation is Warren Nord and Charles Haynes, *Taking Religion Seriously Across the Curriculum*, jointly published by the Association for Supervision and Curriculum Development and the First Amendment Center, 1998.
60. This document is available by writing to Religion in the Public Schools, 15

East 84th St. Suite 501, New York, NY 10028. A directive based on this consensus is available from the US Department of Education, and *A Parents Guide to Religion in the Public Schools* is available from the First Amendment Center, Freedom Forum, 1101 Wilson Blvd., Arlington, VA 22209.

61. See Mary Michell Upson Hirschoff, "Parents and the Public School Curriculum: Is There a Right to have ones Child Excused from Objectionable Instruction?" *Southern California Law Review* 50 (1997), 871. For an excellent discussion by an advocate of excusal, see John W. Whitehead, *The Rights of Religious Persons in Public Education* (Wheaton, IL: Crossway Books, 1994), 177–97.

62. Title 20 USC Sec. 1232h (b) gives parents right to inspect any instructional materials used in the schools in connection with "any program or project in any applicable program designed to explore or develop new or unproven methods or techniques."

63. In *Hardwick v. Fruitridge Board of School Trustees* 205 P. 49 (Cal. 1921). Public school required to exempt dissenting children from dancing classes. In 1970, a school district that required ROTC training was ordered to give a diploma to a student who had absented himself from ROTC training on religious grounds *Spence v. Bailey* 325 F. Supp. 601 (1971); aff'd 465 F. 2d 796 (6th Cir.) (1972). In 1978, a public school system was ordered to exempt from coeducational physical education classes members of the United Pentecostal Church who objected to interacting with members of the opposite sex wearing immodest attire. *Moody v. Cronin* 484 F. Supp. 270 (C.D. Ill.) (1979). Not all excusal attempts had been successful. In the mid-1970s, a federal court turned down a request from members of the Apostolic Lutheran Church, who objected to exposing their children to audio-visual projections, drama, music, and dance, the study of evolution, "humanist" philosophy, discussion of personal and family matters, the role of guidance counselors, and sexually oriented materials. The court refused to order the school district to excuse the children, finding the free exercise rights of the students and their parents subordinate to the state's interest in education. *Davis v. Page* 385 F. Supp 395, 404–05 (D.N.H. 1974).

64. *Minersville School District v. Gobitis* 310 US 568 (1940).

65. *West Virginia Board of Education v. Barnette* 319 US 624 (1943).

66. 647 F. Supp. 1194 (E.D. Tenn. 1986), 827 F. 2d 1058 (6 Cir. 1987). See James Harkins IV, "Of Textbooks and Tenets: *Mozert v. Hawkins County Board of Education* and the Free Exercise of Religion," *American University Law Review* 37 (1988), 985, and Hugh Bryer, "Cinderella, The Horse God and the Wizard of Oz: *Mozert v. Hawkins County Public Schools*," *Journal of Law and Education* 20 (1991), 63.

67. Mark Tushnet, "Thinking about the Constitution at the Cusp, Symposium: Education and the Constitution: Shaping Each Other and the Next Century," *Akron Law Review* 34 (2000), 32–33.
68. Ibid., 33.
69. 827 F. 2d 1058 (7th Cir. 1987). While the decision was unanimous, this case produced three separate opinions. Chief Judge Lively ruled that exposure to ideas in conflict with ones religious beliefs does not unconstitutionally burden public school students' Free Exercise rights. Exposure does not constitute compulsion to believe or to act contrary to ones beliefs. Because religious free exercise was not burdened, the compelling state interest test applied by the district court was not necessary. Judge Kennedy's concurring opinion applied the compelling state interest test and found the state's interest in educating children for life in a pluralistic society sufficient to outweigh any Free Exercise burdens. Judge Boggs reasoned that being compelled to read offensive texts did burden the children's free religious exercise, but "reluctantly" concluded that such a burden was not unconstitutional according to Supreme Court precedents.
70. Very specific instructions for using opt-out strategies are given in John Whitehead, *The Rights of Religious Persons in Public Education* (Wheaton, IL: Crossway Books, 1994).
71. See for example Ethel Herr, *Schools: How Parents Can Make a Difference* (Chicago: Moody Press, 1981); Connaught Marsher, *Blackboard Tyranny* (New Rochelle, NY: Arlington House, 1978) and Mel and Norma Gabler, "Mounting the Offensive Against Undesirable Texts," in *A Parent's Guide to Textbook Reform, Special Supplement to Education Update* (Heritage Foundation, 1978). All of these sources provide very specific strategic advice to parents on organizing a campaign against curricular materials in order to appear to be a grassroots reaction.
72. Perhaps the most thorough advice is Mel and Norma Gabler's instructions for "Mounting the Offensive Against Undesirable Texts." For one description of the Gablers, see Provenzo, 32–40.
73. 827 F. 2d 684 (11th Cir. 1987.) This case grew out of the original litigation challenging the moment of silence laws in *Wallace v. Jaffre*, but was separated early in the litigation. For arguments that secular humanism constitutes a religion, see John Conland and John Whitehead, "The Establishment of the Religion of Secular Humanism and its First Amendment Implications," *Texas Tech Law Review* 10 (1978), 1–66; Nadine Strossen, "Secular Humanism and Scientific Creationism: Proposed Standards for Reviewing Curricular Decisions Affecting Students' Religious Freedom," *Ohio State Law Journal* 47 (1986), 222–307; "Note: Humanistic Values in the Public School Curriculum: Problems in Defining an Appropri-

ate Wall of Separation," *Northwestern University Law Review* 61 (1966), 795–816; B. Douglas Hayes, "Secular Humanism in Public School Textbooks: Thou Shalt Have No Other God (Except Thyself)," *Notre Dame Law Review* 63 (1988), 358–79; James Hitchcock, "Church, State, and Moral Values: The Limits of American Pluralism," *Law and Contemporary Problems* 44 (1981); Martha M. McCarthy, "Secular Humanism and Education," *Journal of Law and Education* 19 (1990), 467–98; Christopher J. Tully, "Public School Curricula, Secularly Humanism and the Religion Clause," *The Journal of Law and Politics* 10 (1994), 413–44; and Kathleen McChehey, "The Public School Curriculum, Secular Humanism, and the Religion Clauses," *Washburn Law Journal* 28 (1998), 380–99.

74. See Justin Watson, *The Christian Coalition: Dreams of Restoration, Demands for Recognition* (New York: St. Martin's, 1997).

75. *Zelman v. Simmons-Harris*, U.S. Supreme Court No. 00–1171, 00–1177, 00–1170 (2002).

Religion, the Family, and the Public School during Non-School Hours: *Good News v. Milford*

R. COLLIN MANGRUM

Introduction

The relationship between religion and the family presents a complex social, cultural, and moral issue, complicated even more whenever the state intervenes in the conflict. Essays in this collection reflect three general views regarding the relationship between religion and the family. First, religion and the family are indistinguishable. In this view religion arises out of and has no discernible content outside the family.[1] Second, the family presents a significant barrier to the realization of religion: true religion requires transcending the parochialism of the family either for a greater good (for example, communion with God) or realization of the existential self (for example, radical feminism).[2] A third, intermediate view is that religion and family are separate but inextricably intertwined.[3] From this perspective, reflected in this essay, the family serves a critical role in realizing religious fulfillment without embodying the entirety of religion.

These three paradigms of the family embodying, obscuring, or serving as an integral part of religion present variant views of the fundamental moral issue of the relationship between religion and the family. Once the issue of the relationship between religion and the family has been identified as a problem for moral development, the role of the state in providing both the ability to act and the freedom to act consistent with one's view becomes critical. This essay considers this "freedom to act" stage of moral development. To what extent does the American constitutional system provide the political freedom within which adherents to each of the respective views of the relationship between religion and the family may realize their vision? What rights does the family have within the American constitutional system that bear directly on the freedom of any actor to achieve his or her vision for prioritizing and reconciling the state, religion, and family?

The Constitutional Issue: The Moral Training of Children

Whatever paradigm one chooses for establishing the proper relationship between religion and the family, the freedom to act consistent with that paradigm depends upon the compatibility of that view with the state's constitutional structure. In review of this issue, this essay examines one of the United States Supreme Court's most recent decision speaking to the relationship between religion, the family, and the state: *Good News Club v. Milford Central School*.[4] *Good News Club* addressed the issue of whether a religious-based club should be permitted to meet after school on public school premises for the purpose of prayer, religious songs, scripture reading, and religious instruction on moral issues. Are such activities within the protected sphere of family rights, or are they proscribed by the Establishment Clause? In deciding this issue, *Good News* provides a window into broader questions related to whether the state's constitutional theory facilitates, undermines, or remains neutral as variant actors within the body politic seek to realize their view of the proper relationship between religion, the family, and the state?

This controversy over religious instruction on school premises after school hours is closely related to a broader controversy over the role of religion within the state generally and the public school in particular. Religious parents who believe that the family serves a critical role in inculcating religious ideas and moral training have expressed disappointment over the dominant influence that epistemic rationality, secular humanism, and liberal morality have had over the public school curriculum.[5] Their concern has been heightened by the United States Supreme Court's prior rulings that the Establishment Clause prohibits regular school prayer,[6] the display of religious symbols within the school,[7] the presence of devotional exercises during school hours,[8] any religious concession on curriculum issues,[9] or even non-routine prayers at either graduation ceremonies[10] or during school athletic events.[11] These parents fear losing control over the moral and religious training of their children as a consequence of the courts prohibiting them from having their children opt out of programs and curriculum that are deemed by religious families to be openly offensive to their religious views.[12]

These parents believe that the Court's persistent sanitizing of the public school's curriculum from everything sacred sends the message that religion is irrational, mythological, nonscientific, or at least irrelevant for the modern world. For many who believe otherwise, including this author, they suggest that these wholesale exclusions are neither legally required nor morally acceptable. For them the consistent exclusion of anything religious from the day-to-day school experience signals the state's hostility toward religion. They would argue that this hostility violates the Establishment Clause by preferring non-religion or secular humanism to traditional religious views thereby effectively establishing the religion of secular humanism.[13] The unacceptability of the Court's apparent hostility to traditional religion within the public school forum and curriculum has prompted many religious families to opt out of public education (a constitutionally protected alternative[14]) in favor of some form of parochial school education or home schooling. This choice may become even more viable for many low-income families because of the Supreme Court's recent validation of Cleveland's school voucher program in the recently decided *Zelman v. Simmons-Harris*.[15] However, if the opt out alternative becomes increasingly available and preferred, would there not be significant social consequences for pluralism if each distinct religious, cultural, or ethnic group chose to opt out of public education in favor of an educational curriculum that accommodated their world view? Are there not constitutional alternatives to the opt-out strategy that would preserve many of the values of public education, including the value of an acceptable level of assimilation?

Permitting after-school religious training on moral issues on school premises (the proposal submitted by the *Good News Club* to Milford School District) may offer a partial alternative solution. While many school districts have been hostile to such proposals, the Supreme Court's holding in *Good News Club v. Milford Central School* permitting such activities will require schools to be more tolerant toward religious speech within the school's limited public forum during non-school hours. *Good News*, in effect, increases the choices of religious families concerned with the pervasive influence of secular education over the minds and spirits of their children.

Good News Club v. Milford Central School

After the Good News Club had unsuccessfully applied for a permit from Milford Central School for the use of the school's facilities during non-school hours for moral training from a religious point of view, the Club filed a 42 U.S.C. Section 1983 action alleging that by refusing the Club's use of the school's facilities, Milford School District had violated the Club's free speech and equal protection rights. Essentially, the Club had proposed providing an important service for the religious families who had become concerned over the secular orientation of the public school's curriculum. This nondenominational, community-based Christian youth organization proposed holding a once-a-week-after-school meeting "to instruct children in family values and morals from a Christian perspective."[16] A typical meeting would include "an opening prayer, singing of Christian songs, memorization, recital, and discussion of biblical verses and scripture, and a closing prayer."[17] The school explained that they had refused the Club's request because the school district "believed that the Club's activities constituted religious worship and instruction," a use prohibited on school premises by both New York Education Law[18] and school policy.[19]

Chief Judge McAvoy agreed with the Milford School District's argument and granted a motion for summary judgment against the Good News Club's civil-rights petition on the reasoning that by including religious exercises as part of the Club's proposed moral training the Club made the use of the school's facilities constitutionally impermissible. Chief Judge McAvoy explained that while the school had created a limited public forum in which other moral development groups had been permitted to use the school's facilities,[20] the Club's activities were, by comparison, "decidedly religious in nature, and not merely a discussion of secular matters from a religious perspective that is otherwise permitted under the District's use policies."[21] The Good News Club appealed arguing that the religious context of the moral training could not cancel out the fact that the training was nonetheless morality centered, and therefore the school's exclusion of the Club's activities constituted viewpoint discrimination.

The United States Circuit Court of Appeals for the Second Circuit affirmed the trial court's granting of summary judgment against the Good News Club.[22] In response to the Club's argument that their exclusion constituted viewpoint discrimination on the teaching of morality from a Christian perspective, the Second Circuit concluded, "that the Good News Club is doing something other than simply teaching moral values."[23] Without mentioning the Supreme Court's clearly most analogous authority, *Lamb's Chapel*, the Second Circuit opined that the "religious instruction and prayer" involved in the Club's meetings took the School's exclusion outside the scope of "viewpoint discrimination" to an exclusion based upon content.[24] In essence, the Second Circuit determined that the worshipful aspects of the Club's speech overwhelmed any argument that the Club's activities pertained to moral development. Religiously inspired moral development simply does not count as moral development.

Circuit Judge Jacobs wrote a dissenting opinion. In response to the majority's view that the School's exclusion could be justified on the basis of the religious subject matter of the Club's activities, Judge Jacobs observed: "when the subject matter is morals and character, it is quixotic to attempt a distinction between religious viewpoints and religious subject matters."[25] The Club appealed to the United States Supreme Court, arguing that Judge Jacob's dissenting opinion more aptly captured the issues than either the Second Circuit majority opinion or the district court's granting of the school's motion for summary judgment.

Justice Thomas, writing for a five justice majority of the United States Supreme Court in *Good News Club v. Milford Central School*,[26] in reversing and remanding[27] held that "[w]hen Milford denied the Good News Club access to the school's limited public forum on the ground that the Club was religious in nature, it discriminated against the Club because of its religious viewpoint in violation of the Free Speech Clause of the First Amendment."[28] The Court also held that such violation was not "required to avoid violating the Establishment Clause."[29]

Justice Thomas began his free speech analysis with an observation that "[w]hen the State establishes a limited public forum, the State is not required to and does not allow persons to engage in every type of speech."[30] However, once it establishes a limited public forum, the state may neither "discriminate on the basis of viewpoint,"[31] nor impose restrictions that are not "reasonable in light of the purpose served by the forum."[32] The Court found that Milford's exclusion of the Good News Club constituted "viewpoint discrimination,"[33] because Milford had opened the school for purposes "'pertaining to the welfare of the community,'"[34] including character and moral development, the very purpose proposed by the Good News Club.[35] The Court disagreed with the lower courts' findings that the context of the moral training, which included prayer, the recitation of biblical verses, religious songs, and the use of biblical stories to inspire the children to act consistent with the morals contained therein,[36] somehow transformed the Club's permissible moral training into an impermissible religious worship.[37] To the contrary, the Court found that under the principle of *Lamb's Chapel*, the religious context of the Club's moral training cannot stand as a justification for viewpoint discrimination.[38] The Court explained:

> The only apparent difference between the activity of *Lamb's Chapel* and the activities of the Good News Club is that the Club chooses to teach moral lessons from a Christian perspective through live storytelling and prayer, whereas *Lamb's Chapel* taught lessons through films. This distinction is inconsequential.[39]

The Court also found *Rosenberger* dispositive on the same issue.[40] Just as the University of Virginia's denial of equal funding to a Christian-oriented student publication constituted viewpoint discrimination, Milford's denial of equal access to the school's facilities after school hours similarly constituted viewpoint discrimination.[41] Contrary to the Court of Appeals for the Second Circuit, "reliance on Christian principles" does not "taint . . . moral and character instruction in a way that other foundations for thought or viewpoints do not."[42]

The Court also rejected Milford's argument that even if their policy constituted viewpoint discrimination, the Establishment Clause justified such discrimination.[43] The Court explained that similar arguments were rejected by the Court in both *Lamb's Chapel* and *Widmar*.[44] The Court explained:

> As in *Lamb's Chapel*, the Club's meetings were held after school hours, not sponsored by the school, and open to any student who obtained parental consent, not just to Club members. As in *Widmar*, Milford made its forum available to other organizations. The Club's activities are materially indistinguishable from those in *Lamb's Chapel* and *Widmar*.[45]

The Court similarly rejected Milford's argument that the elementary-school age of the students made it likely that the "children will perceive that the school is endorsing the Club and will feel coercive pressure to participate."[46] With regard to the endorsement issue and the correlative "neutrality principle" commonly associated with Establishment Clause analysis, the Court observed:

> Milford's implication that granting access to the Club would do damage to the neutrality principle defies logic. For the "guarantee of neutrality is respected, not offended, when the government, following neutral criteria and evenhanded policies, extends benefits to recipients whose ideologies and viewpoints, including religious ones, are broad and diverse.". . . The Good News Club seeks nothing more than to be treated neutrally and given access to speak about the same topics as are other groups.[47]

In response to the possibility that elementary school children might misperceive free speech neutrality as establishment endorsement, the Court noted: "Any bystander could conceivably be aware of the school's use policy and its exclusion of the Good News Club, and could suffer as much from viewpoint discrimination as elementary children could suffer from perceived endorsement."[48] The Court added: "We decline to employ Establishment Clause jurisprudence using a modified heckler's veto, in which a group's religious activity can be proscribed on the basis of what the youngest members of the audience might misperceive."[49]

On the related issue that the children may feel coercive pressure to participate in the Club's activities, the Court held:

> the relevant community would be the parents, not the elementary school children. It is the parents who choose whether their children will attend the Good News Club meetings. Because the children cannot attend without their parents' permission, they cannot be coerced into engaging in the Good News Club's religious activities.[50]

While Justice Scalia joined the majority opinion, he also wrote a concurring opinion to explain both his free speech and establishment rationale for joining. With regard to the issue of free speech, Justice Scalia explained that "'because it's religious'" cannot provide a reasonable basis for discriminating against religious speech.[51] Rejecting the view that the presence of religious conviction somehow taints a free speech analysis,

Justice Scalia reasoned to the contrary: "[j]ust as calls to character based on patriotism will go unanswered if the listeners do not believe their country is good and just, calls to moral behavior based on God's will are useless if the listeners do not believe that God exists."[52]

Justice Scalia, also joining the Court's opinion dismissing the Establishment Clause justification for Milford's viewpoint discrimination, reasoned that "to the extent" that "considerations of coercive pressure" and "perceptions of endorsement" are relevant factors, such factors had "zero" presence in this case.[53] He explained that "peer pressure" arising from private association is a consequence of free speech and free association and, therefore, does not arise to unconstitutional coercion.[54] Similarly, allowing a "priest . . . as much liberty to proselytize as a patriot" in a limited public forum open to all on equal terms cannot signify an unconstitutional endorsement and "erroneous conclusions [about endorsement] do not count."[55]

Justice Breyer agreed with the Court's conclusion that the exclusion of the Good News Club constituted viewpoint discrimination, but wrote a concurring opinion to express concern over the majority's preoccupation with the neutrality principle as an almost exclusive factor in establishment analysis. He insisted that "the government's 'neutrality' in respect to religion is one, but only one, of the considerations relevant to deciding whether a public school's policy violates the Establishment Clause."[56] Rather than focusing exclusively on the parent's perceptions with regard to the endorsement issue, Justice Breyer suggested that "the critical Establishment Clause question here may well prove to be whether a child, participating in the Good News Club's activities, could reasonably perceive the school's permission for the club to use its facilities as an endorsement of religion."[57] In this regard the question is whether in the children's minds "'a formal policy of equal access is transformed into a demonstration of approval.'"[58] He concluded that because the issue of "children's perceptions" had not been determined below, the Court should have remanded this issue for determination prior to deciding the Establishment issue.[59]

Justice Stevens wrote a dissenting opinion criticizing the majority's free speech analysis. Justice Stevens, the champion of free speech when nude dancing is in the spotlight,[60] contended that the state in a limited public forum may discriminate against religious speech if the speech is "worshipful" or "proselytizing."[61] Justice Stevens explained that "such recruiting meetings may introduce divisiveness and tend to separate children into cliques that undermine the school's educational mission."[62] Justice Stevens refused to consider the Establishment issue because establishment "was not addressed by either the District Court or the Court of Appeals."[63]

Justice Souter wrote a dissenting opinion in which Justice Ginsburg joined, criticizing both the majority's free speech and establishment arguments. According to Justice Souter, in designating a limited public forum the Milford School District could properly exclude "religious use" generally on the basis of subject matter. As with Justice Stevens, because the "Good news activities may be characterized as proselytizing and therefore as outside the purpose of Milford's limited forum,"[64] they could be excluded even though the activities also could be characterized as "'teaching of morals and character, from a religious standpoint.'"[65]

Speaking to "the doubtful underpinnings of the majority's [Establishment] conclusion,"[66] Justice Souter observed: "[t]his Court has accepted the independent obligation to obey Establishment Clause as sufficiently compelling to satisfy strict scrutiny under the First Amendment."[67] He offered the opinion "Milford's actions would offend the Establishment Clause if they carried the message of endorsing religion under the circumstances as viewed by a reasonable observer."[68] According to Justice Souter, the facts of temporal and physical continuity of Good News' after-school meetings involving "the minds of young children" suggest, "there is a good case that Good News' exercises blur the line between public classroom instruction and private religious indoctrination, leaving a reasonable elementary school pupil unable to appreciate that the former instruction is the business of the school while the latter evangelism is not."[69]

Analysis of the Constitutional Entitlement Issues

In evaluating whether entitlement claims justify preferential, neutral, or prohibited treatment of religious activities in the school's limited public forum, the constitutional parameters of free exercise, free speech, family rights, and equal protection must be considered. A review of each of these entitlement claims in the context of the issues involved in *Good News* provides substantial constitutional support of the Supreme Court's holding in this case.

The Free Exercise Clause and Preferred Status

The Free Exercise Clause provides the most likely justification for extending preferential status to the Good News Club's religiously based moral training.[70] The free exercise argument suggests that the fact that the Good News Club's activities involve family-chosen religious training states a basis for preferring such activities over competing secular activities. The Court's first significant interpretation of the Free Exercise Clause came in the context of a politically driven assault on the nineteenth-century Mormon practice of polygamy in particular[71] and the Mormon Church in general.[72] Nearly a century later several Supreme Court cases seemed to breathe life into the Free Exercise Clause, made moribund by *Reynolds* and *Beason*, by requiring that the state prove a compelling state interest to justify interfering with the free exercise of religion.[73] Justice Scalia squelched the embryonic development of a free exercise jurisprudence in *Employment Div. v. Smith*,[74] wherein he rejected the notion that the Free Exercise Clause requires the state to prove a compelling state interest before infringing free exercise claims. He stated that, "the right of free exercise does not relieve an individual of the obligation to comply with a 'valid and neutral law of general applicability on the ground that the law proscribes (or prescribes) conduct that his religion proscribes (or prescribes).'"[75] Justice O'Connor recognized in her concurring opinion in *Smith* that Justice Scalia's interpretation of the free exercise clause limits its protection to "the extreme and hypothetical situation in which a State directly targets a religious practice" and thereby relegates free exercise protection "to the barest level of minimum scrutiny that the Equal Protection Clause already provides."[76]

Given Justice Scalia's holding in *Smith*, if a religious claimant such as the Good News Club would seek protection for religious practices, then he or she must look to constitutional principles other than the Free Exercise Clause.[77] Of the alternative sources of rights that have afforded religious activities a modicum of protection, the Free Speech Clause has offered the most hope.

Free Speech as an Alternative Basis for Preserving Entitlement Claims for Religious Activities

The nineteenth century denial of any free exercise protection for the "unchristian" Mormon beliefs and practices[78] left free exercise claims in a constitutional vacuum. If the Free Exercise Clause protected only belief, could the state proscribe all religious activities, including worship and other forms of religious speech? The answer came in several closely related mid-twentieth century cases involving Jehovah's Witnesses conducting door-to-door evangelical distribution of religious literature and solicitation of donations. In these cases the Court acknowledged that even while the Free Exercise Clause only protects belief, it protects religious-oriented conduct that can be characterized as speech.[79] Scholars and jurists have ever since debated whether these "hybrid"[80] cases provide either a case for a "preferred" category of "worshipful" speech or a "reductionist" argument that religious speech receives free speech protection but no more.[81] In recent years many of the early cases extending "preferred" status to worshipful speech either have been forgotten or consciously ignored, but religious speech has received protection under the neutrality principle.

For the purposes of the Court's analysis in *Good News*, the two most important "neutral" free speech cases are *Lamb's Chapel* and *Rosenberger*. The Court in *Lamb's Chapel v. Center Moriches Union Free School Dist.*,[82] without any dissent, held that once a school district had opened the school's facilities for after-school-hour use to a wide range of community groups and purposes, any attempt to exclude participation by comparable speakers from a religious perspective would amount to unconstitutional view point discrimination. The Court held that the government could not "permit school property to be used for the presentation of all views about family issues and child rearing except those dealing with the subject matter from a religious standpoint."[83]

The Court reaffirmed *Lamb's Chapel* neutrality principle in *Rosenberger v. University of Virginia*.[84] In *Rosenberger* the Court considered whether the University of Virginia could discriminate against religiously inspired speech by a Christian student group at the university. Specifically, the university had denied a Christian-oriented student newspaper funding on equal terms with its secular counterparts because of the blatant evangelical message. Indeed, Justice Souter dissented in *Rosenberger* specifically because the paper described its mission as "encourag[ing] students to consider what a personal relationship with Jesus Christ means."[85] Nonetheless, the Court held that once the state university opened a limited forum, the state could not discriminate on the basis of the content of the speech (viewpoint discrimination) even to avoid the establishment specter of evangelical speech.

Contrary to this neutrality principle, the dissenting opinions in *Good News* would discriminate against any religious speech having a worshipful or evangelical context. For these justices, the very speech the Court in *Cantwell, Jamison,* and *Murdock* extended a preferred status because of the added significance of the free exercise of religion, should receive less constitutional protection than all other speech. These justices would make the free exercise context of religious speech a justification for prohibition rather than preference. This contradicts the Court's religious free speech cases, and flies in the face of the Court's separate authority both reserving to the family special rights connected with the religious training of children and proscribing invidious discrimination against religion.

Religion Protected as an Aspect of Family Rights

Although not discussed in *Good News,* family rights provide an independent basis for upholding the Court's result in *Good News*. The right of the family to control the religious training of their children has ancient roots. Under Roman civil law, the doctrine of *patria potestas* established in the father extensive power over both his wife and children. Paternal control over religious training, *religio sequitur patrem*, followed naturally from this more general rule of *patria potestas*. The English common law, influenced not only by the Roman civil law but also by feudalism and the patriarchal orientation of Christianity, adopted the Roman doctrine of both *patria potestas* and *religio sequitur*. Consequently, under English common law the power of the father over religious issues facing the family "was viewed as absolute, proprietary, and God-given, and consequently unalterable by man."[86]

Even though American family law did not develop within the feudal system that gave meaning to the doctrine of *patria potestas*, the American common law adopted the doctrine. Consistent with English law, the state remained nearly powerless to dictate the religious training of children. Parental control over the moral and religious training of children was so well accepted that an early twentieth century scholarly observer remarked "our courts have been remarkably free from litigation over the religious education of children."[87]

The right of the family to control matters related to religious and moral training not only finds support in American tradition[88] and common law, the United States Supreme Court also has recognized these rights as so basic and fundamental as to not require specific constitutional enumeration.[89] The United States Supreme Court first recognized as fundamental the constitutional right of the family to control the religious training of their children in *Meyer v. Nebraska*.[90] In *Meyer* the Court considered whether the State of Nebraska could prohibit by statute the teaching of foreign languages in either public or private schools to children in kindergarten through seventh grade.[91] Nebraska defended the English-only requirement on grounds of national security, reasoning that "the language first learned by a child remains his mother tongue and the language of his heart."[92] To the contrary, the Lutheran parents insisted that their fundamental right to control the religious training of their children, including the education of their children at the Zion Parochial School so they would be able to read the Bible in German, took precedence over the state's vague claims of national security. Upholding the priority of the parent's entitlement claim, the Court held that under the Due Process Clause of the Fourteenth Amendment the parents had a fundamental right to control the religious worship of their children.[93] According to the Court, this right to control the religious training of children justified overriding the "desire of the legislature to foster a homogeneous people with American ideals prepared readily to understand current discussions of civic matters."[94]

The Court reaffirmed the substantive due process right of the parents to control the religious upbringing of their children in *Pierce v. Society of Sisters*,[95] when the Court invalidated Oregon's compulsory public school requirement, which invalidated an Oregon statute compelling attendance at public school at the expense of competing parochial and private schools. The Old Order Amish pushed the limits of this entitlement claim by successfully seeking to opt out of formal education entirely after the eighth grade in *Wisconsin v. Yoder*.[96] There the Court exempted the children of the Old Order Amish from compulsory school requirements after the eighth grade on the grounds of the fundamental rights of Amish parents to raise their children in accordance with the Amish tradition, something formal education after the eighth grade threatened to extinguish. This fundamental right of the family to control the moral and religious training of children has been repeated so often by the Supreme Court as to place the issue beyond dispute.[97]

These family-rights cases establish the constitutional principle that parents who "nurture and direct" their children are constitutionally protected in choices for their children relative to religious views and life styles that may be at odds with the views of the secular state. Undoubtedly, the families who chose to have their children participate in the Good News Club's after-school activities were concerned with the constant drone of secular humanism pervasive in the public school's secular curriculum on their children's religious beliefs, and chose to have their children participate in the Good News Club's religious-oriented moral training to restore some balance to their children's moral upbringing. This choice to have their children exposed to "evangelical" moral training fits well within the established principle that the parents have a fundamental right to control the religious and moral training of their children. The resolution permits the parents to have their children in the public school system, an even less radical step than afforded the Catholic children in *Pierce* and the Old Order Amish children in *Yoder*, without completely abandoning their family's religious insights regarding the moral training of their children.

Analysis of the Establishment Issue

Despite the strong constitutional arguments favoring the entitlement claims of the Good News families, the constitutional viability of *Good News* depends upon reconciling such an entitlement claim with the Court's establishment jurisprudence. The most critical difference between the majority and dissenting opinions in *Good News* is the effect of the Establishment Clause on the entitlement claims. For the majority, Establishment Clause jurisprudence is compatible with extending religious free speech equal protection and neutral treatment. To the contrary, the dissenting justices argue that the Establishment Clause justifies, if not demands, discrimination against religious speech. These disparate establishment views as applied to the after-school use of the public schools are not surprising given that there are few areas of constitutional law in which the Supreme Court has been more inconsistent and more ambivalent than cases involving the Establishment Clause. According to the Supreme Court's own critical self-assessment, "our Establishment Clause jurisprudence is in hopeless disarray."[98] In *Good News* the Court's uncertainty regarding both the identity and relative weight of the critical factors relied upon in determining an establishment violation reflects this disarray. The variant establishment factors discussed by the various justices include "neutrality," "endorsement," "coercion," and "separatism."

Reconciling the state's establishment principles under any of these paradigms with the entitlement claims of the families is the real challenge of the *Good News* case.

The Neutrality or Nondiscriminatory Principle

In recent years the neutrality principle has become the dominant establishment factor for the majority of the present Supreme Court justices. According to the neutrality principle, the state cannot target religion for either benefits or detriments. Religion must be treated neutrally. If the state pursues a legitimate policy or entitlement objective, then any incidental impact on religion following from the policy or entitlement claim, whether for good or ill, does not violate the Establishment Clause.

Several members of the present Court have expressed the view that the neutrality principle represents an analytical advance on the wall-of-separation establishment rhetoric for establishment that many jurists have mentioned in the past. Indeed, much of the impetus for the neutrality principle has been a reaction to confusion wrought by misuse of the wall-of-separation metaphor.[99] As discussed above, the same neutrality principle has come to dominate the Court's analysis of entitlement issues associated with both free speech and state aid to religion.[100] This same neutrality paradigm also dominates Justice Thomas's majority opinion with respect to whether extending entitlement protection to the free speech of the Good News Club would violate the Establishment Clause. Justice Thomas in his majority opinion explains that protecting free speech for religious activities cannot signal an establishment violation:

> Milford's implication that granting access to the Club would do damage to the neutrality principle defies logic. For the "guarantee of neutrality is respected, not offended, when the government, following neutral criteria and evenhanded policies, extends benefits to recipients whose ideologies and viewpoints, including religious ones, are broad and diverse.". . . The Good News Club seeks nothing more than to be treated neutrally and given access to speak about the same topics as are other groups.[101]

The neutrality principle appears so outcome determinative to the majority in *Good News* that Justice Breyer felt compelled to express his concern that the neutrality principle has become too dominant an establishment factor. He explained that while the Club's use of the facilities appeared neutral, "the government's 'neutrality' in respect to religion is one, but only one, of the considerations relevant to deciding whether a public school's policy violates the Establishment Clause."[102] His added consideration is whether the support endorses religion. He would have preferred remanding the case to determine whether "a child, participating in the Good News Club's activities, could reasonably perceive the school's permission for the club to use its facilities as an endorsement of religion.[103] Restated, Justice Breyer recommended that the neutrality principle be subject to the constraint of the endorsement test.

Endorsement

The "endorsement" factor identified by Justice Breyer in his concurring opinion as an important qualifier to the neutrality principle has also played an important role in the Court's recent establishment cases. Although the different justices in *Good News* offer differing views regarding whether the appropriate "endorsement" observer is the parents who signed the consent forms, the students attending the Good News Club activities, or the students roaming the halls during the after-school hours, all the justices who discuss the establishment issue concede that the endorsement analysis is relevant to the establishment issue.[104]

Justice O'Connor originally coined the "endorsement test"[105] as a coherent alternative to the traditional *Lemon* standard for establishment reasoning. Since that time Justice O'Connor has repeatedly recommended the test as an important establishment insight. In *Jaffree* Justice O'Connor went out of her way to explain the advantages of the endorsement test:

> The endorsement test is useful because of the analytical content it gives to the *Lemon*-mandated inquiry into legislative purpose and effect. In this country, church and state must necessarily operate within the same community. Because of this coexistence, it is inevitable that the secular interests of government and the religious interests of various sects and their adherents will frequently intersect, conflict, and combine. A statute that ostensibly promotes a secular interest often has an incidental or even a primary effect of helping or hindering a sectarian belief. Chaos would ensue if every such statute were invalid under the Establishment Clause. . . The endorsement test does not preclude government from acknowledging reli-

gion or from taking religion into account in making law and policy. It does preclude government from conveying or attempting to convey a message that religion or a particular religious belief is favored or preferred. Such an endorsement infringes the religious liberty of the nonadherent, for "[w]hen the power, prestige and financial support of government is placed behind a particular religious belief, the indirect coercive pressure upon religious minorities to conform to the prevailing officially approved religion is plain."[106]

Justice O'Connor also has made it clear that in making an "endorsement" determination,[107] the test's beholder is not "the perceptions of particular individuals" or "isolated non-adherents,"[108] but "rather a personification of a community ideal of reasonable behavior, determined by the [collective] social judgment . . . [who is] aware of the history and context of the community and forum in which the religious display appears."[109]

In the *Good News* case, the majority held that the parents who signed the consent form to permit the participation of their children were the appropriate observers. According to the majority, the necessity of parents' informed consent negates any likelihood that they will misperceive the relative roles of the Good News Club and the school district. Their informed choice reaffirms the control the families constitutionally have over the religious and moral training of their children. Contrary to the traditional control of the parents over such religious and moral issues, Justice Breyer, concurring, would have preferred remanding the case to determine whether "a child, participating in the Good News Club's activities, could reasonably perceive the school's permission for the club to use its facilities as an endorsement of religion."[110] He argued the endorsement issue from the perspective of the involved students was critical because "the government's 'neutrality' in respect to religion is one, but only one, of the considerations relevant to deciding whether a public school's policy violates the Establishment Clause."[111]

In response to Justice Breyer's argument that the elementary school children might misperceive free speech neutrality as establishment endorsement, Justice Thomas in his majority opinion remarked: "Any bystander could conceivably be aware of the school's use policy and its exclusion of the Good News Club, and could suffer as much from viewpoint discrimination as elementary children could suffer from perceived endorsement."[112] He added: "We decline to employ Establishment Clause jurisprudence using a modified heckler's veto, in which a group's religious activity can be proscribed on the basis of what the youngest members of the audience might misperceive."[113]

Coercion as a Separate Establishment Factor

While the principles of neutrality and endorsement dominate the majority and concurring opinions in *Good News,* Justice Kennedy's coercion factor also finds it way into the Court's consideration as a relevant factor. Justice Kennedy, often a supporter of both Justice O'Connor's endorsement test and the majority's neutrality principle, first raised coercion as an independent establishment factor in his majority opinion in *Lee v. Weisman*.[114] In *Lee* Justice Kennedy expressed the view that the City of Providence, Rhode Island's practice of inviting clergy from various religious communities to offer prayer at school graduation ceremonies violates the Establishment Clause both because it endorses a form of a civic religion[115] and coerces participation in a civic religious exercise.

According to Justice Kennedy, the graduation prayer entailed "subtle coercive pressure" to participate or give the appearance of participating in state directed prayer. The Court explained that "[t]he undeniable fact is that the school district's supervision and control of the high school graduation ceremony places public pressure, as well as peer pressure, on attending students to stand as a group or, at least, maintain respectful silence during the Invocation and Benediction."[116] Even though attendance at the ceremony as well as participation in the prayer were both voluntary, the state's choice to have the prayer constituted illegitimate "social pressure to enforce orthodoxy."[117] Coercion, in this sense, arises from peer pressure inviting conformity in a religious exercise.

Out of deference to Justice Kennedy's coercion factor, Justice Thomas in *Good News* addressed the coercion factor, denying that the children may feel coercive pressure to participate in the Club's activities. He explained that from the perspective of both endorsement and coercion,

> the relevant community would be the parents, not the elementary school children. It is the parents who choose whether their children will attend the Good News Club meetings. Because the children cannot attend without their parents' permission, they cannot be coerced into engaging in the Good News Club's religious activities.[118]

This obeisance to the coercion factor, perhaps to secure Justice Kennedy's joining the majority opinion, completes the establishment factors relied upon by the majority and concurring opinions.

Strict Separationism

The unspoken establishment paradigm underlying the dissenting opinions in *Good News* is that permitting a religious-affiliated club to use the school's facilities even on an equal access basis encroaches upon a wall-of-separation that ought to be maintained between church and state. This separationist perspective colors the analysis of each of the dissents. According to a simplistic separationist theory, the Establishment Clause creates a wall of separation between church and state. For these separationists, nowhere is the wall of separation more important than the public school context (especially during the early years) where impressionable children may misinterpret any attempt neutrally to accommodate religious beliefs or practices.

The strict separation paradigm builds upon the wall-of-separation metaphor, disingenuously first expressed by the Supreme Court in *Reynolds v. United States*:

> I contemplate with sovereign reverence that act of the whole American people which declared that their legislature should "make no law respecting an establishment of religion, or prohibiting the free exercise thereof," thus building a wall of separation between church and state.[119]

The Court in *Reynolds* excerpted the "wall of separation" quote from a reply letter written by Thomas Jefferson to the Danbury Baptist Association, eighteen years after the First Amendment had been enacted.[120] In *Reynolds* the nineteenth-century Court invoked the wall-of-separation metaphor in connection with an *ad terrorem* argument to justify their attack on the despised practice of polygamy practiced by the Mormons. If the free exercise of religion were to be given more protection than belief alone, then the wall of separation between church and state would insulate religious practitioners in performing unspeakable acts. As explained in the discussion of free exercise issues, this early narrowing of the Free Exercise Clause has ever since forced religious claimants to look to other constitutional sources for protection of religious practices, such as free speech, family rights, or equal protection.

The wall-of-separation metaphor first became part of the establishment rhetoric in *Everson v. Board of Education*.[121] Despite invoking the metaphor as a paradigmatic explanation of the Establishment Clause, the Court in *Everson* upheld local legislation permitting parents of both private and public schools to be reimbursed for fares paid for the transportation of their children to school by public buses.[122] Apparently, whatever the wall-of-separation placed out of bounds for the state did not include indirect state financial aid of religion.[123] But if the wall of separation does not prohibit indirect financial aid, what does it prohibit? Does the wall prohibit police and fire protection to religious institutions? How do zoning issues play for religious property in the separation debate? How does the metaphor provide any analytical clarity to these issues and the myriad ways religious activities and institutions interact within the state? In reality the complex interrelationship between religious activities and state action necessarily provides more gaps than the wall-of-separation metaphor can ever explain. Further elucidation simply is necessary even for the separationists.

Of the present justices committed to the building a viable strict separationist chorus, Justice Stevens has served as the lead singer,[124] with Justices Ginsburg,[125] and Souter[126] serving as backup singers. The challenge for these would-be-separationists is fashioning a paradigm for establishment cases that realistically accounts for the inevitable interaction between religion and the state[127] without abandoning completely their aspiration of a wall of separation.

The Court announced the most persistent (and also the most maligned)[128] version of qualified separationism in *Lemon v. Kurtzman*.[129] According to what has become known as the *Lemon* test, the constitutionality of any interaction between religion and the state should be judged by a tri-part-test:

> First, the statute must have a secular legislative purpose; second, its principal or primary effect must be one that neither advances nor inhibits religion; finally, the statute must not foster an excessive government entanglement with religion.[130]

Wall-of-separationists often have offered the *Lemon* test to challenge any apparent incursion to the wall-of-separation. Separationists rely upon the *Lemon* test in criticizing the alternative "endorsement," "neutrality," and "coercion" factors relied upon by the majority in *Good News*. The dissenting opinions in *Good News* typify the wall-of-separation sentiments that these justices have consistently expressed in earlier cases. Justice Souter, who was joined by Justice Ginsburg, dissented from the Court's refusal to remand the Establishment issue, reasoning that the majority placed too little weight on the establishment issues in the case.[131] Citing dicta in both *Widmar v. Vincent* and *Lamb's Chapel*, Justice Souter observed: "[t]his Court has accepted the independent obligation to obey Establishment Clause as sufficiently compelling to satisfy strict scrutiny under the First Amendment."[132] For Justice Souter "Milford's actions would offend the Establishment Clause if they carried the message of endorsing religion under the circumstances as viewed by a reasonable observer."[133] In this regard, Justice Souter disputes the majority's view that "the context is 'materially indistinguishable' from the facts in *Lamb's Chapel* and *Widmar*,"[134] because Lamb's Chapel involved a film series opened to the general public in the evening, and the school property had been used repeatedly by other groups making an endorsement unlikely,[135] and *Widmar* involved "university students, a large number of student groups, and a written disclaimer.[136] In comparison, Justice Souter pointed out that in *Good News* the subjects were elementary-age students, a limited number of groups had chosen to take advantage of the limited public forum provided by the school district, and the meetings were held immediately after school.[137]

While Justice Stevens in his dissent refused to address the Establishment issue because the issue "was not addressed by either the District Court or the Court of Appeals,"[138] his answer is predictable. He undoubtedly would have held that the wall-of-separation standard justified the free speech discrimination consistent with his dissent in *Mergens* and his free speech analysis in *Good News*.

Moral Analysis: the Family's Control Over the Religious Training of Their Children

Ultimately the continued viability of the legal and constitutional doctrines related to the family's right to control the religious training of their children depends upon the moral underpinnings of family rights. How should conflicts between the state's interest in cultivating worthy citizens and claimed family rights be resolved from a moral perspective?

From the perspective of public policy, an argument could be made that children should be removed from their parents both because they lack professional training in child psychology, child rearing techniques, and child education and they are subject to parochial biases and religious, cultural, and ethnic prejudices. For these radical critics of traditional family rights the family stands for and perpetuates parochial self-interestedness if not error in judgment and value choices. If social equality is ever to be achieved or a higher consciousness ever attained, then the family must be abolished or transcended for this higher relationship. For these critics of the family, in place of child rearing by parents who lack training and a proper sense of communal responsibility, the state should intervene on the basis of an egalitarian social agenda. Only the state can effectively elevate a moral commitment to liberal values and *e pluribus unum* over conflicting belief systems perpetuated by parents. Many of these critics have argued that the possibility of establishing an egalitarian society, devoid of parochial biases and cultural peculiarities, depends on either the eradication of the family as a protected institution or the subordination of family rights to the public interest. For these reasons permitting the public school to co-opt all moral training of children consistent with epistemic rationality, secular humanism, and democratic morality would serve important policy interests. If so, then permitting the families to supplement the liberal moral training of the public school curriculum by after-school religious programs would send conflicting messages to the children to the detriment of the unified community. These moral arguments weigh against permitting the Good News Club to participate within the school's limited public forum.

Contrary to these radical criticisms of the family, the moral right of the family to retain control over choices of the theory of the good for family members has been a persistent concern for philosophical liberalism. For many liberals preserving freedom of thought within the inevitably coercive context of state education remains an important objective of a truly liberal state. John Stuart Mill, in his famous essay *On Liberty*, anticipated this very dilemma. His answer parallels the solution adopted in *Good News*:

> All that has been said of the importance of individuality of character, and diversity of opinions and modes of conduct, involves, as of

the same unspeakable importance, diversity of education. A general [s]tate education is a mere contrivance for molding people to be exactly like one another; and as the mold in which it casts them is that which pleases the predominant power in the government . . . it establishes despotism over the mind . . .

There would be nothing to hinder them from being taught religion, if their parents chose, at the same schools where they were taught other things. All attempts by the [s]tate to bias the conclusions of its citizens on disputed subjects are evil . . .[139]

Mill is not alone in recommending the preservation of the family's sway over the moral development of children. For example, John Rawls in his defense of philosophical liberalism contained in his famous book *On Justice* recommends preserving the moral development that occurs within the family despite the parochial biases the family may engender. Thus Rawls argues that even though the liberal "principle of fair opportunity can be only imperfectly carried out, at least as long as the institution of the family exists,"[140] the family should be preserved because it cultivates moral appreciation for the difference principle, an aspect of the principle of fraternity, which favors distributing benefits in favor of the least advantaged group. By teaching the principles of love, sacrifice and service the family serves as a foundation for the child's development of self respect and lays the groundwork for further moral development. For Rawls, the "affection, example, and guidance" of loving parents is crucial to the child's moral development. Such feelings cannot be effectively substituted by "loveless relationships maintained by coercive threats and reprisals."[141] As parental love and example teaches associational rights and duties, the child learns to work out his or her own standards of cooperation adapted to the particular complex social relations he or she experiences. By providing the forum within which the child's moral autonomy effectively can be developed, the family justifies its preservation within the liberal state.

While Rawls' defense of the family ironically appears utilitarian in preservation of conditions necessary to cultivate the difference principle, the libertarian Robert Nozick articulates a natural rights defense of the family. Nozick critically notes the ambivalent position of radicals toward the family. Its loving relationships are seen as a model to be emulated and extended across the whole society, at the same time that it is denounced as a suffocating institution too be broken and condemned as a focus of parochial concerns that interfere with achieving radical goals.[142]

For Nozick the historical relationships of love and care within the family are protectable on the libertarian principle that one has a right not to be interfered with so long as one is not interfering with anyone else.[143] The family arises naturally as part of our biological and social capacity. The state, as a result, has no grounds for intervention. Nozick does recognize that once the child exists he or she has claims even against those who created him.[144] He argues, however, constraints on parental discretion, especially in matters of training, care and support, cannot be justified in the broad name of the public interest. Rather, only the competing rights of others, especially the child, can justify overriding parental autonomy.

According to the liberal writings of Charles Fried, family rights follow from the fundamental right to personal privacy: "The guiding conception, I suggest, is that the right to form one's child's values, one's life plan and the right to lavish attention on that child are extensions of the basic right not to be interfered with in doing these things for oneself."[145] The parent's preferred position over the state in determining the child's best interest is "based on the facts of human reproduction,"[146] the significance of family relations to our sense of personal integrity, and the connection between creation and overcoming the fact of mortality.

Fried views the recognition of parental control over the child's moral development as a foundational basis for the child's sense of personal autonomy: "Belonging at first to our parents, whom we will replace, we have a chance of believing we belong to ourselves."[147] For Fried while there is "no right to harm your children," and "no right not to provide for one's children, not to assure they have proper schooling, and so on,"[148] otherwise the "child's most intimate values and determinants" are the prerogative of the parents because the "society has no special right to choose them, since society, after all, is only the hypostasis of individual, choosing persons."[149]

Contrary to this persistent theme of broad family rights characteristic of philosophical liberalism, many liberals express illiberality toward religion generally and also illiberality toward attempts by families to preserve their control over religious and moral training. Professor Carter, considering the persistent intolerance liberalism often displays toward religion, asks:

> [W]hy is it that contemporary liberalism, which proclaims the freedom of individual conscience, values conscience less when an individual chooses to discover the world through faith rather than through reason? What is it about religious belief that liberalism so fears?[150]

Kent Greenawalt, addressing this same issue of the intolerance of liberalism toward religion, posits: "[o]nly a society that was actually hostile to religion or riven by religious strife could think it preferable for people to rely on nonreligious, nonrational judgments rather than open religious convictions."[151]

While the majority justices in *Good News* appear sympathetic to the prior moral claim of the family over the religious and moral training of their children, the dissenting justices typify the intolerance some liberals express towards religion issues. Contrary to their view, the constitutional answer favoring tolerance given by the majority of the justices in *Good News* not only provides a coherent answer to the task of reconciling free speech and establishment principles, it also provides a morally defensible answer to the dilemma of liberal toleration of religion.

Conclusion

The Supreme Court's holding in *Good News* answers two very significant issues that have perplexed many families, religious communities, school boards, and courts that bear directly on the family's constitutional right to control the moral and religious development of their children. First, the family's right to religious speech, including worshipful speech, is entitled to the same constitutional protection as any other speech. Families who are concerned over public school's secular curriculum constitutionally may choose to have the curriculum supplemented if the school has established a limited public forum wherein other after-school activities are justified as teaching moral lessons. Second, the Establishment Clause does not provide an acceptable basis for justifying viewpoint discrimination against religious speech. The wall-of-separation view of the dissenters, an establishment paradigm epitomized by the long-standing

Lemon v. Kurtzman test,[152] has been abandoned in favor of a more tolerant (neutral) perspective toward religious activities within limited public forums. By upholding the constitutionality of after-school religious-moral training, the Court has validated an important alternative for religious families who are considering opting out the public school system entirely. Such an alternative is indeed good news for religious families who are concerned with the overwhelming influence of secular humanism that defines the public school curriculum. The decision in *Good News*, in essence, increases the viability of the public schools for these families who closely correlate religion and the family.

Notes

1. See Raymond Bucko, "Sacred Kinship: Creating and Extending Family Among the Lakota of Pine Ridge"; Ronald Simkins, "Competing Portraits of the Israelite Family"; John Calvert, "Reshaping Family in Egypt: The Islamist Discourse."
2. See Susan Calef, "The Shape of Family and Family Values: 'The Bible Tells Us So,' or Does It?"; David Hunter, "An Early Christian Debate on Marriage and Family: The Jovinianist Controversy."
3. See Charles Harper, "Religion and Family in America: A Socio-Historical Reconnaissance."
4. 121 S.Ct. 2093, 2097 (2001). Chief Justice Rehnquist, and Justices O'Connor, Scalia, and Kennedy joined Justice Thomas's majority opinion. Justice Breyer also joined the conclusion, and joined the majority's opinion to the extent consistent with his establishment concerns. Ibid., 2111 (Breyer, J. concurring in part).
5. See Bette Novit Evans, "Kids Caught in the Crossfire: Reflections on the School Wars," in this volume.
6. *Engle v. Vitale*, 370 U.S. 421 (1962).
7. *Stone v. Graham*, 449 U.S. 39 (1980).
8. *Abington Township School District v. Schempp*, 374 U.S. 203 (1963).
9. *Epperson v. Arkansas*, 393 U.S. 97 (1968) (invalidating an Arkansas statute than banned the teaching of evolution in state schools); *Edwards v. Aguillard*, 482 U.S. 578 (1987) (invalidating a law requiring a "balanced treatment" of evolutionary theory and "scientific creationism" which supported divine creation).
10. *Lee v. Weisman*, 505 U.S. 577 (1992).
11. *Sante Fe Independent School District v. Doe*, 530 U.S. 290 (2000).
12. See *Mozert v. Hawkins County Bd. of Educ.*, 827 F.2d 1058, 1062 (6th Cir. 1987).
13. The Court in *Torcaso v. Watkins*, 367 U.S. 488, 495 n. 11 (1961), in defining re-

ligion as encompassing belief systems that do not include traditional belief in God, observed that "among religions in this country which do not teach what would generally be considered a belief in the existence of God are Buddhism, Taoism, Ethical Culture, Secular Humanism and others."

14. *Pierce v. Society of Sisters*, 268 U.S. 510 (1925).
15. 70 *Law Week* 4683 (2002) (decided June 27, 2002, after the symposium and, as a consequence, not discussed in the body of the essay).
16. *The Good News Club v. Milford Central School*, 21 F.Supp. 2d 147, 149 (N.D. N.Y. 1998).
17. Ibid.
18. Ibid., 149, citing Section 414 New York Education Law.
19. Ibid. Section 414 of the New York Education law authorized the use of local school facilities for uses pertaining to the community welfare, but prohibited the use by a religious sect or denomination. Ibid., n 2. Milford's "Community Use of School Facilities Policy" specifically prohibited use for religious purposes. Ibid., n. 3.
20. Ibid., 153.
21. Ibid., 154.
22. *The Good News Club v. Milford Central School*, 202 F.3d 502 (2nd Cir. 2000).
23. Ibid., 510.
24. Ibid., 511.
25. Ibid., 512 (Jacobs, J., dissenting).
26. 121 S.Ct. 2093, 2097 (2001). Chief Justice Rehnquist, and Justices O'Connor, Scalia, and Kennedy joined Justice Thomas's majority opinion. Justice Breyer also joined the conclusion, and joined the majority's opinion to the extent consistent with his establishment concerns. Ibid., 2111 (Breyer, J. concurring in part).
27. Ibid., 2107.
28. 121 S.Ct. 2107.
29. Ibid., 2102.
30. Ibid.
31. Ibid., citing *Rosenberger v. Rector and Visitors of Univ. of Va.*, 515 U.S. 819, 829 (1995); *Lamb's Chapel v. Center Moriches Union Free School Dist.*, 508 U.S. 384, 392–93 (1993).
32. Ibid., at 2100, citing *Cornelius v. NAACP Legal Defense & Ed. Fund, Inc.*, 473 U.S. 788, 806 (1985).
33. Ibid., 2100 (also finding that because the school's exclusion constituted viewpoint discrimination, "we need not decide whether it is unreasonable in light of the purposes served by the forum").
34. Ibid., 2100, citing App. to Pet. for Cert. D1.

35. Ibid., citing App. N10–N11.
36. Ibid., 2098, citing App. in No. 98-949 (CA2) at A30.
37. Ibid., 2101.
38. Ibid., 2100. The Court found it "remarkable that the Court of Appeals majority did not cite *Lamb's Chapel*, despite its obvious relevance to the case." Ibid., n. 3.
39. Ibid., 2101.
40. Ibid., 2101–02.
41. Ibid., 2101–02, citing *Rosenberger* at 826, 831.
42. Ibid., 2102.
43. Ibid., 2103.
44. Ibid.
45. Ibid., 2103.
46. Ibid., 2103.
47. Ibid., 2104.
48. Ibid.
49. Ibid., 2106, citing cf. *Capitol Square* (O'Connor, J., concurring in part and concurring in judgment) ("the endorsement inquiry is *not about the perceptions of particular individuals* or saving isolated nonadherents from . . . discomfort . . . It is for this reason that the reasonable observer in the endorsement inquiry must be deemed aware of the history and context of the community and forum in which the religious [speech takes place]").
50. Ibid., 2104.
51. Ibid., 2108 (Scalia, J., concurring), citing *Church of Lukumi Babalu Aye, Inc. v. Hialeah*, 508 U.S. 520, 532–33, 546 (1993); Employment Div., Dept. of Human Resources of Ore. Smith, 494 U.S. 872, 877–78 (1990).
52. Ibid., 2109.
53. Ibid., 2107.
54. Ibid.
55. Ibid., 2108, quoting *Capitol Square Review and Advisory Bd. v. Pinette*, 515 U.S. 753, 765 (1995) and citing *Lamb's Chapel*, 508 U.S. 384, 401 (Scalia, J., concurring judgment).
56. Ibid. 121 S.Ct. 2093, 2111 (Breyer, J., concurring in part), citing *Mitchell v. Helms*, 530 U.S. 793, 839 (O'Connor, J., concurring in judgment); *Capitol Square Review and Advisory Bd. v. Pinette*, 515 U.S. 753, 774, 777 (O'Connor, J., concurring in part and concurring in judgment).
57. Ibid., 2111 (Breyer, J., concurring in part).
58. Ibid., 2111, quoting *Capitol Square Review and Advisory Bd.*, 515 U.S. 753, 777(1995) (O'Connor, J., concurring in part and concurring in judgment).

59. Ibid., 2111–12 (Breyer, J., concurring in part).
60. *City of Erie v. Pap's A.M. d.b.a. "Kandyland,"* 529 U.S. 277 (2000) (Stevens, J. dissenting, joined by Ginsburg, J.) (arguing that the erotic message of nude dancing is constitutionally protected even against arguments of adverse "secondary effects" such as an increase in prostitution, sexually transmitted disease, debasement of women and crime).
61. *Good News Club,* 121 S.Ct. at 2112–13.
62. Ibid., citing in support only "Cf. *Lehman v. Shaker Heights,* 418 U.S. 298 (1974) (upholding a city's refusal to allow 'political advertising' on public transportation)."
63. Ibid., 2115.
64. Ibid., 2117, citing Stevens' dissent at 2114.
65. Ibid., 2117, quoting the Court's opinion at 2101.
66. Ibid., 2117 (J. Souter, dissenting).
67. Ibid., 2118 (J. Souter, dissenting), citing *Widmar v. Vincent* 454 U.S. 263, 271 (1995) and *Lamb's Chapel,* 508 U.S. at 394.
68. Ibid., 2118 (J. Souter, dissenting), citing *Capitol Square Review and Advisory Bd. v. Pinette,* 515 U.S. 753, 777 (O'Connor, J., concurring).
69. Ibid., 2119–20 (Souter, J., dissenting).
70. See Michael W. McConnell, "The Origins and Historical Understanding of Free Exercise of Religion," *Harvard Law Review* 103 (1990), 1409–1517, who provides historical support for the proposition that the Framers intended that the Free Exercise Clause would protect religion against interference by the state.
71. *Reynolds v. United States,* 98 U.S. 145 (1878) ("Congress was deprived of all legislative power over mere opinion, but was left free to reach actions which were violative of social duties or subversive of good order").
72. *Davis v. Beason.* 133 U.S. 333 (1890) (wherein the Court upheld an Idaho territorial statute that not only disfranchised polygamists, but also prohibited all "members" of the Mormon Church from either voting or holding public office, because the Church encouraged the "belief" in the practice of polygamy). For a more complete analysis of the national assault on Mormon society in general and the institution of polygamy in specific, see Edwin B. Firmage and R. Collin Mangrum, *Zion in the Courts: A Legal History of the Church of Jesus Christ of Latter-Day Saints, 1830–1900* (Urbana: University of Illinois Press, 1988), 128–260.
73. See *Sherbert v. Verner,* 374 U.S. 398 (1963); *Thomas v. Review Board of Indiana Employment Security Division,* 450 U.S. 707 (1981); *Hobbie v. Unemployment Appeals Commission,* 480 U.S. 136 (1987).
74. 494 U.S. 872 (1990).

75. *Smith*, 494 U.S. 879 (quoting Justice Steven's concurring opinion in *United States v. Lee*, 455 U.S. 252, 263 n.3 (1982)).
76. 494 U.S. 894 (Justice O'Connor, concurring).
77. *Smith*, 494 U.S. 881 ("The only decision in which we have held that the First Amendment bars application of a neutral, generally applicable law to religiously motivated action have involved not the Free Exercise Clause alone, but the Free Exercise Clause in conjunction with other constitutional protections, such as freedom of speech and of the press").
78. Justice Field in *Davis v. Beason* noted that "[b]igamy and polygamy are crimes by the laws of all civilized and Christian countries." Ibid., 341.
79. *Lovell v. City of Griffin*, 303 U.S. 444 (1938) (where the Court invalidated a Jehovah Witness challenge on free speech grounds of a city ordinance that required colporteurs first obtain permission from the city manager before distributing or selling religious circulars, magazines, pamphlets or handbooks); *Cantwell v. Connecticut*, 310 U.S. 296, 303–04 (1940) (invalidating on free speech grounds the conviction of a father and his two sons, each ordained ministers for the Jehovah's Witnesses, for their door-to-door missionary efforts on the streets of New Haven, Connecticut in violation of a city ordinance requiring that they obtain a certificate from the secretary of the public welfare council prior to conducting such activities); *Jamison v. Texas*, 318 U.S. 413, 416 (1943) ("one who is rightfully on a street which the state has left open to the public carries with him there as elsewhere the constitutional right to express his views in an orderly fashion. This right extends to the communication of ideas by handbills and literature as well as by the spoken word"); *Murdock v. Pennsylvania*, 319 U.S. 105, 107, 110–111 (1943) (while "[t]he states can prohibit the use of streets for the distribution of purely commercial leaflets, even though such leaflets may have a 'civic appeal, or a moral platitude' appended" . . . They may not prohibit the distribution of handbills in the pursuit of a clearly religious activity merely because the handbills invite the purchase of books . . . or . . . seek in a lawful fashion to promote the raising of funds for religious purposes").
80. *Employment Div., Dep't of Human Resources v. Smith*, 494 U.S. 872, 881–82 (1990).
81. William P. Marshall, "Solving the Free Exercise Dilemma: Free Exercise as Free Expression," *Minnesota Law Review* 67 (1983), 575–94. See a characterization of Marshall's thesis as the "reduction principle" in Stanley Ingber, "Religion or Ideology: A Needed Clarification of the Religion Clauses," *Stanford Law Review* 41 (1989), 241. For a criticism of the incompleteness of this reductionist strategy, see Marci A. Hamilton, "The Belief/Conduct Paradigm in the Supreme Court's

Free Exercise Jurisprudence: A Theological Account of the Failure to Protect Religious Conduct," *Ohio State Law Journal* 54 (1993), 737–42.
81. 113 S.Ct. 2141, 2146 (1993).
82. *Lamb's Chapel*, 508 U.S., 393–94.
83. 515 U.S. 819 (1995).
84. 515 U.S. 819, 865 (1995) (Souter, J., dissenting).
85. Zainaldin, "The Emergence of a Modern American Family Law: Child Custody, Adoption, and the Courts, 1796-1851," *Northwestern University Law Review* 73 (1979), 1045.
86. Friedman, "The Parental Right to Control the Religious Education of a Child," *Harvard Law Review* 29 (1916), 498.
87. For an extended discussion of Roman, Germanic, Anglo-Saxon, and Judeo-Christian tradition of family autonomy, see Christopher L. Blakesley, "Family Autonomy," in *Contemporary Family Law: Principles, Policy & Practice*, L. D. Wardle, C. L. Blakesely, and J. Y. Parker, eds. (Deerfield, IL: Callaghan, 1988), 1–16.
88. The notion of fundamental rights as a source of constitutional limitation on the power of the state is at least as old as the Slaughter House Cases, 83 U.S. (16 Wall.) 36, 76 (1872). The same notion of fundamental rights arising out of common law recognition based on "time immemorial" or natural law reasoning antedating and surviving the enactment of the constitution finds support in Coke's famous dictum in Dr. Bonham's case, 8 Coke 107, 118 and James Otis' Writs of Assistance case argument in 1761. Indeed, fundamental rights reasoning comprised one of the persistent revolutionary themes. See Bernard Bailyn, *The Ideological Origins of the American Revolution* (Cambridge, MA: Belknap, 1967), 175–229.
89. 262 U.S. 390 (1923).
90. The Court noted at the time of Meyer that twenty one other states had similar laws proscribing the teaching of foreign languages in schools to children. 262 U.S. 395.
91. 262 U.S. 394, 398.
92. 262 U.S. 399.
93. Ibid., 402.
94. 268 U.S. 510 (1925).
95. 406 U.S. 205 (1972).
96. *Smith v. Organization of Foster Families*, 431 U.S. 816, 845 (1977) ("The individual's freedom to marry and reproduce is 'older than the Bill of Rights,' . . . the liberty interest in family privacy has its source, and its contours are ordinarily sought, not in state law, but in intrinsic human rights, as they have been under-

stood in "this Nations's history and tradition") (footnote and citations omitted); *Moore v. City of East Cleveland*, 431 U.S. 494 (1977) (plurality opinion) ("Our decisions establish that the Constitution protects the sanctity of the family precisely because the institution of the family is deeply rooted in this Nation's history and tradition. It is through the family that we inculcate and pass down many of our most cherished values, moral and cultural"); *Stanley v. Illinois*, 405 U.S. 645, 651–52 (citations omitted) ("The Court has frequently emphasized the importance of the family. The rights to conceive and to raise one's children have been deemed 'essential,' . . . 'basic civil rights of man,' . . . and '[r]ights far more precious . . . than property rights,' . . . 'It is cardinal with us that the custody, care and nurture of the child reside first in the parents, whose primary function and freedom include preparation for obligations the state can neither supply nor hinder'").

97. 15 S.Ct. 2510, 2532 (1995) (Thomas, J., concurring).

98. On the issue of relevancy of the Jefferson wall-of-separation metaphor on the issue of the Framer's intent, Chief Justice Rehnquist (then Justice) observed that "Thomas Jefferson was of course in France at the time the constitutional Amendments known as the Bill of Rights were passed by Congress and ratified by the States. His letter to the Danbury Baptist Association was a short note of courtesy, written 14 years after the Amendments were passed by Congress. He would seem to any detached observer as a less than ideal source of contemporary history as to the meaning of the Religion Clauses of the First Amendment." *Wallace v. Jaffree*, 472 U.S. 38, 92 (1985) (J. Rehnquist, dissent) ("It is impossible to build sound constitutional doctrine upon a mistaken understanding of constitutional history, but unfortunately the Establishment Clause has been expressly freighted with Jefferson's misleading metaphor for nearly 40 years").

99. *Westside Community Bd. of Ed. v. Mergens*, 496 U.S. 226 (1989) (upholding the constitutionality of the Equal Access Act permitting religious extracurricular groups to use school facilities on an equal access or neutral principle basis); *Lamb's Chapel v. Center of Moriches School Dist.*, 508 U.S. 384 (1993) (permitting an evangelical church to use school facilities during nonschool hours to show to the public a film series on Christian family values); *Witters v. Dept. of Services for Blind*, 474 U.S. 481 (1986) (unanimously upholding on grounds of neutrality the State of Washington's funding of vocational assistance to a blind person even though he was studying at a private Christian college to become a pastor, missionary, or youth director); *Zobrest v. Catalina Foothills School Dist.*, 509 U.S. 1 (1993) (upholding the constitutionality of a neutral distribution of benefits to the handicapped under the Disabilities Education Act (IDEA) even to the extent of providing a sign-language interpreter to accompany a deaf child even though

the classes were held at a Roman Catholic high school); *Rosenberger v. Rector & Visitors of Univ. of Va.*, 515 U.S. 819 (1995) (holding that the University of Virginia could not discriminate against a student "'journal pervasively devoted to the discussion and advancement of an avowedly Christian theological and personal philosophy,'" because "[a] central lesson of our decisions is that a significant factor in upholding government programs in the face of Establishment Clause attack is their neutrality towards religion"); *Agostini v. Felton*, 521 U.S. 203 (1997) ("We therefore hold that a federally funded program providing supplemental, remedial instruction to disadvantaged children on a neutral basis is not invalid under the Establishment Clause when such instruction is given on the premises of sectarian schools by government employees pursuant to a program containing safeguards . . ."); *Mitchell v. Helms*, 530 U.S. 793, 839 (in upholding the constitutionality of funds distributed by the federal government to state and local agencies that were in turn used to finance the lending of educational materials and equipment to both public and private schools, the Court held: "if the government, seeking to further some legitimate secular purpose, offers aid on the same terms, without regard to religion, to all who adequately further that purpose . . . then it is fair to say that any aid going to a religious recipient only has the effect of furthering that secular purpose").

100. Ibid., 2104.
101. Ibid. 121 S.Ct. 2093, 2111 (Breyer, J., concurring in part), citing *Mitchell v. Helms*, 530 U.S. 793, 839 (O'Connor, J., concurring in judgment); *Capitol Square Review and Advisory Bd. v. Pinette*, 515 U.S. 753, 774, 777 (O'Connor, J., concurring in part and concurring in judgment).
102. Ibid., 2111–12 (Breyer, J., concurring in part).
103. Although Justice Kennedy relies heavily on the endorsement test, he has added a "coercion" factor as well in some cases as illustrated by his opinion in *Lee v. Weisman*.
104. Justice O'Connor's endorsement test is a variation on the neutrality paradigm, first suggested by Professor Kurland. The endorsement test asks whether the questioned policy constitutes an endorsement (statement of preference) of religion or simply an adoption of a neutral policy that benefits religion equally and indirectly. Kurland, "Of Church and State and the Supreme Court," *University of Chicago Law Review* 29 (1961), 2. Philip B. Beschle views Justice O'Connor's endorsement test as an improvement on Kurland's neutrality policy because it allows the investigation to go beyond the apparent neutrality of the text or expressed policy to see whether a message of approval or disapproval is being conveyed. If no endorsement is manifest then religion can be indirectly supported as

part of a broader public policy agenda. He explains that "[w]hen neutrality among and legal equality of value systems becomes the goal of the inquiry, we can abandon the foundation of separationism, that all contact between church and state is suspect and to be only reluctantly tolerated when absolutely unavoidable." Donald L. Beschle, "The Conservative as Liberal: The Religion Clauses, Liberal Neutrality, and the Approach of Justice O'Connor," *Notre Dame Law Review* 62 (1987), 175–76.

105. *Jaffree*, 472 U.S. 69–70 (J. O'Connor, concurring), quoting *Engel v. Vitale*, 370 U.S. 421, 431 (1962). See also *Lynch*, 465 U.S. at 690, 693–94 (O'Connor, J., concurring) ("The purpose prong of the Lemon test asks whether government's actual purpose is to endorse or disapprove of religion. The effect prong asks whether, irrespective of government's actual purpose, the practice . . . in fact conveys a message of endorsement or disapproval. An affirmative answer to either question should render the challenged practice invalid"); *Wallace v. Jaffree*, 472 US. 69; *Corporation of Presiding Bishop v. Amos*, 483 U.S. 327, 346-48 (1987) (O'Connor, J. concurring) ("On the one hand, a rigid application of the *Lemon* test would invalidate legislation exempting religious observers from generally applicable government obligations. By definition, such legislation has a religious purpose and effect in promoting the free exercise of religion." On the other hand, judicial deference to all legislation that purports to facilitate the free exercise of religion would completely vitiate the Establishment Clause. Any statute pertaining to religion can be viewed as an 'accommodation' of free exercise rights.'").

106. *Capitol Square Review and Advisory Bd. v. Pinette*, 115 S.Ct. 2440 (1995) (O'Connor, J, concurring) (permitting the Ku Klux Klan to display a Latin cross on Capitol Square, a 10–acre, state-owned plaza surrounding the Statehouse in Columbus, Ohio, which had been used for over a century as a gathering place for public speeches and festivals advocating and celebrating a variety of secular and religious causes).

107. Ibid., 2455.

108. Ibid., 2455.

109. Ibid., 2111–12 (Breyer, J., concurring in part).

110. Ibid. 121 S.Ct. 2093, 2111 (Breyer, J., concurring in part), citing *Mitchell v. Helms*, 530 U.S. 793, 839 (O'Connor, J., concurring in judgment); *Capitol Square Review and Advisory Bd. v. Pinette*, 515 U.S. 753, 774, 777 (O'Connor, J., concurring in part and concurring in judgment).

111. Ibid.

112. Ibid., 2106, citing cf. *Capitol Square* (O'Connor, J., concurring in part and concurring in judgment) ("the endorsement inquiry is *not about the perceptions of par-*

ticular individuals or saving isolated nonadherents from . . . discomfort . . . It is for this reason that the reasonable observer in the endorsement inquiry must be deemed aware of the history and context of the community and forum in which the religious [speech takes place]").

113. 1192 U.S. Lexis 4364.
114. The "endorsement" in *Lee* came as a result of the school's participation in (1) deciding that an invocation and benediction be given; (2) choosing the religious participant, here a rabbi; and (3) giving the rabbi directions and guidelines that the prayer should be nonsectarian. This "degree of school involvement here made it clear that the graduation prayers bore the imprint of the State and thus put school-age children who objected in an untenable position." Ibid., 10.
115. Ibid., 11.
116. Ibid.
117. Ibid., 2104.
118. Justice Rehnquist, in dissent, in *Wallace v. Jaffree*, 472 U.S. 38, 91–92 (1985) (J. Rehnquist, dissent), quoting 8 *Writings of Thomas Jefferson* 113 (H. Washington ed. 1861).
119. 98 U.S. 145, 164 (1878), quoting 8 *Writings of Thomas Jefferson* 113 (H. Washington ed. 1861).
120. 330 U.S. 1, 16 (1947).
121. Justice Rutledge, in his dissent in *Everson v. Board of Education*, 330 U.S. 1, 31–32 (Rutledge, J., dissenting), argued that the majority had failed to enforce the Establishment Clause's wall-of-separation which was intended "to create a complete and permanent separation of the spheres of religious activity and civil authority by comprehensively forbidding every form of public aid or support for religion."
122. Justice Jackson, dissenting in *Everson*, observed that the Court's words of separation "seem utterly discordant with its conclusion yielding support to their commingling in educational matters." 330 U.S. at 19 (Jackson, J., dissenting).
123. See, e.g., *Board of Ed. of Westside Community Schools (Dist. 66) v. Mergens*, 496 U.S. 226, 285 n. 21 (J. Stevens, dissenting) (1989) (the Equal Access Act's requirement that public schools give religious student groups equal access to the public school for extracurricular activities violates the Establishment Clause because Congress passed the Act for the illegitimate purpose of giving religious speech equal status to other speech). Justice Stevens separationist tendencies can be illustrated by his two-paragraph concurring opinion in *City of Boerne v. P. F. Flores, Archbishop of San Antonio*, 521 U.S. 507, 537 (J. Stevens, concurring). Justice Stevens opined that the Religious Freedom Restoration Act violates the

Establishment Clause because it seeks to afford religion some protection, subject to a compelling state interest standard, from otherwise generally applicable laws. Following this rationale, the Free Exercise Clause itself would violate the Establishment Clause because its raison d'etre must be affording religion some level of protection against the state than otherwise would be available. Such an interpretation of the religion clauses that totally ignores one of the clauses in favor of the exclusive priority of the other makes no sense.

124. See, e.g., *Capitol Square Review and Advisory Bd. v. Pinette*, 515 U.S. 753, 817, (1995) (J. Ginsburg, dissenting) (discrimination against even private religious speech displayed on public property is necessary for disestablishment purposes "to uncouple government from church . . .").

125. *Rosenberger v. Rector & Visitors of Univ. of Va.*, 515 U.S. 819, 864 (1995) (Souter, J. dissenting) (direct subsidization of religious activity is categorically forbidden under the Establishment Clause); *Agostini v. Felton*, 521 U.S. 203, 246 (1997) (Souter, J. dissenting) (the presence of state employees teaching within the walls of sectarian schools creates a "symbolic union" between church and state and therefore, an impermissible effect of endorsement).

126. *Agostini v. Felton*, 521 U.S.203, 233 (1997) ("Interaction between church and state is inevitable . . . and we have always tolerated some level of involvement between the two").

127. Justice Blackmun's concurring opinion in *Lee v. Weisman*, responding to the persistent assault on *Lemon*, reminded the Court of the frequency of which the Court has regularly applied the test despite all the criticism it has received. 505 U.S. 577, 599 (1992) (Blackmun, J., concurring)..

128. *Lemon v. Kurtzman*, 403 U.S. 602 (1971).

129. Ibid., 612–13.

130. Ibid., 2117 (J. Souter, dissenting).

131. Ibid., 2118 (J. Souter, dissenting), citing *Widmar v. Vincent* 454 U.S. 263, 271 (1995) and *Lamb's Chapel*, 508 U.S. at 394.

132. Ibid., 2118 (J. Souter, dissenting), citing *Capitol Square Review and Advisory Bd. v. Pinette*, 515 U.S. 753, 777 (O'Connor, J., concurring).

133. Ibid., 2118 (Souter, J., dissenting).

134. Ibid., 2119 (Souter, J., dissenting).

135. Ibid., 2118–19 (Souter, J., dissenting).

136. Ibid., 2119–20 (Souter, J., dissenting).

137. Ibid., 2115.

138. John Stuart Mill, *On Liberty* (New York: Liberal Arts, 1956), 129–31.

139. Ibid., 74.

140. Ibid., 466.
141. Robert Nozick, *Anarchy, State and Utopia* (New York: Harper and Row, 1974), 167.
142. Ibid., 168.
143. Ibid., 38–39, 287–91.
144. Ibid., 152.
145. Ibid., 153.
146. Ibid., 155.
147. Ibid., 152.
148. Ibid., 154.
149. Stephen L. Carter, "Evolutionism, Creationism and Treating Religions as a Hobby," *Duke Law Journal* (1987), 984–85.
150. Kent Greenawalt, "Religious Convictions and Lawmaking," *Michigan Law Review* 84 (1985), 379.
151. 403 U.S. 602 (1971).

Culture Wars, Family Wars?
The Political Mobilization of Clergy on Family Issues[1]

SUE E. S. CRAWFORD
MELISSA M. DECKMAN
LAURA R. OLSON

In his book, *Culture Wars: The Struggle to Define America*, sociologist James Davison Hunter (1991) argues that political debates about issues concerning family are part of an overarching "culture war" that is transforming American politics. This supposed war features two opposing camps fighting to define cultural views about family and morality. Although the culture wars thesis has been heavily criticized by a range of scholars, political and social debates about appropriate family arrangements and gender roles, and government responsibility for supporting or regulating such matters, nevertheless figure prominently in American politics. A sampling of culture war debates ranges from the family rights of gays and lesbians, the state's role in reducing divorce rates, the implications of federal tax laws and welfare policies for married and unmarried people, and the ways local schools should respond to the needs of working parents. The politics of family-related issues often necessitates debate about morality, which brings the views of clergy to the political fore.

This essay reports on a study that examines the extent to which the clergy of one mainline Protestant denomination,[2] the Disciples of Christ, engage in public debate about family politics and the extent to which their engagement may be explained by a broad version of the culture wars theory. First, we examine whether family politics appears to be a priority for these clergy, or if other political issues are more likely to attract their attention. We then investigate whether these clergy address family issues *in public*. Do liberal clergy speak out on family issues, or do they cede that civic space to conservative clergy? Do patterns in civil discourse match predictions of the culture war theory, or do clergy engage in a dialogue about family issues that fits a different agenda or mold?

Clergy, Family, and Politics

A study of clergy engagement in public discourse about family politics offers a rich view of the nexus of religion, politics, culture, and family life since their work involves the interplay of these domains. They lead religious organizations that help shape cultural norms through extensive socialization of both children and adults via sermons, instruction, study groups, and other educational programs. They are granted civil authority to create legal family unions and provide counseling and advice regarding a wide range of challenges that families face. Their work with congregants and their families routinely links religion and family issues.

Clergy engagement in public discourse about the American family is a classic example of how leaders of civic institutions that are not explicitly political in nature (by virtue of being designed for a primary purpose other than politics) come to understand how their leadership responsibilities require them to engage in politics (Crawford 1995; Olson 2000). Through their work with families in the congregational setting, some ministers may conclude that a larger political or cultural reality must be changed for the sake of families. Similarly, through their work with families who ask the church for assistance, clergy may see firsthand shortcomings of their community's social services networks. In their efforts to teach and instruct families, clergy may recognize key cultural beliefs that frustrate their efforts to help families develop "Godly" family practices or behaviors. In these ways, clergy may serve as mediators between government and private citizens and become key players in the negotiation of religion and family life.

Clergy often work with broader civic groups to educate the public about family issues and encourage particular family practices. Examples of their engagement in civic associations concerning family include marriage preparation, parenting courses, community divorce mediation, support organizations for single parents, and Parents, Families, and Friends of Lesbians and Gays (PFLAG). Clergy may also lobby government about policies concerning family, ranging from advocacy for or against same-sex marriage laws to advocacy for living wage laws. Through their advocacy in the civic and governmental realms, clergy can shape the influence of religion on family and on social structures that bear on family life. Clergy are often viewed as religious experts, representatives of religion, and moral leaders. Their statements about religion and family can, therefore, shape society's understanding religious prescriptions about appropriate family behavior *and* about appropriate government policy concerning family.

Clergy as Political Actors

Early studies of clergy involvement in politics (Hadden 1969; Quinley 1974; Stark, Foster, Glock, and Quinley 1971) were designed to document and explore the radicalization of mainline Protestant clergy during the civil rights movement. Only recently has scholarly attention again been paid to the political involvement of clergy. James Guth and colleagues (1997; see also Guth 1983, 1996, 2001; Guth, Green, Smidt, and Poloma 1991; Penning and Smidt 2001) have amassed and analyzed the results of a wide variety of surveys about clergy's political beliefs and practices, while other scholars (Cavendish 2001; Day 2001; Jelen 1993; Olson 2000; Olson, Crawford, and Deckman forthcoming) have undertaken pioneering ethnographic work by interviewing clergy and visiting their churches.

Persistent patterns in this research on clergy show that mainline Protestant clergy have liberal political views rooted in a longstanding tradition that emphasizes proactive roles for government in reducing poverty and enhancing civil rights. Further, mainline Protestant theology encourages engagement in the public sphere and abiding concern about the morality of social structures (Niebuhr 1951; Wuthnow and Evans 2002), and mainline Protestant clergy have a long history of active participation in civic discourse concerning a wide range of social issues. Recent studies demonstrate that a strong emphasis on prophetic social witness in mainline Protestantism continues to push clergy, particularly those with liberal views, to speak out (Djupe and Gilbert 2003; Olson, Crawford, and Deckman forthcoming). Little attention has been paid, however, to their discourse concerning family issues (but see Cadge 2002; Olson and Cadge 2002; Wilcox 2002, 2004).

Culture Wars and Religious Discourse

Hunter's (1991) culture wars thesis asserts that American politics has shifted toward a new alignment of cultural conflict that will supersede existing alignments and cut across existing religious divisions, separating Catholics, liberal and conservative Protestants, and Jews (see also Wuthnow 1988). This new cultural conflict pits the "orthodox," who believe in a fixed, divinely established truth, against "progressives," who fundamentally disagree. Progressives instead affirm the role of science and human reason alongside divine revelation as important sources for moral reasoning and are open to changes in the moral order over time. According to Hunter, the orthodox-progressive dichotomy ultimately will push all other political conflict to the margins, yielding an intractable division that will escalate into intolerable conflict. Since this orthodox-progressive divide rests on fundamentally irreconcilable views of moral authority, he argues that extreme conflict is inevitable—hence the term culture "war." Culture wars theorists expect debates concerning gender roles, appropriate sexual behaviors, and government policies concerning marriage, child care, reproduction, and sexual orientation to be central to the struggle to define American culture. Family issues are the expected frontlines of the battle, so religious elites are expected to be key players. Hunter's book highlights specific stories of culture "warriors" to illustrate the strident nature of the political debates and the difficulty of finding compromise. He notes that conflict is primarily the domain of political activists, not the mass public, who instead hover in the middle between the two camps.

The notion of a culture war captured the imagination of conservative activists (Carney and Hawkins 1999; Rabkin 1999) and spurred scholarly interest in the mobilization of the religious Right (Green, Guth, Smidt, and Kellstedt 1996; Wilcox 1992). By the late 1990s, however, critiques of the culture wars thesis had become a cottage industry. The U.S. Senate's failure to remove Bill Clinton from the presidency was cited by some pundits as a sign that conservatives had "lost" the culture war, or as evidence that conservatives need to change their battle strategy (Carney and Hawkins 1999).

On the academic side, scholars of public opinion consistently demonstrated that while an orthodox-progressive cleavage could be found on some issues, it was clearly not the case that this cleavage had superseded other cleavages (Davis and Robinson 1997; Demerath and Yang 1997; Jelen 1997; Williams 1997a, 1997b). Nor was there convincing evidence of a consistently increasing polarization of political views in the mass public (DiMaggio, Evans, and Bryson 1996; Evans, Bryson, and DiMaggio 2001;

Miller and Hoffman 1999). In all fairness to Hunter, challenges based on studies of mass behavior perhaps miss his point: the culture war is a war between *activists* who wish to shape the culture. Those on the sidelines of the battle should not be expected to show either the same single-purposed dedication or polarization. Clergy, however, are an example of the very people Hunter argues would be engaged in the culture war.

Much of the academic criticism of the culture wars thesis emphasizes qualifications of Hunter's basic thesis. Chief among these caveats are arguments that the orthodox-progressive cleavage does not operate for all issues, nor does it erase other cleavages (Davis and Robinson 1997; Demerath and Yang 1997; Jelen 1997; Williams 1997a, 1997b), and that the schism between the orthodox and progressives will be repaired peaceably, much like other political conflicts, instead of escalating into violence (McConkey 2001; Miller and Hoffman 1999; Rabkin 1999; Williams 1997b).

On the other hand, studies do find evidence of two other components of Hunter's thesis, especially surrounding family issues, and especially for Protestants. A few public opinion studies identify strong orthodox-progressive cleavages and some level of polarization over family and gender issues (Davis and Robinson 1997; DiMaggio, Evans, and Bryson 1996). Jelen (1997) also notes that patterns in party identification for Protestants lend credibility to the culture wars theory for that segment of the population.

Other scholars have confirmed the existence of an orthodox-progressive split among religious individuals that cuts across denominational lines (Guth and Green 1991; Wuthnow 1988). In one of the more comprehensive studies of clergy politicization, Guth and colleagues (1997) note an orthodox-progressive split among Protestant clergy on numerous political and social issues. A cursory overview of political news coverage within Protestant denominations also yields various examples of orthodox-progressive conflict between activists, who are often clergy, within denominations, particularly over questions involving sexual orientation. In their study of political activists, Guth and Green (1996) find mainline Protestants heavily involved on both the "religious left" *and* the "religious right." In another study, Guth and colleagues (1996) find that progressive religious activists have dense religious ties and obtain information from religious sources, including clergy, at rates similar to their orthodox colleagues. This same study confirms another key role that clergy play in culture wars debates, as activists say they often look to clergy cues for guidance and information (Guth et al. 1996).

Despite criticisms of some aspects of the culture war theory, therefore, consistent patterns in studies of religion and clergy lend credence to the value of a "broad" (Williams 1997b) version of the culture wars theory as a lens through which to view the involvement of mainline Protestant clergy in debates about family politics. This broad version of the theory retains the idea that debates about various cultural values (including social definitions of family and government policies concerning families) consistently pit orthodox and progressive factions against one another; that these debates stem from fundamentally different understandings of what sources of moral authority should guide cultural and political decisions; and that the orthodox and progressive camps cut across religious and party lines. On this last point, it is of particular interest that the camps cut across denominational lines, pitting progressive and orthodox factions against each other *within* many denominations. However, this broad version of the theory recognizes that culture wars have *not* taken over politics and erased all old divisions.

Culture War Expectations

If we use this broad version of the culture wars as our primary lens for examining clergy involvement in political debates over family issues, we are led to expect that (1) clergy will give high priority to political issues that are central to definitions of cultural family norms (such as sexual orientation, gender role, reproductive choice, and domestic violence); (2) clergy will be engaged in public debates over these cultural family issues; (3) clergy in the same denomination will be split along orthodox-progressive lines; and (4) this orthodox-progressive split will influence the choices clergy make about how to get involved in political debates over family issues.

When clergy are asked to list the political issues that matter most to them, we expect that culture wars issues will be high on their lists. Since we are adopting the broader version of the culture wars theory, we do not expect clergy to list *only* culture wars issues. Their actual prioritization of culture wars issues vis-à-vis other matters provides an indication of the overall salience of culture wars issues for mainline Protestant clergy. If culture wars issues top their lists, then we conclude that such issues are among their central political concerns.

The second expectation assumes that clergy will also be engaged in public debate on culture wars issues. This follows from the expectation that clergy should care about these issues from the culture wars perspective. However, elites who play key roles in shaping cultural norms (such as the media, interest groups, academia, and, importantly for this study, clergy) should be embroiled most heavily in these struggles. We do not expect clergy to be engaged in public debate *only* about family issues that fit into the culture wars schema. The level of clergy engagement in debates over culture wars issues, compared to the time and attention that they give other social issues, provides another measure of the salience of culture wars issues.

The third expectation—that orthodox-progressive splits will divide denominations—means that we should find an orthodox-progressive split within any given religious denomination. The denomination that we study here, the Christian Church (Disciples of Christ), could well be fertile ground for this sort of division among clergy, especially because its denominational tradition and structure lend themselves to political and cultural diversity. The core theme of Disciples theology is acceptance of theological diversity. A non-creedal faith, Disciples stress that they have "no creed but Christ," and they embrace elements of the diverse traditions of Presbyterians, Baptists, Methodists, and Roman Catholics.[3]

The first three expectations put the pieces in place for culture wars political conflict among clergy—interest and activity on culture wars issues and an orthodox-progressive divide. The fourth expectation ties these pieces together and anticipates that clergy's interest in and activity surrounding culture wars issues will be shaped by their views of moral authority (their orthodox or progressive beliefs). Central to the culture wars theory is the image of zealous elites on the orthodox and progressive sides battling it out over issues such as abortion, sexual orientation, and women's roles in the family and workplace. So, we expect clergy who are most polarized politically to be embroiled most heavily in family politics. Adherents of a stricter view of the culture wars thesis would argue that the orthodox-progressive split would shape views on *all* political issues on which clergy take action. We test for the influence of orthodox or progressive views to see whether holding such views shapes political debate on *all* family issues, or just on family issues most central to culture wars debates.

Other Influences on Religious Family Discourse

Although the recent attention to culture wars highlights the political implications of fundamental views of moral authority, this is by no means the only moral dimension we expect to find underlying clergy engagement in family politics. Since we adopt a broader version of the culture wars theory, we assume that other longstanding political commitments will continue to influence clergy's choices on political issues, especially on issues that are not on the frontlines of culture war battles. One could hardly discuss the political views and actions of mainline Protestant clergy without giving some attention to the strong social justice tradition in those denominations. The emphasis on social justice, particularly surrounding racial and economic justice, pervades many mainline Protestant denominations (Wuthnow and Evans 2002). Historically, this emphasis has been linked to mainline activism in the early Progressive movement, the New Deal, and the antipoverty campaigns of Lyndon Johnson's Great Society programs (Guth et al. 1997). Linked to the historic social justice theology is a longstanding concern about human rights. Mainline Protestant ministers were among the most actively involved in the civil rights movement of the 1950s and 1960s (Findlay 1993; Friedland 1998) and the sanctuary movement of the 1980s, which was designed to protect illegal immigrants who had fled oppressive Latin American regimes supported by the anticommunist Reagan administration (Smith 1996). The result of such a history might be that clergy, particularly those who feel most committed to the social justice tradition, place a higher priority on race, poverty, and education than they do on the issues of the culture wars agenda, such as moral decay and gay rights.

Clergy work in the realm of religion and morality, so one also expects this occupational focus to color their politics, particularly when it comes to making public statements on political issues, the main mode of political activity that we study here. Clergy, however, are also fellow human beings whose political decisions are influenced not only by their work context but also by their community, family, and personal concerns. Although these other influences are not central to this chapter, we can measure the influence of the moral dimensions on clergy's political choices only if we account for these other influences in our statistical models. Consequently, our models include factors that measure organizational encouragement of political activity (*organizational mobilization*) and organization-led restraints on political action (*organizational demobilization*), as well as measures of protection that clergy might have from organizational demobilization such as lengthy tenure.[4] Political behavior literature shows us that political engagement for all individuals is often a function of education level, ideology, party identification, and interest in politics (Rosenstone and Hansen 1993; Verba and Nie 1972; Verba, Schlozman, and Brady 1995; Wolfinger and Rosenstone 1980). Another key personal influence on politics is *issue mobilization* (Rosenstone and Hansen 1993). People who care passionately about a particular issue are more likely to engage in politics to address that issue than are those with lukewarm feelings, including clergy (Crawford, Olson, and Deckman 2001; Guth 2001). Our data allow us to test for the influences of these factors, as well as orthodoxy, on the choices that clergy make concerning public discussion of family issues.[5]

Political Concerns

To determine their political priorities, we asked Disciples ministers to name, in their own words, the three biggest problems facing the United States today.[6] We use their responses to this question to create a list of Disciples clergy's chief issue concerns. Recall our expectation that culture wars issues would rank high, but that other issues would also emerge as important.

Our results reveal a mix of culture wars issues (family decay, moral decay, spiritual problems) and social justice issues (civil rights, healthcare, poverty, greed) among the clergy's top priorities (see Table 1). Not surprisingly, Disciples clergy are most concerned about social justice-related issues, the bread and butter of mainline Protestant politics. Distributive justice concerns (poverty, income gap, greed) stand out as the most common priority. Concern for basic social-service structures (education, healthcare, and social security) comprises a second tier, with more than one in four clergy rating concern with these institutions as the biggest problem facing the United States today.

Education concerns, such as those discussed in Evans' essay in this volume, and efforts to fight conservative movements in education policy fall into the culture wars category, whereas concerns about the basic quality of education or unjust distribution of educational resources fit more appropriately into the social justice category. We expect much more concern about the latter among these clergy and thus consider education issues to fall into the social justice category.

TABLE 1. Top Issue Concerns of Disciples Ministers

Issue	Percentage
Poverty, income gap, greed	38.0%
Healthcare, social security	26.3
Education	26.0
Civil rights, racism	21.8
Moral decline, spiritual problems	21.0
Drugs, crime, and violence	13.3
Family problems, family decline	9.1

Overall, the standard economic justice issues dominate clergy's personal issue priorities. However, they have almost as much concern about moral decline as they do civil rights. Family decline also emerges as an important priority for some clergy. Clearly, these clergy have not pushed aside more traditional economic- and justice-related concerns in favor of an exclusive emphasis on culture wars concerns, but neither do they dismiss culture wars outright. Their concern about families manifests primarily as care about the economic well-being and security of families, with a sizable minority worrying about the erosion of moral norms (moral decline and family decline) or the impact of discrimination (civil rights, racism) on families and family structures.

Civic Speech

Clergy are in a position to marshal the resources of religious institutions to address the family-relevant problems that they identify. They may also use their standing as civic leaders to call others to address these concerns. It is to this civic leadership that we now turn.

Our survey asked clergy how often they made their views about a series of issues known in any public forum (very often, often, seldom, or never). The list on the survey included 22 issues such as abortion, hunger, poverty, family decline, gay rights, and healthcare. If we look at these issues in terms of how they relate to families, two broad categories emerge: *structural support* for families and *moral codes* for families.

Again we see evidence of both social justice and culture wars politics

TABLE 2. Frequent Public Discussion of Family-Relevant Issues

Structural Support for Families	Percentage
Hunger, poverty	89.1%
Race relations, civil rights	82.4
Environment	57.2
Aging	53.6
Healthcare	51.9

Moral Codes for Families	Percentage
Gender equality	77.8%
Alcohol, drug abuse	66.0
Domestic violence	61.3
Family decline	45.7
Gay rights, homosexuality	44.8

(see Table 2). Social justice issues relate to *structural support* for families—hunger and poverty, race relations and civil rights, aging, environmental problems, and healthcare. Gender equality, alcohol and drug abuse, domestic violence, decline of the nuclear family, and gay rights—all issues that fall specifically under the culture wars rubric—relate to appropriate *moral codes* for families. Gender equality and gay rights are issues that many conservatives perceive as threats to traditional family structures, while substance abuse and domestic violence cause overt damage to families.

Clergy seem to speak out on culture wars issues more frequently than their personal issue prioritizations would predict. This may reflect a concern among mainline clergy to respond to political statements by religious groups on the right. Left-leaning clergy may feel the need to expend time and energy trying to provide more balance in discussions of "Christian" or "religious" views of family issues in civic discourse despite the fact that these issues are not top personal priorities for them. Gender equality, which is a key point of contention in the culture wars, is the third most frequently discussed issue for these clergy, and nearly half of the ministers say they discuss family decline and gay rights, respectively. Again, evidence exists that these clergy engage in culture wars debates, but the evidence does *not* indicate that they focus their energies on these issues to the exclusion of family-related issues of the old social justice variety.

Note that clergy who list gender equality as a top priority may represent a mix of ministers arguing for greater equality for women and those who advocate more traditional gender roles. Similarly, clergy who rate gay rights highly undoubtedly include ministers who are supportive of gay rights and those who oppose them. Our analysis here is not concerned with which *side* clergy take on family issues, but instead with the specific *kinds* of family issues they debate and the factors that lead them to discuss these issues in public.

Clergy Orthodoxy

Central to the question of whether clergy's family debates make sense in light of culture wars dynamics is analysis of the role of *orthodoxy* as a factor that shapes clergy's choices. Two expectations are central to this analysis: (1) orthodox and progressive ministers may both be found among Disciples clergy; and (2) orthodoxy leads clergy to be engaged on culture wars issues but not on social justice issues.

Because the orthodox-progressive dimension plays such a central role in our analysis, the specifics of the measure bear further explanation here. Modeled after a similar measure developed by Guth and colleagues (1997), our orthodoxy variable identifies the placement of ministers on a dimension that ranges from strong allegiance to the "orthodox" camp of the culture wars to strong allegiance to the "progressive" camp. This scale is based on three theological measures that tap Christian beliefs about the sources and boundaries of moral authority in order to distinguish clergy who view moral authority as coming from a fixed divine source (orthodox) from those who take a broader view (progressives). We asked survey respondents if they strongly agree (coded 1), agree (coded 2), are not sure about (coded 3), disagree (coded 4), or strongly disagree (coded 5) with the following three statements: (1) "The Bible is the inerrant Word of God, both in matters of faith and in historic, geographical, and other secular matters"; (2) "There is no other way to salvation but through belief in Jesus Christ"; and (3) "The Devil actually exists." Agreement with each statement is an indication of orthodoxy, whereas disagreement is an indication of progressiveness. Added together, the scale ranges from 3 to 15. Given the coding of the questions, high scores indicate strong disagreement with the statements and thus progressiveness. Clergy with the lowest scores are the most orthodox, and clergy with middling scores would be considered moderates on the orthodox-progressive dimension.

As expected, Disciples clergy differ on orthodoxy. The sample includes a mix of highly orthodox clergy, highly progressive clergy, and clergy with moderate views. When we break our orthodoxy scale into four categories (most orthodox, orthodox, progressive, most progressive), over twenty percent of Disciples clergy fall into each category. The strong openness to theological diversity ("no creed but Christ') across the denomination appears alive and well. Indeed, the orthodox-progressive variation among clergy in this denomination is striking. Conventional wisdom would tend to place Disciples clergy firmly in the progressive camp. Yet we find that progressive or modernist views of moral authority do not dominate, even among Disciples clergy.

Influences on Civic Speech

In order to assess the influence of orthodoxy on issues clergy discuss, we first need to measure the level of clergy debate on different types of family issues. Principal components factor analysis provides a tool that translates clergy's responses concerning how frequently they discuss issues into a smaller number of variables that indicate the extent to which they discuss different *types* of family issues. This analysis yields measures of three specific kinds of civic speech concerning families: *structural support*, *family definition*, and *moral decay*. Structural support measures the extent to which clergy discuss hunger, poverty, civil rights, aging, environmental problems, and healthcare. The family definition measure captures the extent to which clergy discuss gender equality and gay rights. Moral decay measures the extent to which clergy discuss additional moral issues, such as family decline, alcohol, drug abuse, and domestic violence (see appendix for discussion and results).

Family definition clearly qualifies as culture wars content. As such, we expect those who are most orthodox and those who are most progressive to be most outspoken on these issues. The moral decay measure could be tied to concern about declining cultural commitment to traditional behavior standards, which orthodox activists see as divinely ordained.

As such, we would expect more orthodox clergy to be more vocal about these issues. However, there is no reason to think that concerns about alcoholism, domestic violence, and drug abuse would be limited to orthodox clergy, so we do not expect orthodoxy to matter as much for these issues as might be the case for family definition. At the other end of the spectrum, we expect orthodoxy to have little to do with engagement on structural support issues.

Through further analyses, we hoped to identify the variables that best explain why some clergy discuss these issues publicly more than other clergy. More specifically, we wished to test whether orthodoxy emerges as a key explanation. Our models included the orthodoxy measure itself and a measure of commitment to social justice, since that should be another key moral dimension of political activism for mainline Protestant clergy. We asked clergy whether they agreed or disagreed with the statement, "Social justice is at the heart of the Gospel." The initial models also included variables that tap into organizational mobilization by interest groups such as Focus on the Family or Bread for the World; measures of possible congregational mobilization or demobilization; measures of issue interest; and personal factors including party identification, political interest, age, and gender (see Tables 4 and 5 in the appendix). The discussion that follows emphasizes only the results for the orthodoxy measure and for the most significant and robust predictors of clergy engagement in public debate on each type of issue.

Since family definition fits most squarely into expectations about culture war debates, we expect that the most orthodox and progressive clergy will be most likely to discuss these issues in public. Our results indicate this is indeed the case, although the results also show that, among Disciples clergy, progressive clergy are most deeply involved in these debates. Moreover, the results indicate that these orthodoxy measures exert a stronger influence on the level of clergy's public discussion of these issues than do any of the other predictors. Since we control for both political and theological views on gender equality and gay rights, these results indicate that one's views on moral authority matter beyond their effects on personal views on gender roles and sexual orientation. These beliefs appear to be indicative of a broad moral vision that motivates clergy to make their views on gender and homosexuality known. As such, our results are consistent with the broad culture wars theory. The most orthodox and progressive clergy are mobilized by their moral views to engage in cultural debates over the definition of family. However, no real basis for conservative mobilization appears in the statistical models. No specific theological or political view nor any specific issue advocacy organization appears to inspire higher levels of civic speech by Disciples clergy who believe in more traditional gender roles and family structures.

The "commitment to social justice" variable exerts only a weak influence on the extent of clergy involvement in debates about family issues. One other religious factor, a variable that measures the extent to which clergy say that their theology motivates them to act politically, is significant in the family definition model, but its relative influence is only slightly stronger than that of commitment to social justice. Other than orthodoxy, theology emerges as the strongest predictor of public speech on family definition. Clergy who support the ordination of gays are those who speak out the most about family definition in public. Likewise, clergy who support women's ordination speak out more on these issues, although openness to women in the pulpit exerts less influence than openness to gays in the pulpit. Of the various political variables tested, only feminist orientation emerges as a strong predictor of civic speech on family definition, and its impact is relatively strong. Feminist orientation, measured by agreement with the statement that more legislation is needed to protect women's rights, exerts more influence than does social justice theology, activist theology, and support of women's ordination.

These results indicate that despite the fact that the most orthodox *and* the most progressive ministers are engaged in debates over family definition, Disciples clergy with liberal views on gender and homosexuality are even more apt to make statements on these issues. Overall, civic speech on family definition among Disciples clergy appears to be driven primarily by progressive theology and feminism and thus likely contributes to arguments for broader legal and social definitions of families and family roles.

Our statistical models have a more difficult time explaining why some Disciples clergy engage in civic speech on moral decay issues. Much of the difference among clergy remains unexplained by these models. The strongest and most robust model, however, shows a mirror orthodoxy effect to that found for family definition. The most orthodox and the most progressive clergy speak out more often on moral decay, but this time the more orthodox clergy are most outspoken (see Table 5 in the appendix).

The mobilization of conservative clergy on these issues appears to be bolstered by their feelings of closeness to Focus on the Family, a large, socially conservative Christian organization that emphasizes traditional moral codes for families (see Apostolidis 2000). This "Focus on the Family effect" is stronger than any of the other factors except for orthodoxy. Since Focus on the Family programs often stress traditional gender roles and condemn homosexual behavior, it seems reasonable that feelings of closeness to Focus on the Family would also bolster conservative civic speech on family definition. However, our analysis does not confirm this suspicion. No statistically significant relationship exists between feelings of closeness to Focus on the Family and speech on family definition. The relationship that does exist suggests counter-mobilization among those who distance themselves from Focus on the Family and its sociopolitical agenda.

Commitment to abstinence-based sex education also exerts a positive influence on the mobilization of clergy voice on moral decay issues above and beyond the "Focus on the Family effect." Progressive mobilization gets a much smaller boost from the positive impact of social justice commitment. The general picture for civic speech on moral decay among Disciples clergy, then, also shows evidence of a culture wars dynamic, albeit a weaker one.

As expected, orthodoxy is statistically weakest in the models that predict civic speech on structural support issues (see Table 3 in appendix). The orthodoxy pattern holds, but we are not as certain that these results are broadly applicable. Evidence of clear orthodoxy mobilization on these issues is much weaker than it is for family definition and moral decay issues.

The structural support issues fit squarely into the longstanding social justice emphasis of the Protestant mainline, so it is not surprising that the four core predictors of civic speech on structural support issues are commitment to social justice, desire for more denominational activism, agreement with the political statement that the federal government needs to do more to solve social problems, and liberal political ideology. This foursome fits the stereotypical image of mainline clergy who have a strong personal commitment to the government safety net and a tendency to push their denominations to be more politically engaged. Disciples clergy who fit this image have engaged in civic speech on structural issues themselves. Recall that more Disciples clergy rank social structure issues among their top personal concerns and that clergy report more frequent discussions of poverty and hunger than discussions of other political issues. Clearly, these mainline Protestant clergy retain a political worldview rooted in the imperative of addressing distributive justice in order to improve the lives of families. This emphasis resonates with the strong social justice theology of the mainline tradition and is likely bolstered by the day-to-day encounters between clergy and families. Culture wars politics has not shifted attention away from the sociopolitical emphasis on structural supports for families.

Political interest does not show up as a significant predictor of civic speech on any of the family issues. This is surprising because political interest has emerged as a strong predictor of political activism in previous studies of clergy (Guth 2001; Guth et al. 1997; Penning and Smidt 2001). Clergy engagement in various debates that touch on family politics appears to be driven more by moral commitments, commitments to policy issues, and organizational mobilization than it is by political interest. Most factors that significantly predict public discussion by Disciples clergy about family issues have a liberal bent, suggesting their public discourse on family issues still takes a liberal tone despite the diversity in orthodoxy and ideology we observed among the clergy.

Conclusion

To what extent do Disciples of Christ clergy appear to be culture warriors? As leaders in a liberal mainline Protestant denomination, they plausibly could be expected to fall into Hunter's progressive camp. Clergy, after all, number among cultural elites, the very population that Hunter argues is on the frontlines of the culture wars. We might, therefore, expect to find that Disciples clergy would enumerate issues that are central to family arrangements and sexuality—the contested ground in the culture wars— among their top personal concerns. We would also expect to find them actively advocating progressive viewpoints on these issues in public forums. Yet results show that Disciples clergy say they are most concerned about social justice issues, such as poverty, hunger, healthcare, racism, and education, and that they discuss precisely those issues in public as much as or more than they discuss culture wars issues. These findings are consistent with mainline Protestantism's longstanding public concern about social justice.

Although mainline Protestant clergy have not abandoned their battle for traditional social justice aims, they have also not ignored civic debates over appropriate family structures moral codes. Patterns in Disciples clergy's civic speech reveal attention to culture war issues and evidence of culture war mobilization dynamics. Their speech is loudest on family definition issues and emphasizes a civil rights mode of social justice advocacy.

The diversity of Disciples clergy suggests that there is also conservative mobilization around issues of gender and sexual orientation, but this potential appears relatively untapped. Whether or not future denominational battles over issues such as sexual orientation will serve to mobilize socially conservative clergy remains to be seen. The absence of strong conservative mobilization on these issues may reflect the denomination's commitment to diversity, which might discourage conservative clergy from speaking out against gay rights. It may also reflect a lack of recruitment by conservative groups that mistakenly assume that all Disciples clergy fall in the progressive camp.

Disciples clergy who promote liberal and conservative family agendas tend to do battle on different issues more than they battle each other. Although the most progressive and the most orthodox clergy speak out on both family definition and moral decay, other factors that mobilize civic speech (issue mobilization, recruitment, and organizational mobilization) tend to encourage liberal clergy to address family definition and conservative clergy to emphasize moral decay. Theological diversity among Disciples clergy manifests itself in different civic speech specializations. Such specialization and their common commitment to structural support issues is likely to ease tensions among clergy. The absence of public discussion of abortion in our findings suggests a reduction in culture wars friction among Disciples clergy. This very divisive moral issue appears to be largely off the table among clergy of this denomination.

Disciples clergy's contributions to debates about family values go beyond the standard litany of abortion, gay rights, divorce, and moral breakdown. Although Disciples clergy are divided over many culture war issues, their divisions seem to result in different priorities for civic speech rather than wars over set issues. The culture war, if one can be said to exist, appears largely to be a war over the appropriate agenda for religious influence on families with economic issues still carrying the day, gender rights and gay rights following close behind. The overall message from this civic speech, then, is characterized by inconsistencies and tensions that emphasize the religious basis of social safety nets, civil rights, and moral codes that enhance healthy social behaviors.

Appendix

Data and Method

Shortly after the General Election in November 2000, we conducted a mail survey of Disciples of Christ clergy. Using the 2000 Yearbook Directory of the Christian Church (Disciples of Christ), we used a stratified, random sample to select 1,000 Disciples clergy who serve as pastors (or associate pastors) in recognized congregations.[7] After two waves of mailing, we received 558 usable responses. Most respondents are white (93%), which reflects the actual percentage (90%) of white Disciples ministers nationwide, and nearly a fourth of the respondents are women (23%). An overwhelming majority (86%) of the ministers are married. The Disciples clergy are also well educated: over 90% have at least a college degree, and more than one-third of all respondents have a postgraduate degree such as a D.Min. or a Th.D. The mean age of our respondents is 51. On average, the clergy surveyed have spent 21 years in the ministry and seven years in their current congregations.

The survey focuses upon clergy's political interests, actions, and attitudes. We also inquire about their theological beliefs, the characteristics of their congregations, and their personal backgrounds.[8] Central to this essay, the survey provides questions that examine the political issues clergy consider most important, the political issues on which they speak publicly, their placement on an orthodox-progressive dimension, their identification with the social justice political tradition, as well as measures of organizational mobilization, organizational demobilization, political interest, party identification, and views on specific political issues.

Factor Analysis

We placed the variables that tap frequency of addressing structural support issues—hunger and poverty, civil rights, aging, environmental problems, and healthcare—in one analysis, which yielded just one underlying factor. We placed variables that tap frequency of addressing moral code issues—gender equality, drugs and alcohol, domestic violence, family decline, and gay rights—into a second factor analysis, from which two underlying factors or types of issues emerged. Gender equality and gay rights clustered together on the first factor, which we shall call the *family definition* factor, because both issues involve debates over new ways of defining families. The remaining three issues—drugs and alcohol, domestic violence, and family decline—loaded on a separate factor, which we refer to as the *moral decay* factor. Factor scores on each of the three dimensions (structural support, family definition, and moral decay) measure the extent to which clergy are involved in public debates concerning political issues of structural support for families, definitions of families, and moral decay, respectively. The factor score described in this section serve as depended variable for the regression models in the next section. The regression models, then, measure the extent to which various other variables influence the levels of each kind of civic discussion of family values.

Regression Analysis

Ordinary least squares multiple regression identifies the expected effect of each of the independent variables on the dependent variable while controlling for all of the other independent variables in the model by simultaneously calculating the linear relationships between the independent variables and the dependent variable that best fits patterns found in the cases in the study. In our regression analysis, the dependent variable is the level of public discussion of the issue.

The other variables tested include interest in politics, ideology, party identification, strength of party identification, various measures of intensity of views on the political issues, feelings of closeness to Bread for the World (a liberal group that emphasizes social justice concerns), feelings of closeness to Focus on the Family (a conservative group that emphasizes traditional moral codes), pastor's perception of whether their congregations are politically united or politically divided, approval of public stands on political issues, age, number of years in the ministry, gender, and race. For results from the full regression model, see Deckman, Crawford, and Olson (2002). The results discussed in this chapter come from smaller models that retain only orthodoxy and the other statistically significant or robust variables. Since each of the civic speech factor variables codes more frequent speech at lower values and less frequent speech at higher values, the signs on the original regression models all reflect predictions about what *decreases* civic speech. To make the results more intuitive for discussions of *mobilization* of civic speech, the signs of the regression coefficients are all changed in the following tables so that the results will be more intuitive, with positive results indicating variables that increase civic speech and negative signs indicating variables that decrease public speech. Signs of coefficients for variables coded in unintuitive directions (such as feelings of closeness to Focus on the Family) were also changed so that the results would reflect the direction of the relationship given the intuitive understanding of the variables.

Regression Results

TABLE 3. Structural Support Regression Model

Variable	Standardized Regression Coefficient
Orthodoxy	−0.35#
Orthodoxy squared	0.31#
Social justice at the heart of the gospel	0.16***
Denomination should be more politically involved	0.20***
Federal government should do more to solve social problems.	0.14***
Ideology	−0.11*
R^2	0.23

# $p < 0.15$; * $p < 0.10$; ** $p < 0.05$; *** $p < 0.01$.

TABLE 4. Family Definition Regression Model

Variable	Standardized Regression Coefficient
Orthodoxy	0.45**
Orthodoxy squared	−0.58***
Social justice is at the heart of the Gospel	0.08**
We need women's rights legislation	0.18***
Theology motivates personal political involvement	0.09**
All clergy positions should be open to women	0.11**
All clergy positions should be open to homosexuals	0.24***
R^2	0.32

* $p < 0.10$; ** $p < 0.05$; *** $p < 0.01$.

TABLE 5. Moral Decay Regression Model

Variable	Standardized Regression Coefficient
Orthodoxy	−0.40*
Orthodoxy squared	0.43*
Social justice is at the heart of the gospel	0.13***
Theology motivates personal political involvement	0.03
Closeness to Focus on the Family	0.28***
Sex education should be abstinence-based.	0.11**
R^2	0.12

* $p < 0.10$; ** $p < 0.05$; *** $p < 0.01$.

Notes

1. This research was funded by grants from the Association for the Study of Religion, the Louisville Institute, the Society for the Scientific Study of Religion, and Washington College, as well as additional financial support from Clemson University. We thank Tracey Stewart, Christy Rowan, and students at Clemson University for excellent research assistance. We thank Corwin Smidt for organizing the cooperative project, as well as Richard Hamm and the Christian Church (Disciples of Christ) for their helpful cooperation with our portion of it.
2. Mainline Protestantism refers to the historically dominant, hierarchically organized denominations of American Protestantism. Mainline Protestants embrace theological diversity and reject literalist interpretations of scripture. Unlike many evangelical Protestants, they envision a broad role for the church in society. In addition to the Disciples of Christ, other major mainline Protestant denominations in the United States include the American Baptist Churches, the Episcopal Church, the Evangelical Lutheran Church in America, the Presbyterian Church (U.S.A.), the Reformed Church in America, the United Church of Christ, and the United Methodist Church.
3. For further information on the Christian Church (Disciples of Christ), see their official denominational web site at http://www.disciples.org/general/whoweare.
4. For a fuller account of organizational mobilization, organizational demobilization, and issue mobilization for clergy see Crawford, Olson, and Deckman (2001).
5. The appendix to this essay provides an overview of the methodology of the study, including sampling methods, variable definitions, and statistical methods.

6. Note that this survey was administered before September 11, 2001, so terrorism, security, and war concerns that have come to dominate the public agenda were not yet salient for the American people.
7. The 2000 Yearbook reports there are 7,113 ordained Disciples clergy in the United States. Most, however, do not serve in a congregation, but have other positions such as Christian educators, missionaries, administrators at the local, regional, and national level, counselors, ministers of music, and other positions. A large number are also retired. We chose active ministers of recognized congregations, which totaled 2,575.
8. We conducted this survey as part of a cooperative project designed to study the political behavior of clergy in nineteen different religious traditions after the 2000 elections. Clergy include a range of religious traditions, from mainline and evangelical Protestants to Roman Catholics, Unitarian Universalists, and Jews.

References

Apostolidis, Paul. 2000. *Stations of the Cross: Adorno and Christian Right Radio.* Durham: Duke University Press.

Cadge, Wendy. 2002. "Vital Conflicts: The Mainline Denominations Debate Homosexuality." In *The Quiet Hand of God: Faith-based Activism and the Public Role of Mainline Protestantism.* Robert Wuthnow and John H. Evans, eds. Berkeley: University of California Press.

Carney, Dan, and David Hawkins. 1999. "Conservative 'Culture War' Pauses for a Reality Check." *CQ Weekly* 57: 738–45.

Cavendish, James C. 2001. "To March or Not To March: Clergy Mobilization Strategies and Grassroots Antidrug Activism." In *Christian Clergy in American Politics.* Sue E. S. Crawford and Laura R. Olson, eds. Baltimore: Johns Hopkins University Press.

Christian Church (Disciples of Christ) web site. http://www.disciples.org.

Crawford, Sue E. S. 1995. "Clergy at Work in the Secular City." Ph.D. diss., Indiana University.

Crawford, Sue E. S., Laura R. Olson, and Melissa M. Deckman. 2001. "Understanding the Mobilization of Professionals." *Nonprofit and Voluntary Sector Quarterly* 30: 321–50.

Davis, Nancy J., and Robert V. Robinson. 1997. "A War for America's Soul? The American Religious Landscape." In *Culture Wars in American Politics: Critical Review of a Popular Myth.* Rhys H. Williams, ed. New York: Aldine de Gruyter.

Day, Katie. 2001. "The Construction of Political Strategies among African American Clergy." In *Christian Clergy in American Politics*. Sue E. S. Crawford and Laura R. Olson, eds. Baltimore: Johns Hopkins University Press.

Deckman, Melissa M., Sue E. S. Crawford, and Laura R. Olson. 2002. "Clergy as Political Mobilizers: Does Gender Matter?" Paper presented at the annual meeting of the American Political Science Association, Boston.

Demerath, N. J. III, and Yonge Yang. 1997. "What American Culture War? A View from the Trenches as Opposed to the Command Posts and the Press Corps." In *Culture Wars in American Politics: Critical Review of a Popular Myth*. Rhys H. Williams, ed. New York: Aldine de Gruyter.

DiMaggio, Paul J., John H. Evans, and Bethany Bryson. 1996. "Have Americans' Social Attitudes Become More Polarized?" *American Journal of Sociology* 102: 690–755.

Djupe, Paul A. and Christopher P. Gilbert. 2003. *The Prophetic Pulpit: Clergy, Churches, and Communities in American Politics*. Lanham. MD: Rowman and Littlefield.

Evans, John H., Bethany Bryson, and Paul DiMaggio. 2001. "Opinion Polarization: Important Contributions, Necessary Limitations." *American Journal of Sociology* 106: 944–60.

Findlay, James F. 1993. *Church People in the Struggle: The National Council of Churches and the Black Freedom Movement, 1950–1970*. New York: Oxford University Press.

Friedland, Michael B. 1998. *Lift Up Your Voice Like a Trumpet: White Clergy and the Civil Rights and Antiwar Movements, 1954–1973*. Chapel Hill, NC: University of North Carolina Press.

Green, John C., James L. Guth, Corwin E. Smidt, and Lyman A. Kellstedt, ed. 1996. *Religion and the Culture Wars: Dispatches from the Front*. Lanham, MD: Rowman and Littlefield.

Guth, James L. 1983. "Southern Baptist Clergy: Vanguard of the Christian Right?" In *The New Christian Right*. Robert C. Liebman and Robert Wuthnow, eds. New York: Aldine de Gruyter.

Guth, James L. 1996. "The Political Mobilization of Southern Baptist Clergy, 1980–1992." In *Religion and the Culture Wars: Dispatches From the Front*. John C. Green, James L. Guth, Lyman A. Kellstedt, and Corwin E. Smidt, eds. Lanham, MD: Rowman and Littlefield.

Guth, James L. 2001. "The Mobilization of a Religious Elite: Political Activism among Southern Baptist Clergy in 1996." In *Christian Clergy in American Politics*. Sue E. S. Crawford and Laura R. Olson, eds. Baltimore: Johns Hopkins University Press.

Guth, James L., and John C. Green, ed. 1991. *The Bible and the Ballot Box*. Boulder, CO: Westview.

Guth, James L. and John C. Green. 1996. "Politics in a New Key: Religiosity and Participation among Political Activists." In *Religion and the Culture Wars: Dispatches from the Front*. John C. Green, James L. Guth, Corwin E. Smidt, and Lyman A. Kellstedt, eds. Lanham, MD: Rowman and Littlefield.

Guth, James L., John C. Green, Lyman A. Kellstedt, and Corwin E. Smidt. 1996. "Onward Christian Soldiers: Religious Activist Groups in American Politics." In *Religion and the Culture Wars: Dispatches from the Front*. John C. Green, James L. Guth, Corwin E. Smidt, and Lyman A. Kellstedt, eds. Lanham, MD: Rowman and Littlefield.

Guth, James L., John C. Green, Corwin E. Smidt, Lyman A. Kellstedt, and Margaret M. Poloma. 1997. *The Bully Pulpit: The Politics of Protestant Clergy*. Lawrence,: University Press of Kansas.

Guth, James L., John C. Green, Corwin E. Smidt, and Margaret M. Poloma. 1991. "Pulpits and Politics: The Protestant Clergy in the 1988 Election." In *The Bible and the Ballot Box*. James L. Guth and John C. Green, eds. Boulder, CO: Westview.

Hadden, Jeffrey K. 1969. *The Gathering Storm in the Churches*. Garden City, NY: Doubleday.

Hunter, James Davison. 1991. *Culture Wars: The Struggle to Define America*. New York: Basic Books.

Jelen, Ted G. 1993. *The Political World of the Clergy*. Westport, CT: Praeger.

Jelen, Ted. G. 1997. "Culture Wars and the Party System: Religion and Realignment, 1972–1993." In *Culture Wars in American Politics: Critical Review of a Popular Myth*. Rhys H. Williams, ed. New York: Aldine de Gruyter.

McConkey, Dale. 2001. "Whither Hunter's Culture War? Shifts in Evangelical Morality, 1988–1998." *Sociology of Religion* 62: 149–74.

Miller, Alan S., and John P. Hoffmann. 1999. "The Growing Divisiveness: Culture Wars or a War of Words?" *Social Forces* 78: 721–46.

Niebuhr, H. Richard. 1951. *Christ and Culture*. New York: Harper and Row.

Olson, Laura R. 2000. *Filled with Spirit and Power: Protestant Clergy in Politics*. Albany: State University of New York Press.

Olson, Laura R., and Wendy Cadge. 2002. "Talking about Homosexuality: The Views of Mainline Protestant Clergy." *Journal for the Scientific Study of Religion* 41: 153–67.

Olson, Laura R., Sue E. S. Crawford, and Melissa M. Deckman. Forthcoming. *Women with a Mission: Religion, Gender, and the Politics of Women Clergy*. Tuscaloosa: University of Alabama Press.

Penning, James M., and Corwin E. Smidt. 2001. "Reformed Preachers in Politics." In *Christian Clergy in American Politics*. Sue E. S. Crawford and Laura R. Olson, eds. Baltimore: Johns Hopkins University Press.

Quinley, Harold E. 1974. *The Prophetic Clergy: Social Activism among Protestant Ministers*. New York: Wiley.

Rabkin, Jeremy. 1999. "The Culture War that Isn't." *Policy Review* 96: 3–20.

Rosenstone, Steven J., and John Mark Hansen. 1993. *Mobilization, Participation, and Democracy in America*. New York: Macmillan.

Smith, Christian. 1996. *Resisting Reagan: The U.S. Central American Peace Movement*. Chicago: University of Chicago Press.

Stark, Rodney, Bruce D. Foster, Charles Y. Glock, and Harold E. Quinley. 1971. *Wayward Shepherds: Prejudice and the Protestant Clergy*. New York: Harper and Row.

Verba, Sidney, and Norman H. Nie. 1972. *Participation in America: Political Democracy and Social Equality*. Chicago: University of Chicago Press.

Verba, Sidney, Kay Lehman Schlozman, and Henry E. Brady. 1995. *Voice and Equality: Civic Voluntarism in American Society*. Cambridge: Harvard University Press.

Wilcox, Clyde. 1992. *God's Warriors*. Baltimore: Johns Hopkins University Press.

Wilcox, W. Bradford. 2002. "For the Sake of the Children? Family-Related Discourse and Practice in the Mainline." In *The Quiet Hand of God: Faith-based Activism and the Public Role of Mainline Protestantism*. Robert Wuthnow and John H. Evans, eds. Berkeley: University of California Press.

Wilcox, W. Bradford. 2004. *Soft Patriarchs, New Men: How Christianity Shapes Fathers and Husbands*. Chicago: University of Chicago Press.

Williams, Rhys H., ed. 1997a. *Culture Wars in American Politics: Critical Reviews of a Popular Myth*. New York: Aldine de Gruyter.

Williams, Rhys H. 1997b. "Is America in a Culture War? Yes—No—Sort Of." *The Christian Century* 114: 1038–39.

Wolfinger, Raymond H., and Steven J. Rosenstone. 1980. *Who Votes?* New Haven: Yale University Press.

Wuthnow, Robert. 1988. *The Restructuring of American Religion: Society and Faith Since World War II*. Princeton: Princeton University Press.

Wuthnow, Robert, and John H. Evans, ed. 2002. *The Quiet Hand of God: Faith-based Activism and the Public Role of Mainline Protestantism*. Berkeley: University of California Press.

The Impact of Religiosity on Marital Stability

LISA A. RILEY

The 2000 Census reported that over half (56.9%) of the U. S. population was married whereas 1.8% were separated, 8.6% divorced, and 2.5% widowed. The remaining one-third (30.3%) had never been married. The projected rate of divorce for those marrying is between 40 and 50%, *given* current social trends. If these trends change, then the projected divorce rate will change.[1] Given the current projected likelihood of divorce, there has been a plethora of research focusing on predictors of marital stability and instability. Although researchers have often studied religious indicators of divorce, few have attempted to measure the many different dimensions of religiosity. In this essay I first summarize the history of the relationship between religiosity and marital stability. Then, I report and discuss the results of a study that explored the impact of personal attributes and religiosity on martial stability.

As is evident from a multitude of research, benefits of marital stability include better physical and mental health, greater satisfaction with life, increased longevity, higher male wages, and better child outcomes (for summaries, see Amato and Booth 1997; Doherty et al. 2002; Gray and Vanderhart 2000; McLanahan and Sandefur 1996; Waite and Gallagher 2000; Wallerstein, Lewis, and Blakeslee 2000). Thus, factors that increase the likelihood of marital stability decrease the likelihood of negative outcomes for spouses, children, and, ultimately, society itself. The ultimate question addressed in this chapter is: What are the factors that increase the likelihood of remaining in a marital relationship? Specifically:

Does marrying later in life increase the likelihood of martial stability?

Does premarital cohabitation increase the likelihood of marital instability?

Does family approval of one's spouse increase the likelihood of marital stability?

Does disagreement over parents or in-laws increase the likelihood of marital instability?

Is there a greater likelihood of marital stability if both spouses are the same race, have similar levels of education, are both in their first marriage, or about the same age?

Does marriage preparation increase the likelihood of marital stability?

Does having a religious wedding ceremony or participating together in religious activities increase the likelihood of marital stability?

Do religious differences or disagreements over religion increase the likelihood of marital instability?

Do differences in religions increase the likelihood of marital instability?

Who has the greatest likelihood of marital stability?

Religiosity and Marital Stability

Researchers have found a relationship between religious characteristics and marital issues. This is not surprising given the fact that both religion and family are institutions that emphasize values and provide socialization for individuals. A large body of literature reports on what is likely to increase marital stability, or decrease the likelihood of divorce. There are also numerous studies about the difference religion and religious influence make in one's life (e.g., Roof and McKinney 1987). During the late 1990s, researchers began to focus on the relationship between different dimensions of religiosity and marital stability. Until this time, a majority of studies used a single dimension, such as church attendance, to measure a person's religiousness or religiosity and, hence, the impact of religiosity on marriage.

For the past 30 years, studies consistently found that religiously homogamous marriages (husband and wife adherents of the same religion) had a lower rate of divorce than religiously heterogamous marriages (husband and wife adherents of different religions) (e.g., Bumpass and Sweet 1992; Heaton and Pratt 1990; Hoge and Ferry 1981; Lehrer and Chiswick 1993). This led many to promote religiously homogamous or *same-church* marriages as one way of lowering the divorce rate. However, other researchers found that the incidence of religiously heterogamous marriages was related to other social trends, such as religious autonomy, individualism, pluralism, privatism, secularism, and voluntarism (e.g., Ammerman and Roof 1995; Hoge, Dinges, and Gonzales 1999; Wuthnow 1993). Hence, these social trends, not only religious heterogamy, may have led to the higher likelihood of divorce for heterogamous marriages. Others have consistently found that religious affiliation is generally associated with a lower risk of divorce. It appears that denominational practices and teachings about marriage and divorce lead to different levels of marital stability (Call and Heaton 1997; Lehrer and Chiswick 1993).

In this essay, religiosity is determined by a variety of measures, such as religious homogamy, participation in joint religious activities, level of religious differences, and whether or not marriage preparation occurred. These measures attempt to provide information on the many different dimensions of religiosity. The term, *interchurch marriage*, refers to religiously heterogamous marriages in which each spouse, however loosely, identifies with a different Christian denomination or church. A large majority (86%) of the United States population consider themselves Christian (Kosmin and Lachman 1993), which allows for basic survey questions about religious beliefs.

Who Are the People Who Responded?

The data reported in this essay is from a study conducted by the Center for Marriage and Family at Creighton University, *Ministry to Interchurch Marriages: A National Study* (1999). The study's respondents were individuals who were married, divorced, or separated and whose most recent marriage occurred within the past twenty years. All respondents and their partners identified with a Christian denomination or church at

TABLE 1. Denominational Representation

Affiliation	Study Sample	Christian Abstract of 1997 Gallup Sample of Religious Affiliation
Baptist	21.2%	22.0%
Catholic	29.4%	26.0%
Christian	7.2%	—
Episcopal	1.7%	2.0%
Lutheran	6.7%	6.0%
Methodist	7.1%	9.0%
Mormon	3.0%	—
Non-denominational	4.4%	3.0%
Pentecostal	2.6%	3.0%
Presbyterian	3.1%	4.0%
Protestant	5.0%	—
Other Denominations	6.0%	5.0%
None/Atheist	2.2%	—

— Not Reported by Gallup

the time of engagement, and that neither had subsequently changed to a non-Christian religion.

Table 1 shows a comparison of the denominational representation of the study sample and a Christian abstract of Gallup's August 1997 national sample of religious affiliation. This clearly shows that the study sample was very similar to the overall population.

Two versions of the interview, one for married persons and a shorter one for divorced persons, were used. (Several questions about marriage and religiosity were not asked of divorced persons because the event of divorce has the potential to alter accurate recall.) Sixty-three percent of those contacted completed the interview. Of the 1512 telephone interviews completed, 1285 were by married persons and the remaining 227 by those who were divorced or separated.

FIGURE 1. Combined Sample Church Type

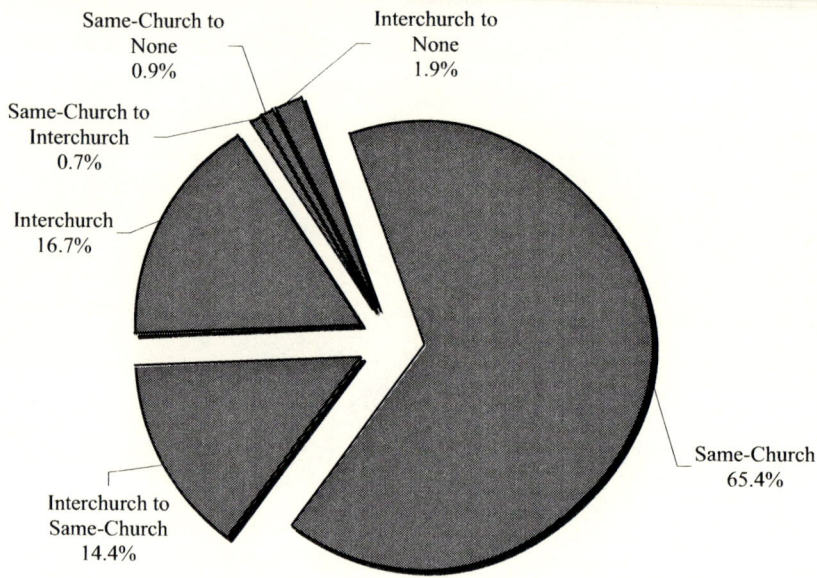

Characteristics of Respondents

Profile: Combined Sample of 1512 Married, Divorced, and Separated Persons

Approximately one-third of those who responded were in an interchurch relationship at the time of engagement, but only 16.7% were in interchurch marriages at time of interview for married individuals or at the time of the divorce or separation for those who were divorced or separated. Another 14.4% had changed from an interchurch relationship to a same-church relationship due to either one spouse or both spouses changing their religious affiliation. Almost two-thirds of those interviewed remained in a same-church relationship from the time of the engagement to the time of interview or divorce/separation. In a few cases, a spouse in an interchurch marriage changed from a religious affiliation to no religious affiliation; a spouse in a same-church relationship changed to no religious affiliation; or a spouse in a same-church relationship changed religious affiliations (Figure 1).

The average age of the respondents was 37.5 years. Fifteen percent were divorced; almost three-quarters were in their first marriage; and

FIGURE 2. Married Sample Church Type

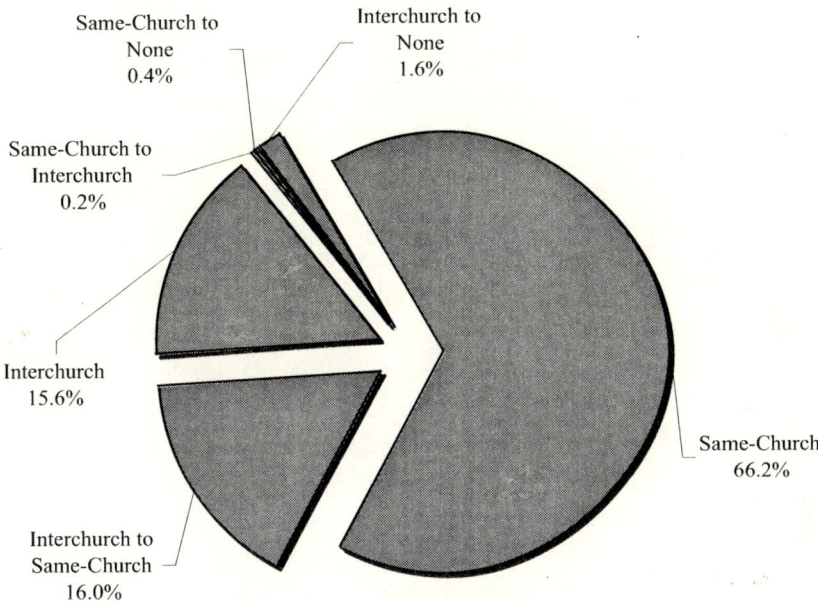

59.8% were female. About one-third had a bachelor's degree or higher educational level and 15% were of a non-White ethnicity or race. The average number of children per family was less than 2.

Profile: Married Sample (1285)

Not surprisingly, the married respondents had a profile similar to the combined sample (see Figure 2). At the time of engagement, one-third were in interchurch relationships, but only half were in interchurch marriages at the time of the interview. The majority of these interchurch relationships had one or both spouses change religious affiliations to create a same-church relationship. The remaining two-thirds began and remained in same-church relationships. At time of interview, only 15.8% of respondents were in interchurch marriages, whereas 82.2% in same-church marriages.

Descriptive statistics of the married sample are similar to those of the combined sample. The average age of respondents was 37.5 years old, nearly three-quarters were reporting on their first marriage, and 60.5% were female. Slightly more than one-third had a bachelor's degree or higher educational level and 13% were of a non-White ethnicity or race. The average number of children per family was slightly more than 2.

Profile: Divorced/Separated Sample (227)[2]

There were some differences between those who were divorced or separated and their married counterparts (see Figure 3). At time of engagement, approximately one-third of the sample were in interchurch relationships; a majority of these remained in interchurch relationships at the time of divorce or separation. Only a few interchurch relationships at engagement became same-church relationships when one or both spouses changed religious affiliation or changed to no religious affiliation. Almost two-thirds of the sample began and remained in same-church relationships. Thus, at time of divorce or separation, slightly more than one-quarter had been in interchurch marriages whereas just over two-thirds had been in same-church marriages.

Descriptive statistics of the divorced and separated sample are as follows. The average age was 37.41, nearly three-quarters were reporting on their first marriage, and 55.5% were female. Slightly less than one-fourth had a bachelor's degree or higher educational level and one-quarter reported a non-White ethnicity or race. The average number of children per family was 1.5 children—slightly less than their married counterparts. It is important to note that any results presented in this essay apply only to Christians. It is unknown if the same or similar findings would apply to those who profess other religions.

Measures of Religiosity[3]

Respondents were asked about a variety of issues concerning religion. Married persons were asked, "How much disagreement have you and your (husband/wife) had over religion? A great deal, a moderate amount, a little bit, or none?" Those who were divorced or separated were read a list of several areas, including religious matters, in which couples may have disagreement. After each statement was read, respondents were to answer whether they disagreed a great deal, a moderate amount, a little bit, or not at all. Based upon responses to these questions, a variable representing the level of disagreement on religion was created. About half reported that they did *not* disagree with their spouse on religion. Additionally, 62% of respondents reported having some type of marriage

FIGURE 3. Divorced Sample Church Type

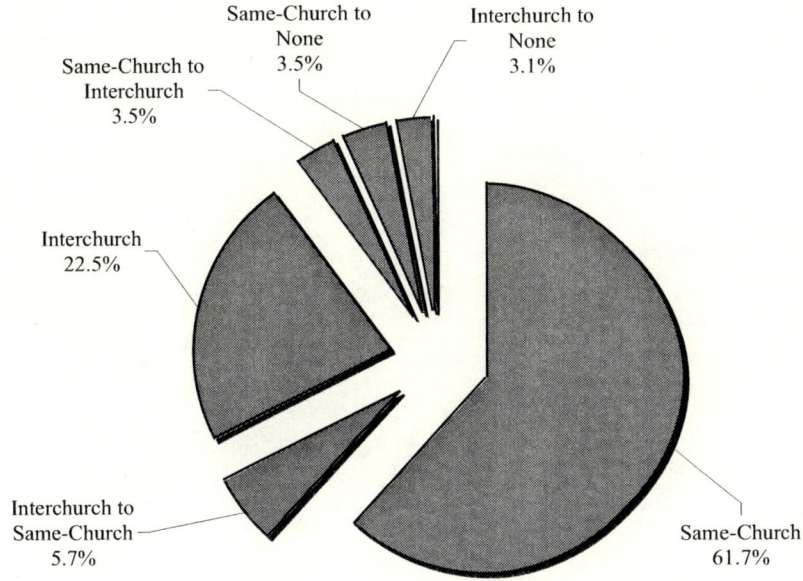

preparation and over three-fourths reported participating in a religious wedding ceremony.

The next three religious variables are scales. The first scale, *joint religious activities*, was computed from six questions. Questions were asked about their current activities or those they "may or may not have done *together as a couple*" when married (for those who were divorced or separated). For each of the following six items, individuals responded: regularly, often, occasionally, or never.

- Attend a church worship service together
- Attend a Bible study or religious education activity together
- Serve or work together on a church project or committee
- Participate together in a church-sponsored social activity
- Pray together
- Discuss religious or spiritual matters together

Since scores ranged from 0–3 (never to regularly) a scale was created by adding the scores of each item together. The range was from a low of

FIGURE 5. Joint Religious Activities Scale

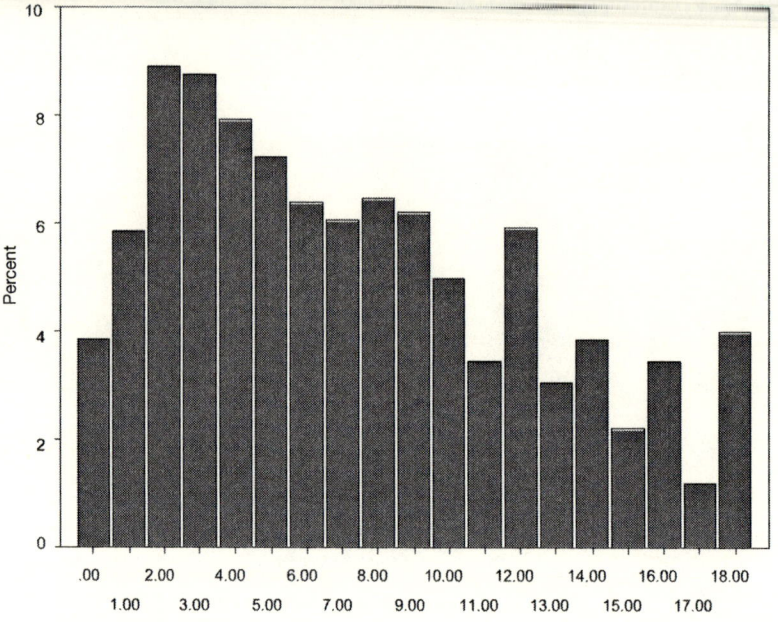

0 to a high of 18 with an average score of 7.41. Those receiving a score of 0 had to have replied "never" to each of the above six items. As shown in Figure 5, a significant percentage fell on the lower side and thus rarely participated in these activities together.

A second scale, *religious differences*, was created from seven questions. Questions were also asked about the ways in which they and their spouse (or ex-spouse) may or may not have been different. For each of the following seven items, individuals responded with very different, somewhat different, or not different.

- What you consider(ed) to be right and wrong
- The church teachings you believe(ed) in
- Your beliefs about what it means to be saved
- The importance of attending church
- Your religious practices
- The importance of the Bible
- The importance of prayer

Scores ranged from 0–2 (not different to very different) for each item

FIGURE 6. Religious Differences Index

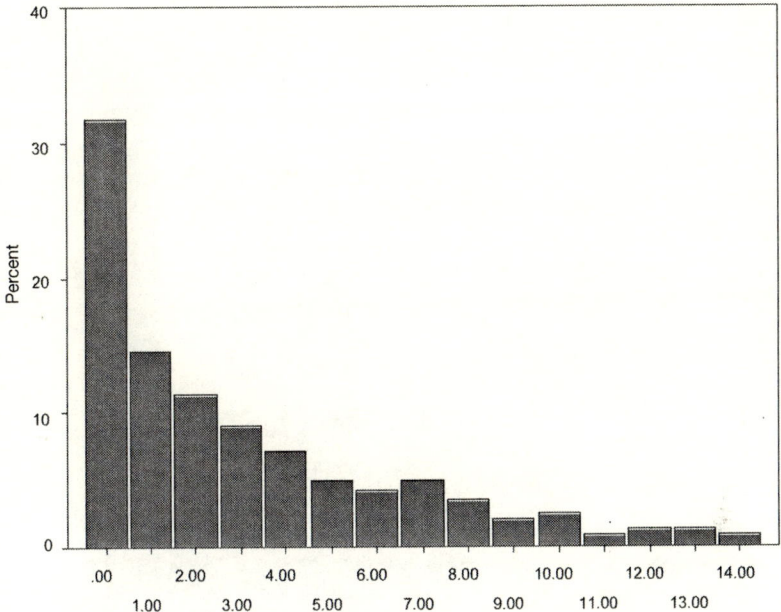

and thus ranged from 0 to 14 for the composite scale. Those with lower scores had fewer religious differences with their spouse or ex-spouse; those with higher scores had more religious differences with their spouse or ex-spouse. The average score was 3.01, indicating that there was a low level of religious differences among spouses. Approximately one-third indicated no differences with their spouses on any of the above items (see Figure 6).

The final scale, *acceptance of other religions*, was created from three questions. Respondents were read areas in which couples sometimes have disagreements. Answers included a great deal, a moderate amount, a little bit or not at all. For each of the following three items, individuals responded: strongly disagree, disagree, agree, or strongly agree.

- The churches you grew up in taught you to accept other religions
- The town or neighborhood you primarily grew up in taught you to accept other religions
- The family you grew up in taught you to accept other religions

Scores ranged from 1–4 (strongly disagree to strongly agree), creating

FIGURE 7. Acceptance of Other Religions Index

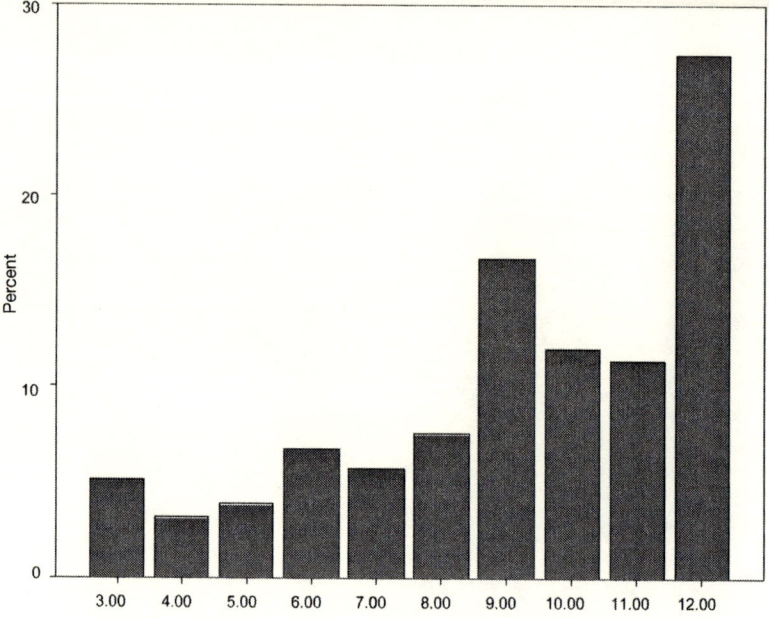

a composite scale from 3 to 12, with higher scores indicating a greater level of acceptance. Those scoring a 3 indicated that they were *not* taught to be accepting of other religions by their childhood churches, towns, or families. The average score was 9. Slightly more than one-quarter strongly agreed with all three statements and thus were taught to be very accepting of other religions (see Figure 7).

Discussion

Since the social world includes many variables, the impact of one variable on another does not usually tell the entire story. However, one should be aware of bivariate (two-variable) relationships. Table 2 presents the relationship between the respondent's church type and marital stability. It reveals that a greater proportion of those who remained in interchurch relationships were divorced (about one-fifth) compared to 14% of those who were in same-church relationships.

Figure 8 presents another way to look at the relationship between church type and marital stability (ignoring those who changed to none or

Table 2. Church Type and Marital Stability

Church-Type	Marital Status		
	Divorced/ Separated	Married	Total
Remain in *Interchurch Relationship*	51	201	252
Change *Interchurch to Same-church Relationship*	13	205	218
Remain in *Same-church Relationship*	140	850	990
Change *Interchurch to No Church Relationship*	7	21	28
Change *Same-church to No Church Relationship*	8	5	13
Change *Same-church to Interchurch Relationship*	8	3	11
Total	227	1285	1512

from interchurch to same-church relationships). When those who were in same-church relationships, whether starting at engagement as same-church or interchurch, were compared to those who remained in interchurch relationships, those in the same-church relationships had a significantly lower percentage of divorce (12.7%) than those who remained in interchurch relationships (20.3%). When those in same-church relationships were divided into two groups based on whether the relationship was initially same-church or interchurch, a significant difference in percentage of divorce in the resulting three groups was revealed. Those who remained in interchurch relationships had the highest percentage of divorce (20.3%), those remaining in same-church relationships had the next highest (14.1%), and those who changed from an interchurch to a same-church relationship had the lowest percentage of divorce (6.0%). The percentage of divorce for those who changed from an interchurch to a same-church relationship was significantly different from those who began and remained in *either* a same-church or interchurch relationship. The difference in the percentage of divorce between those who remained

FIGURE 8. Marital Stability by Church Type

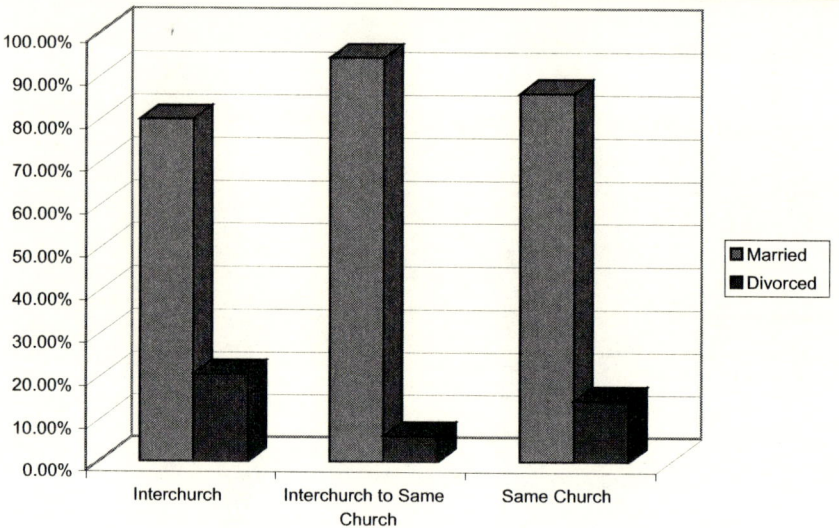

in same-church relationships and those who remained in interchurch relationships was only marginally significant.

The previous analysis of the relationship between church type and martial stability excluded the impact of other social variables. The remaining sections of this essay focus on the effect of multiple factors on marital stability. The issue is whether interchurch status *per se* increases the likelihood of divorce/separation when other factors, including personal characteristics, homogamy, family of origin variables, and religious variables, are taken into account.

In order to answer effectively the questions listed at the beginning of the essay, it is important to look at more than just the bivariate, or two variable, relationship.[4] Thus, each question will be answered by using a statistical technique that allows for multiple impacts on the likelihood of marital stability.[5] Personal characteristics, such as gender, race, level of education, age at marriage, and whether or not one had children, were always taken into consideration. For this sample, being female, white, older at time of marriage, and having children all increased the likelihood of marital stability. When looking solely at the effect of the personal characteristics on the likelihood of marital stability, neither gender nor level of education significantly impacts the likelihood of marital stability (see

Appendix C, column 1). However, when the homogamy and/or religious variables are added to the personal characteristics, being female and having less education increased the likelihood of marital stability (see Appendix C, column 3).

Does marrying later in life increase the likelihood of martial stability?

Being older at marriage had a significant positive effect on marital stability. In other words, the older the person was at the time of marriage, the greater the likelihood that the marriage was intact. Researchers have recently reported that there is a 24% point decrease in the risk of divorce or separation for women during the first ten years of marriage if she marries at age 25 or older (as compared to under 18) (Bramlett and Mosher 2002). Raley (2000) and Fitch and Ruggles (2000) both find that the average age at first marriage is rising.

Does premarital cohabitation increase the likelihood of marital instability?

Cohabitation did not emerge as a significant predictor of marital instability for this sample, however, it was not ascertained if the cohabitation came prior to or after engagement. New studies are finding that those who cohabit after their engagement do not have the negative aspects previously associated with cohabitation (e.g., negative communication, higher divorce rate, etc.). It is possible that respondents in this sample may be different due to the fact that they all identified with a Christian denomination at the time of engagement. Thus, the religious character of the sample and the possibility that religion affects attitudes towards cohabitation may be another possible explanation as to why cohabitation was not a significant predictor (see Lye and Waldron 1997:199–225; Sweet 1989; Sweet and Bumpass 1990; Thornton, Axinn, and Hill 1992:628–51).

Does family approval of one's spouse increase the likelihood of marital stability?

Having a higher level of family approval of one's spouse at the time of the marriage increased the likelihood of marital stability.

Does disagreement over parents or in-laws increase the likelihood of marital instability?

Disagreements over parents or in-laws did not impact the likelihood of divorce. Couples who agreed over parents or in-laws were just as likely to get divorced as those who disagreed.

Is there a greater likelihood of marital stability if both spouses are the same race, have similar levels of education, are both in their first marriage, or about the same age?

Being the same race, having both spouses in their first marriage, and being similar in age did not significantly increase or decrease the likelihood of marital stability. In other words, couples who were the same race were no more or less likely to divorce than those who were not the same race. The same is true for couples who were both in their first marriages (as compared to couples in which one or both spouses were in their second or subsequent marriage) and those who were similar in age. However, having both spouses sharing the same level of education significantly increased the probability of marital stability.

Does marriage preparation increase the likelihood of marital stability?

Although it is unknown as to what kind of marriage preparation a couple had, those who reported having marriage preparation had a higher likelihood of marital stability than those who did not report having marriage preparation. This supports previous findings from the Center for Marriage and the Family (1995) about the importance of marriage preparation.

Does having a religious wedding ceremony or participating together in religious activities increase the likelihood of marital stability?

Having a religious wedding ceremony did not increase the likelihood of marital stability. In other words, those who had religious weddings were just as likely to divorce as those who did not have religious weddings. One of the most significant indicators of marital stability was joint participation in religious activities. Individuals who reported higher levels of participating together in religious activities had a much higher likelihood of marital stability than those who reported lower levels of doing religious activities together.

Do religious differences or disagreements over religion increase the likelihood of marital instability?

Although disagreements over religion did not impact the likelihood of divorce, there was a large impact of religious differences on marital stability. Spouses who reported fewer religious differences had a much lower likelihood of marital instability than those who reported more religious differences.

Do differences in religions increase the likelihood of marital instability?

First, recall the previous discussion on the bivariate relationship between spouses being the same religion and marital stability. Those who were in interchurch relationships had a higher percentage of divorce than those who were in a same-church relationship. When those who were in a same-church relationship were divided into those who began and remained in a same-church relationship and those who began in an interchurch relationship and became same-church, differences appeared. Those in interchurch to same-church relationships had a significantly lower percentage of divorce (only 6.0%) than those who remained in same-church relationships (14.1%). Thus, couples who began in interchurch relationships had both the highest and the lowest levels of marital stability, depending upon whether the relationship remained interchurch or became same-church. That individuals were willing to change religious affiliation may reflect a high level of commitment to marriage, which is perhaps related to the lower percentage of divorce in marriages that began as interchurch but became same-church marriages. On the other hand, those who remain in interchurch relationships may have less regard for social norms favoring religious homogamy. A diminished concern for social norms could be related to a greater acceptance of divorce. Although respondents in interchurch relationships had a higher percentage of divorce, it should be emphasized that almost 80% remained married.

Conclusion

An important finding is that when other variables are included, remaining in an interchurch marriage was not a predictor of marital instability. This suggests that it is not the interchurch status of marriage *per se* that puts interchurch couples at risk for instability, but the other factors such as a lower level of joint religious activities or a higher level of religious differences. Regardless of whether or not a couple is in a same-church or interchurch marriage, it is the extent to which spouses perceive greater religious differences and have a lower level of joint participation in religious activities that puts the marital relationship at risk. It is *not* the fact that there is an interchurch marriage.

Who has the greatest likelihood of marital stability?

If one waits to get married until s/he is older, attends marriage preparation, has one's family's approval of his/her spouse, marries someone with a similar level of education, participates with one's partner in religious activities, has few religious differences, and *if* in an interchurch relationship one or both change religious denominations to create a same-church relationship, then one's chances of remaining married is very high indeed.

When looking at how marital instability may be impacted by church type (same-church or interchurch) as well as other variables, an interesting picture emerged. Factors that increased the likelihood of marital stability were: older age at marriage, being a parent, being female, being white, and having a lower level of education in addition to being in an interchurch-to-same-church marriage, participating in joint religious activities, having fewer religious differences, similar levels of education, having marriage preparation, and having one's family approval of spouse at time of marriage.

Based on this study, it appears that marital stability is impacted by a number of factors, not all of them tested here, working together. Those factors within an individual's control include being older when one marries, choosing to have children, choosing the same religion *if* one is in an interchurch relationship at time of engagement, choosing to participate together in joint religious activities, going through marriage preparation, making sure one's family approves of one's spouse, and marrying someone with a similar educational level.

The consistent negative predictor for educational level supports recent findings. With greater levels of education, divorce may become more acceptable and available given greater financial stability. However, marrying someone at a similar educational level did increase the likelihood of marital stability. Other homogamy variables did not seem to increase the likelihood of marital stability, besides being in a same-church marriage.

These findings suggest that marriage preparation and enrichment programs would be beneficial. By making couples aware of their religious differences and perhaps lessoning those differences through education or at least a greater understanding and acceptance of the differences, marital stability should increase. Likewise, strong encouragement of couples' participating together in religious activities may well result in greater marital stability. In marriage preparation or enrichment, family of origin issues, and especially family approval of one's future spouse could be important issues.

Appendix

A. Non-Religious Variables

Socio-Demographic Variables: These are sometimes referred to as control variables. That is, in regression analysis, one controls for variables that may be impacting the dependent variable (marital stability in this case) and preventing a different variable (religious one) to have a significant effect when there really is no effect. In other words, by excluding the effect of these variables, then the effect of the other variables becomes clearer. Married persons were asked their gender. Almost 60% reported their gender as female. Additionally, they were asked "Do you consider yourself to be White, Black, Hispanic, Asian, or of another ethnic group?" The majority (83.9%) reported their race/ethnicity as White. When asked "What is the highest level of education of education you have achieved (at time of divorce or separation)?", 38.1% had a high school degree or less whereas almost one-third had at least a Bachelor's degree. Based on current age and the year married, an individual's age at time of marriage was computed. The average age at marriage was 27.5 ranging from 16 years to 60 years. The average age for females was 26.5 and their husband's age at marriage was almost 29. This was similar to male reports of their own and their wives age at marriage. Four fifths were parents.

Homogamy Variables: Questions were asked about one's self and one's current or ex-spouses. Variables were created to determine whether homogamy or heterogeny on race/ethnicity, whether or not it was both parties' first marriage, age, education, and church type. Most (91.3%) couples were *not* or had not been in an interracial marriage. Hence, the majority were currently or had been in racially homogamous marriages. Almost two-thirds of the couples were both in their first marriages. As for age, 69% were married to someone within four years of their age. Almost half reported the same level of education for one's spouse and one's self (recall, that if one was divorced or separated, they used the time of divorce as the time of truncation). Finally, a variable, church type (whether or not a couple was in a same-church relationship at the time of interview for those married or at time of divorce/separation for the rest) was computed. Although this is also a religious variable, all homogamy variables were kept together. Four-fifths were in a same-church marriage (belonged to the same Christian denomination) at time of interview or divorce.

Family of Origin: Questions were asked about one's parents and childhood. For family approval of spouse at marriage, they were asked whether they strongly agreed to strongly disagreed with the following statement: "Your family approved of your spouse/ex-spouse when you first got married." Almost nine-tenths agreed or strongly agreed with this statement. Similarly, they were read areas in which couples sometimes have disagreements. Answers included a great deal, a moderate amount, a little bit or not at all. They were asked about their ways of dealing with parents or in-laws. Nine percent reported a great deal of disagreement over parents/in-laws whereas about three quarters reported none or a little bit.

Cohabitation: Approximately two-thirds did not cohabit with their spouse prior to marriage. However, there is a difference between those who were married and divorced/separated. About half (49.8%) of those who were divorced or separated reported cohabiting with one's spouse prior to marriage whereas slightly more than a third (36.7%) of those married reported cohabiting with one's spouse.

Marital Stability: Of those who responded, 85% were married and the remaining 15% were divorced or separated at time of interview. Of these, 11.1% were divorced and the remaining 3.0% were separated.

B. Variables Used in Analyses

Variable Name	% or Mean (Average)
Independent Variables	
Sociodemographic	
Female	59.8%
White	83.9%
Education Level	
11th grade or less	5.7%
High School	32.4%
Trade School	3.3%
Some College	25.9%
Bachelor's Degree	20.4%
Some Grad School	2.4%
Master's Degree	8.0%
Ph.D., M.D., J.D.	1.9%
Age at Marriage	27.41 (range=16 to 60)

Parent	80.5%

Homogamy (spouses are/were same)
- Race Homogamy — 91.3%
- First Marriage Homogamy — 61.7%
- Age Homogamy — 69.0%
- Educational Homogamy — 49.3%
- Church type Homogamy — 79.9% (SC 65.5%; IC-SC 14.4%)

Family of Origin
- Family Approval of Spouse @ Marriage
  - 7.7% Strongly Disagree
  - 4.5% Disagree
  - 13.1% Agree
  - 74.7% Strongly Agree
- Disagreement over Parents/In-laws
  - 36.6% None
  - 36.6% Little
  - 18.1% Moderate
  - 8.7% Great deal

Cohabitation with Spouse before Marriage — 38.6%

Religious
- Disagreement over Religion
  - 43.7% None
  - 36.3% Little
  - 13.4% Moderate
  - 3.6% Great deal
- Marriage Preparation — 62.3%
- Religious Wedding Celebration — 78.5%
- Joint Religious Activities — 7.41
- Religious Differences — 3.01
- Religious Acceptance — 9.15

Dependent Variable
- Marital Stability
  - Married — 85.0%
  - Divorced and Separated — 15.0%

C. Predictors of Marital Stability for all respondents (stepwise logistic regression)

	Control Variables	Homogamy Variables	Religious and Family Variables
	B	B	B
Female	.24	.30*	.54***
White	.93***	.85***	.59**
Education Level	−.04	−.01	−.13*
Age at Marriage	.04***	.04***	.05***
Parent	.47**	.46**	.40*
Educational Homogamy		.48**	.35*
Change from SC-to-IC		.88**	.93**
Remain IC		−.43*	.08
Change to None or SC-to-IC		−1.56***	−.87**
Joint Religious Activities			.58***
Religious Differences			−1.01***
Marriage Preparation			.37*
Familial Approval of Spouse when married			.79***
Constant	−.61	−.94	−1.82***
Model χ^2/df	44.00***/5	98.18***/9	236.24***/13

* $p < .05$, ** $p < .01$, *** $p < .001$

Variables excluded from column 2: race homogamy, first marriage homogamy, and age homogamy.

Variables excluded from column 3: cohabitation, religious acceptance, disagreement over parents-in-laws, disagreement over religion, and religious wedding ceremony.

Notes

1. In the 1990s, the divorce rate had leveled off and presented a slight decline, although no one would suggest that it is "low."
2. The percentage of divorce found in this sample is lower than the percentages commonly reported for divorce between 1977 and 1997, the study's time-frame (see Martin and Bumpass 1989: 37–51; Cherlin 1992; Glenn 1997). One possible reason for this is that every person in this study had to identify with a Christian denomination at the time of their engagement. Thus, the sample may be more religiously oriented than the general married population.
3. Appendix A provides the non-religious variable definitions.
4. See Appendix B for the variables and the percent or mean (average score) for each variable used.
5. See Appendix C for the logistic regression analyses. All non-significant variables were dropped from each analysis unless they were control variables.

References

Amato, Paul R. and Alan Booth. 1997. *A Generation at Risk: Growing Up in an Era of Family Upheaval*. Cambridge: Harvard University Press.

Ammerman, Nancy Tatum and Wade Clark Roof. 1995. *Work, Family, and Religion in Contemporary Society*. New York: Routledge.

Bramlett, Matthew D. and William D. Mosher. 2002. *Cohabitation, Marriage, Divorce and Remairriage in the United States*. National Center for Health Statistics, Vital and Health Statistics 23 (22).

Bumpass, Larry L. and James A. Sweet. 1972. "Differentials in Marital Instability: 1970." *American Sociology Review* 37:754–66.

Call, R. A. Vaughn and Heaton, Tim B. 1997. "Religious Influence on Marital Stability." *Journal for the Scientific Study of Religion* 36:382–92.

Center for Marriage and Family. 1995. *Marriage Preparation in the Catholic Church: Getting it Right*. Omaha, NE: Creighton University.

Center for Marriage and Family. 1999. *Ministry to Interchurch Marriages: A National Study*. Omaha, NE: Creighton University.

Doherty, William J., William A. Galston, Norval D. Glenn, John Gottman, Barb Markey, Howard J. Markman, Stephen Nock, David Popenoe, Gloria Rodrigues, Isabel V. Sawhill, Scott M. Stanley, Linda J. Waite and Judith Wallerstein. 2002. *Why Marriage Matters: Twenty-One Conclusions for the Social Sciences. A Report from Family Scholars*. New York: Institute for American Values.

Fitch, Catherine A. and Steven Ruggles. 2000. "Historical Trends in Marriage Formation: The United States 1850–1990." In *The Ties that Bind: Perspectives on Marriage and Cohabitation*. Linda J. Waite, ed. New York: Walter de Gruyter.

Gray, Jeffrey S. and Michel J. Vanderhart. 2000. "On the Determination of Wages: Does Marriage Matter." In *The Ties that Bind: Perspectives on Marriage and Cohabitation*. Linda J. Waite, ed. New York: Walter de Gruyter.

Heaton, Tim B. and Edith L. Pratt. 1990. "The Effects of Religious Homogamy on Marital Satisfaction and Stability." *Journal of Family Issues* 11:191–207.

Hoge, Dean R., William D. Dinges, and Juan L. Gonzales, 1999. *Religion in the Culture of Choice*. New York: Doubleday.

Hoge, Dean R. and Kathleen M. Ferry. 1981. *Empirical Research on Interfaith Marriage in America*. Washington, DC: United States Catholic Conference.

Kosmin, Barry A. and Seymour P. Lachman. 1993. *One Nation Under God: Religion in Contemporary American Society*. New York: Harmony Books.

Lehrer, Evelyn L. and Carmel U. Chiswick. 1993. "Religion as a Determinant of Marital Stability." *Demography* 30:385–404.

Lye, Diane N. and Ingrid Waldron. 1997. "Attitudes Toward Cohabitation, Family, and Gender Roles: Relationships to Values and Political Ideologies." *Sociological Perspective* 40:199–225.

McLanahan, Sarah and Gary Sandefur. 1996. *Growing up with a Single Parent: What Hurts, What Helps*. Cambridge: Harvard University Press.

Raley, R. Kelly. 2000. "Recent Trends and Differentials in marriage and Cohabitation: The United States." In *The Ties that Bind: Perspectives on Marriage and Cohabitation*. Linda J. Waite, ed. New York: Walter de Gruyter.

Roof, Wade C. and William McKinney. 1987. *American Mainline Religion: It's Changing Shape of the Religious Establishment*. New Brunswick: Rutgers University Press.

Sweet, James. 1989. *Differentials in the Approval of Cohabitation*. NSFH Working paper No. 8. Madison: Center for Demography and Ecology, University of Wisconsin.

Sweet, James and Larry L. Bumpass. 1990. *Religious Differentials in Marriage Behavior and Attitudes*. NSFH Working Paper No. 14. Madison: Center for Demography and Ecology, University of Wisconsin.

Thornton, Arland. 1988. "Reciprocal Influences of Family and Religion in a Changing World." In *The Religion and Family Connection: Social Science Perspectives*. Darwin L. Tomas, ed. Provo: Religious Studies Center, Brigham Young University.

Thornton, Arland, William G. Axinn, and Daniel H. Hill. 1992. "Reciprocal Effects of Religiosity, Cohabitation, and Marriage." *American Journal of Sociology* 98:628–51.

Waite, Linda and Maggie Gallagher. 2000. *The Case for Marriage.* New York: Doubleday.

Wallerstein, Judith S., Julia M. Lewis, and Sandra Blakeslee. *The Unexpected Legacy of Divorce: The 25 Year Landmark Study.* New York: Hyperion.

Wuthnow, Robert. 1993. *Christianity in the Twenty-First Century.* New York: Oxford University Press.

The Shape of Family and Family Values: "The Bible Tells Us So," or Does It?

SUSAN A. CALEF

Contemporary family values discourse is marked by an intense nostalgia for and advocacy of the family form portrayed in popular television shows of the nineteen fifties—*Leave It To Beaver, Ozzie and Harriet, Donna Reed,* and the title most telling of all, *Father Knows Best.* The message of these sitcoms, according to a recent study, was clear and enticing: "you too can escape from the conflicts of race, class, and political witch-hunts into harmonious families where father knows best, mothers are never bored or irritated, and teenagers rush to the dinner table each night, eager to get their latest dose of parental wisdom."[1]

Nostalgic Christian discourse often assumes that the family form typified by these television households originated not in the nineteen fifties but in the Garden of Eden at the dawn of creation, when God "split the Adam," so to speak, the resultant couple eventually producing a pair of brothers, hence, the first family unit composed of a heterosexual couple (Adam and Eve) and their sons (Cain and Abel; Gen 2:18–25; 4:1–2). For "family values" advocates,[2] the biblical creation account is the basis for two further assumptions, namely, that the patriarchal nuclear family is "traditional," having existed from time immemorial;[3] moreover, that it is "natural," as natural as rain falling or the sun rising and setting.[4]

It is hardly surprising that the Bible features prominently in the rhetoric of the family values campaign. The Bible, after all, as "the Word of God" for Christians, is the foundation of faith for the multiple denominations and has been described as "the soul of theology".[5] Jesus himself set the precedent in this regard, frequently citing the Hebrew Scriptures in support of his teachings.[6] Moreover, the claim that something is biblical, hence, divinely-ordained, makes for potent ammunition in the battle over family that is part of the culture war currently being waged in America.[7] It is easy to see why "the Word of God" would be the weapon of choice in the rhetorical arsenal of those fighting to "take back" America for "traditional," i.e., Christian, values.

The rhetoric employed by those enlisted in the current campaign gives the impression that the Bible speaks univocally on the subject of family. The Bible, it is claimed, establishes a single family form, the patriarchal nuclear family, and a particular set of values embedded in that form, male headship, female submission, and obedience on the part of children, as universally and eternally normative;[8] hence, the contention, "You just cannot improve on God's formula for the family: one man, one woman, for one lifetime. Any other formula leads to broken hearts and broken homes."[9]

In this essay I intend to problematize this rhetoric and its claims by exposing the inadequate reading of the Bible on which it is based. Specifically, I will demonstrate that the reading of the Bible practiced by family values proponents, insofar as it fails to engage the whole of the biblical witness on the subject of family, is partial and simplistic.[10] To that end, three points will be made. First, what may be termed "the Bible tells me so" approach ignores the evidence that biblical families were actually quite different from ours in form, function, and values. Second, the campaign's view of the so-called "biblical family" amounts to a romanticization, obscuring the reality, amply attested throughout the Bible, that biblical families, including "the first family," could be as dysfunctional, even deadly, as any modern, and now, post-modern, family can be.[11]

Third, in adopting the principle "the Bible tells me so," family values discourse seemingly ignores that what the Bible tells us about family life and ties is hardly consistent, even quite diverse. In the New Testament, for example, three distinct strands of tradition are obviously relevant to Christian reflection on family. One of them, comprised of texts attributed to the apostle Paul, presumes the patriarchal (although not nuclear) family form and advocates male authority, female submission, and obedience on the part of children and slaves (Col 3:18–4:1; Eph 5:21–6:9; 1 Tim 2:8–15; 5:1–2; 6:1–2; Titus 2:1–10).[12] It is these "household codes," as they are termed by scholars, which are privileged in family values discourse.[13] Paul's counsel on matters of marriage and sexuality in 1 Corinthians 7 comprises a second strand of tradition pertinent to our topic.

Significantly, in its somewhat deprecating view of marriage, its explicit preference for the unmarried state (7:7–8, 27, 37–38, 40), and its remarkable lack of reference to procreation and child-rearing, this Pauline tradition appears to be at odds, or at least in considerable tension, with the household code tradition.[14] Gospel testimony to the words and deeds of Jesus constitute a third strand of tradition. Because Christianity has its historical source in the teachings and praxis of Jesus, what Jesus himself said and did with respect to "family", it could be argued, should enjoy pride of place in Christian faith and practice. This third strand of tradition, however, is conspicuously absent from family values discourse.

Constraints of space prohibit discussion of all three strands of New Testament tradition here. Critical consideration of the Gospel traditions exposes the inadequacy of the "the Bible tells me so" approach to family. To problematize, as this essay aims to do, is a necessary first step but in itself insufficient to move us forward in the search for solutions to the problems of the contemporary family. Therefore, the final section concludes with observations regarding the Gospel traditions that contribute to Christian reflection on family.

Biblical and Contemporary "Family": A Word Worlds Apart

Recent studies of family in the Bible ask, what does the Bible tell us about family life and ties? One is immediately confronted by the problem of terminology.[15] In the contemporary cultural context of the United States, "family" has meant, first and foremost, a husband, wife, and their biological and/or adoptive children, i.e., the nuclear family. In the ancient Mediterranean cultural context from which the New Testament comes, however, there were a number of terms relevant to "family," most notably, Hebrew *beth*, Greek *oikos* and *oikia*, Latin *domus* and *familia*, none of which refers to the nuclear family unit. The husband-wife-children configuration existed, but did not function in isolation from the larger kin group to which it belonged. The ancients apparently assigned it no nomenclature of its own.[16] This difference in terminology reflects the vast cultural and temporal distance between modern readers and ancient authors, and so, too, the many differences between ancient biblical and modern American families that have been identified by recent research.

Patterns of kinship in contemporary U.S. culture and the ancient Mediterranean have been analyzed in relation to a number of variables: family form, spousal choice, marriage strategy, marriage arrangement, post-marital residence, and economic function. Until the 1970s when changes began to occur, the nuclear dual-generational family form (parents and their own children) predominated in twentieth century America.[17] This family form was built on the marriage of two heterosexual individuals whose free choice to commit themselves to one another was based on mutual attraction and romantic love and formalized by a custom known as engagement. Marriage in the United States is exogamous by law (outside the kin group) and usually neolocal (a new residence is established by the bride and groom). Because the industrial U.S. operates on a sharp division between the public and the private, the family home is considered a refuge or haven from the public world of work.[18] Within its confines the family performs two major functions: consumption and the nurture of children toward autonomous adulthood, resulting in the eventual "empty nest." Privacy, emotional and psychological support, material comfort and convenience, entertainment, and individual achievement are among the pre-eminent values of the contemporary family in the United States.

By contrast, the family form predominant in the ancient Mediterranean was the multi-generational extended family.[19] In addition to spouses and their children, household and family units included unmarried relatives as well as persons related in other ways, e.g., patronage, business, and ownership, thus, clients, freedmen and freedwomen, and slaves. Although the legal structure of households was patriarchal, there is evidence of variety in the composition of actual households.[20] Marriages, in this context, were between extended families, not individuals, and were paternally arranged with a view to the interests of the larger kin group. Spousal selection had nothing to do with notions of individual choice and romantic love but everything to do with preserving the resources and honor status of the kin.[21] In pre-industrial agrarian societies, because goods were in limited supply and the family was the producing unit, the loss of a family member through marriage had serious economic consequences. Therefore, patriarchs adopted defensive strategies to prevent the loss of family members, especially males, to another family.[22] Marriage was patrilocal (the bride moved in with her husband's family) and endogamous (marrying as close to the conjugal family as incest laws permitted), with cross-cousin marriages on the paternal side of the family as the ideal. The home, for the ancients, was not a refuge from the world of work but the locus of production. The predominant values of the family were not the privacy, emotional and psychological support, and individual achievement prized by modern Americans, but honor and shame, loyalty to the kin group, and interdependence.

It is also worth noting that the Bible tells readers, without any hint of moral scruple, of families whose way of life included at various times polygamy, concubinage, and slavery.[23] Mark 12:18–23 illustrates just how different family life and customs in the biblical world were from those of modern Americans. A group of Sadducees, citing the case of a widow whom seven brothers of her deceased husband had married, ask Jesus, "At the resurrection, whose wife will she be? For all seven had been married to her" (12:23). This hypothetical scenario, immensely perplexing to modern readers, presupposes that brothers of a deceased man are obliged to provide him with heirs by intercourse with his widow, a custom known as levirate marriage.[24] Clearly, the families and family life depicted in biblical accounts are far too foreign to serve as models for contemporary families. Indeed, as the words for "family" in the various ancient languages and modern English suggest, ancient biblical and contemporary American families are "worlds apart" in form, function, and values.

The Biblical Family: From Romance to Reality

Recent studies have also confirmed what many have suspected, that the depiction of family life in the 1950s sitcoms was more romance than reality.[25] The same can be said of the so-called "biblical family"; for indeed, much material on family in the Bible is far from idyllic or edifying. Notorious examples may be cited: the first fraternal relationship ended in fratricide (Gen 4:3–8); Jacob tricked Esau out of his heritage (Gen 27); Joseph's brothers attempted to kill him (Gen 37); David had Uriah killed so that he could marry his wife Bathsheba (2 Kgs 11); Amnon raped his half-sister Tamar, for which he was then killed by her avenging brother Absalom (2 Kings 13); Jephthah sacrificed his virgin daughter to fulfill an oath he had made (Judg 11:29–40). Because the biblical tradition is androcentric, stories of women's familial and household interactions feature less prominently; still, they are not altogether absent. One reads of in-house nastiness between the female rivals Sarah and Hagar, resulting in banishment to what could have meant death to Hagar and her young son Ishmael (Gen 16; 21:19–21); of the wily ways of Rebecca who manipulates her blind husband Isaac on behalf of her favorite son Jacob (Gen

27); of Tamar who lures her father-in-law Judah into sexual intercourse in order to do her duty to her deceased husband (Gen 38).[26]

Family life struggles also appear in stories about Jesus. We hear of sons fighting over family inheritance, a squabble in which Jesus is asked to referee (Luke 12:13–14); of sisters' squabbles over household duties (Luke 10:38–42); of sibling rivalry and sons' bitterness over their father's judgments (Luke 15:11–32); of a mother seeking to advance her sons' careers, much to the chagrin of their fellow disciples (Matt 20:20–24); of the notorious Herodias and daughter, masterful manipulators of an honor-drunk husband, whose collusion puts the head of John the Baptist on a platter in revenge for the prophet's stance on wife-swapping between brothers (Mark 6:17–29).

Thus, the biblical families are *not* the nuclear family championed by family values advocates; they are also far from inspiring. Not even the Holy Family, traditionally the object of sentimental romanticizing by Catholics in particular, represents a suitable ideal. Close scrutiny of the Gospels reveals that much of Jesus' teaching, as well as his attitude and conduct toward his own and other families, were troubling, even scandalous, in the eyes of his own and other families of the time.[27]

Jesus and Family: Good News or Bad?

The goal and sentiments of the family values campaign and the prominent place of the Bible in its self-understanding and rhetoric are illustrated in the following description of one of its popular pro-family movements: "[Focus on the Family] attempts to 'turn hearts toward home' by reasonable, biblical and empirical insights so people will be able to discover the founder of homes and the creator of families—Jesus Christ."[28] In the midst of the deterioration of family life in contemporary America, one might well query, what Christian could possibly object to such a sentiment and agenda? None perhaps. But the Jesus of the Gospel tradition, I contend, is quite another matter.[29]

All four canonical Gospels remember Jesus as having had things to say about family life, including his own, and as interacting with his own family and with members of other families in various ways. Significantly, however, he has comparatively little to say about family life and ties, which makes the few things that he does say the more noteworthy. In the following examination of Gospel traditions of Jesus' words and deeds in relation to "family", I pose two questions. First, in his own historical and cultural context, was Jesus himself a good family man? Second, in his context, was he good for the family life of others? Much of what Jesus says and does, as we will see, belies the characterization of him as "founder and creator of every family" and reveals that "turning hearts toward home" was clearly not part of Jesus' agenda, for himself or for his disciples.

In both Matthew and Luke, for example, Jesus declares, without apology or hint of regret, that the purpose, not just the consequence, of his mission is to set the members of a family against one another:

> Do you think that I have come to establish peace on the earth? No, I tell you, but rather division. From now on a household of five will be divided, three against two and two against three; a father will be divided against his son and a son against his father, a mother against her daughter and a daughter against her mother, a mother-in-law against her daughter-in-law and a daughter-in-law against her mother-in-law (Luke 12:51–53).[30]

Such enmity between family members is a foretaste of the eschatological tribulations soon to come. In the apocalyptic discourse in Mark, Jesus warns of persecution by political and religious authorities (13:9) and of the betrayal by family members that such persecution will precipitate: "Brother will hand over brother to death, and the father his child; children will rise up against parents and have them put to death" (13:12).[31]

The divisive effect of Jesus' mission on families that is in view in the preceding quotes is the consequence of the fundamental transfer of allegiance to which Jesus called his contemporaries. In the "hard" saying on discipleship Jesus in effect pits discipleship against family loyalty, admonishing the crowds that follow him, "If anyone comes to me without hating his father and mother, wife and children, brothers and sisters, and even his own life, he cannot be my disciple" (Luke 14:26–27). Elsewhere Jesus' reply to two persons whom he calls to follow him (Luke 9:57–62) highlights the urgency of response to the kingdom of God and insists on the absolute priority of discipleship over blood kin obligations. The first responds to Jesus' invitation with a request to perform a sacred duty, "let me go first and bury my father" (9:59). Shockingly, Jesus dismisses the priority of the duty to kin, commanding, "Let the dead bury their dead. But you, go and proclaim the kingdom of God" (9:60). Likewise, in an exchange reminiscent of the prophet Elijah's call of Elisha (1 Kgs 19:19–21), a second would-be disciple requests, "first let me say farewell to my family at home" (9:61). In stark contrast to Elijah, however, who permitted Elisha to provide for his family before departing to follow the prophet, Jesus' response is curt and uncompromising, "No one who sets a hand to the plow and looks to what was left behind is fit for the kingdom of God" (Luke 9:59–60).[32]

That discipleship of Jesus meant abandonment of family and property is attested by Gospel narratives of the call of the first disciples.[33] When Jesus calls James and John to follow him, they leave behind their boat, hence, their occupation and source of livelihood, and their father, Zebedee, in the boat (Matt 4:21–22).[34] In a society in which all goods were limited and the family was the locus of production, loss of a productive male entailed severe economic cost. Furthermore, a son's abrupt abandonment of family and property constituted shameless disregard of the divinely ordained obligation to honor parents.[35] The likely sentiments of those left behind are represented in a fictional portrayal of one Susannah, a resident of Nazareth whose son abandoned the family in order to follow Jesus.

> This Jesus is bad and leads people astray. He corrupts the young people. It all sounds fine: Blessed are you who weep, for you will laugh. But what does he actually do? He makes parents weep over their lost sons. He promises that everything will change. But what actually changes? Families are destroyed because children run away from their parents.[36]

The family members who had been abandoned were not the only ones to "pay the price." In a culture in which personal identity and status were defined by and dependent on kinship, renunciation of blood kin ties proved costly to disciples themselves. That this was the case is attested by a telling exchange between Peter and Jesus in the Gospel of Mark. Jesus' declaration, "How hard it is for those who have wealth to enter the kingdom of God!" evokes Peter's affirmation, "We have given up everything and followed you" (Mark 10:28).[37] Jesus' reply to Peter's anxious self-promotion acknowledges the high price paid by disciples but promises hundred-fold compensation:

Amen, I say to you, there is no one who has given up house or brothers or sisters or mother or father or children or lands for my sake and for the sake of the gospel who will not receive a hundred times more now in this present age: houses and brothers and sisters and mothers and lands, with persecutions, and eternal life in the age to come (Mark 10:29–30).

Gospel traditions also attest that Jesus' relation to his own family was strained and for good reason. To abandon family and property for an itinerant lifestyle, as Jesus does, in utter disregard of familial obligations was deviant behavior on the part of a son, hence, a threat to family honor, one to which Jesus' family apparently felt it necessary to respond. When his relatives hear of the crowds coming to Jesus, they set out to seize him, thinking that he is out of his mind (Mark 3:20–21). "Just as one might today hurry an eccentric relative out of public scrutiny because of public perception and guilt by association, Jesus' family was concerned about their honor rating."[38] Later in the scene, upon hearing that his mother and brothers had arrived and were summoning him, Jesus retorts, "Who are my mother and brothers?" and then, pointing to those around him, declares, "Here are my mother and my brothers. Whoever does the will of God is my brother and sister and mother" (Mark 3:31–35). That his family took offense at this dismissal of the priority of blood kin bonds is suggested by their virtual disappearance from the narrative after this point.[39]

Still more evidence that Jesus' family misunderstood, even rejected, him is found in Mark 6:1–6. A crisis is precipitated when Jesus, returning to his hometown accompanied by an entourage of disciples, teaches in the synagogue, apparently with astounding authority (6:2). The question posed by his audience, "Is he not the carpenter, the son of Mary and the brother of James and Joses and Judas and Simon? And are not his sisters with us?" (6:3), suggests that, in their estimation, the hometown boy, son of a manual laborer, is out-of-line in arrogating to himself the prerogative to teach in synagogue. Offended by his inappropriate claim to an honor status that is not rightly his, they aim to cut him down to size. The proverb that Jesus cites in response to them attests the dishonorable status that his conduct earned him, "A prophet is not without honor except in his native place and among his kin and in his own house" (6:4).

The overall image of Jesus with which Gospel traditions leave readers is startling indeed. In his own person Jesus modeled an unconventional, even iconoclastic, relation to the institutions of family and household of his time and culture. He did not marry; he did not conceive children; he did not assume the headship of a patriarchal household. Remarkably, he did not heed the ancient command, "be fruitful and multiply" (Gen 1:28). Rather, in order to pursue an itinerant ministry on behalf of the reign of God (Mark 1:14–15), Jesus abandoned his household and its work and uttered an uncompromising call to others to do the same. In cultural context, such conduct represented a serious breach of filial duty on the part of an eldest son; consequently, he was, as the proverb that he cites self-referentially suggests, "a prophet without honor among his kin" (Mark 6:4). By the standards of his time and culture, clearly, the Jesus of the Gospels was hardly a good family man. Moreover, the radical demands of discipleship that he laid down for those whom he called to follow him were hardly beneficial to their family life.

Does this mean that Jesus was "anti-familial," as some scholars have concluded? The choice of the term "anti-familial" is misleading for a number of reasons. First, to claim that the Jesus of the Gospels was anti-familial is to overlook the traditions in which Jesus offers teachings that support families and/or takes action on behalf of family members, thereby affirming the continuing validity of family life and ties. According to Mark (7:9–13) and Matthew (15:3–6), for example, Jesus attacks religious leaders for failing to uphold the divinely sanctioned obligation to care for elderly parents (Exod 21:17; Lev 20:9; Deut 5:16). Elsewhere, in his interaction with a man concerned to inherit eternal life, Jesus reaffirms God's prohibition of adultery and the obligation to honor parents (Luke 18:18–23); and his prohibition of divorce by either partner (Mark 10:1–12) strongly reaffirms marital relations.

In addition, numerous Gospel narratives recount Jesus' compassionate outreach to families in need. Frequently, for example, he responds to distraught parents of a sick child, e.g., raising Jairus' daughter (Mark 5:21–24, 35–43); exorcising the Canaanite woman's daughter (Matt 15:21–28); healing a royal official's son (John 4:46–54); raising a widow's son (Luke 7:11–17). He also responds to sisters, Mary and Martha, grieved by the death of their brother, Lazarus (John 11:1–44) and heals Simon Peter's mother-in-law (Mark 1:29–31).[40]

The claim that Jesus was anti-familial also fails to recognize the highly rhetorical nature of the "hard" sayings on discipleship.[41] Using the hyperbolic speech typical of prophets, Jesus clearly intends to compel a definitive choice for his cause, the kingdom of God, on the part of his contemporaries. Indications that their discipleship did not involve *permanent* abandonment of family and property may be found in New Testament traditions.[42] In Mark 1:29–31, for example, Jesus enters the house of his disciple, Simon, where he performs a healing, and Paul refers to Peter traveling with his wife (1 Cor 9:5). Moreover, the pervasive use of kinship terminology to describe Jesus' relation with God as Son to Father and early Christians' relation with each other as brothers and sisters is difficult to explain if Jesus had been truly "anti-family."[43]

The Jesus of the Gospels, then, is not anti-familial. Rather, rhetorically his "hard" sayings on discipleship compel a radical re-prioritization on the part of his contemporaries, with Jesus and his cause, the reign of God, displacing blood kin as the ultimate and defining priority of one's identity and way of life.[44] Family life is not rejected or negated; the reprioritization to which disciples are called in view of the nearness of the kingdom involves incorporation into a new family ("Here are my mother and my brothers. [For] whoever does the will of God is my brother and sister and mother," Mark 3:34–35).[45] That the radical reprioritization to which Jesus called his contemporaries is followed by redefinition of family strongly affirms that family, whether based on biological or marital bonds or fictive kinship, is fundamental and necessary in the life of Christian disciples.[46]

Concluding Reflections: The Bible in Christian Reflection on Family

Disturbed by the breakdown of the family and the moral decline of contemporary American society, family values advocates frequently cite the second creation account (Gen 2) and the New Testament household codes in support of their contention, that there is need to restore the patriarchal nuclear family which, they claim, was established by God at creation and which, they assume, reigned supreme until the feminist movement of the nineteen sixties and seventies destroyed the domestic harmony of American households.[47]

This essay has sought to problematize this rhetoric and its claims by demonstrating that its reading of the Bible is selective and partial, even simplistic. A more thorough reading of biblical materials compels very different conclusions. The families in the Bible are not of the nuclear variety that dominated the American landscape for a few brief decades of the twentieth century; rather, what we find in the Bible are shifting family forms that included, at various times, polygamy, concubinage, and slavery.[48] The Bible does not establish the patriarchal nuclear family, or any other particular family structure for that matter, as normative for Christians of all times and places.[49] There was no golden age of "the biblical family," just as there was no golden age of American families, the current nostalgia for the nineteen fifties notwithstanding.[50] Like it or not, the Bible does not provide a neat and simple family model or ideal that, by simple imitation, can solve our current problems.

Do such conclusions mean that the Bible has nothing to contribute to Christians' search for guidance in the midst of the current crisis? Surely not. But the diversity and complexity of the biblical witness must first be acknowledged, and the host of questions to which this realization gives rise must be addressed. For example, where teachings are divergent, which are normative? How do we discern which are normative? Is it even appropriate to ask and expect counsel about family life and ties from the Bible? Which material in the Bible is and should be relevant to contemporary discussions of family life? These questions indicate the need to develop hermeneutical principles by which to interpret the Bible for contemporary Christian life.[51] To ask what the Bible tells us about family is simply the wrong starting-point because it bypasses a prior, more fundamental question, namely, the question of what the Bible is, thus, what kind of wisdom it imparts, and how the Bible speaks.[52] Indeed, the Bible is Word of God for Christians; but it must be asked, how does God speak to us in and through the Scriptures? In the absence of reflection on this question and without the explicit articulation of hermeneutical principles to which such reflection should lead, Christians, be they Right, Left, or somewhere between, are doomed to engage in proof-texting wars that have more to do with our own word than God's word, more to do with self-serving ideological agendas than with God's agenda for the human family.[53]

As we have seen, the Bible sets before the reader families whose life together is marked by jealousy and rivalry, selfishness and infidelity, families as flawed and fallible as any we might be or know. Even such accounts, however, for all their awful and unedifying realism, can contribute to Christian reflection on family because they attest to a sobering truth: families can either be spirited and life-giving or dispirited and deadly. Biblical accounts serve as potent correctives to the false sentimentality about family life that can render one blind to sinful realities within family life—domination, egocentrism, physical and emotional neglect and/or abuse—and thus, to the need for God's redeeming grace; blind to families in crisis who need, not self-righteous judgment by others but the compassion of the Living Body of Christ; blind to others—the single, the divorced, childless couples, sexual minorities—so often excluded or ignored by the Christian family for "failing" to be family in the single form deemed normative.

Curiously, the words and deeds of Jesus with respect to family are for the most part absent from family values discourse. What might the Gospel traditions, and in particular, the hard sayings of Jesus to which this essay has drawn attention, contribute to Christian reflection on the family? Only a few preliminary suggestions may be offered here. Most importantly, biological family ties and harmonious family relations are not ultimate values, according to the Jesus of the Gospels. Rather, blood kin ties and obligations are subordinated to a higher priority, the reign of God, and the new eschatological family of disciples dedicated to that reign. This bears significant implications for Christians. First, it means that every Christian family belongs to and participates in the extended "eschatological" family of disciples that is "church." It is within this family that Christians, "discipled" to Jesus, should be able to learn the values of the kingdom and cultivate the virtues of the new covenant upon which that kingdom is based. Second, for Christian disciples, the family is not an end in itself. Rather, in calling those who would be his disciples to a radical re-prioritization, and so, a redefinition of their identities in terms not of blood but allegiance to the reign of God, Jesus has reconfigured family in such a way that families are to be about a higher and self-transcendent end. That is, Christians, as members of the new family of Jesus, share in his prophetic vocation and way of life.

What might Christian family life in the prophetic mode entail? What might its form, function, and values be? The form of the Christian family is constituted not by a specific structure—heterosexual couple and their offspring—as if a particular constellation of persons insures satisfying family life, but by covenant commitment rooted in love (*agape*), and is marked, not by hierarchical relations of dominance and submission patterned after the fall from grace, but by a partnership in the mutual self-giving love characteristic of the new creation effected by the Christ-event.[54] The chief function of this covenant community, determined by the priority of its discipleship, is to live by and witness to the values of the reign of God, justice and mercy, for which Jesus gave himself, and to nurture and reflect in all its relationships the virtues of the covenant God who, according to biblical testimony, is merciful, gracious, slow to anger, rich in kindness and fidelity (Exod 34:6). These values and virtues were embodied by the Gospel of Jesus, who, in word and deed, emphasized forgiveness and reconciliation, neighborliness and hospitality, service of the needs of others, including families in crisis, and outreach to the poor and marginalized.

To "turn hearts toward home" as family values advocates propose to do, although understandable in view of the deterioration of the social and moral fabric of contemporary America, smacks of a kind of sentimentality that hardly accords with the prophetic consciousness and praxis of the Gospel Jesus. Moreover, in a rabidly individualistic American culture, such an agenda could well tempt Christians to a familial self-absorption that is contrary to the gospel of Jesus. Securing "the good life" now and for one's own family, which since the nineteen eighties has often meant a self-indulgent materialism dictated by Madison Avenue and the entertainment industry, is not a kingdom value, and so, not a Christian family value. Nor is its religious variation, securing "salvation" for one's own family while sitting in moral judgment of and/or ignoring the needs of other families, especially the poorest.[55]

Rather, the biblical witness to the prophetic ministry of Jesus compels would-be disciples in any age to the realization that the problems of "our family" are not bounded by genetics or laws, by shared religious affiliation, socio-economic status, ethnicity or race, but only by our common kinship as members of the human race, the family of the Creator God. Thus, it challenges Christians to stretch the boundaries of our concern in the kind of inclusive outreach to others modeled by Jesus.

The work of the Christian family, then, is not to turn hearts toward home but to nurture the hearts of its members in *agape*, the other-centered love that is God (1 John 4:8, 16), and to school hearts and minds in the values of the kingdom of God. It is a work that perforce impels family members outward in service to the world, to the most needy members of the human family. By virtue of its discipleship to the prophet Jesus, the Christian home is to be, not a haven from the world but a school for service to the world, not a place of refuge from "others" but of hospitality to others, most notably, the modern counterparts of "the widow, the orphan, the stranger" who, by stipulation of the God of the covenant, are entitled to others' care.

When such nurturance and schooling occurs, Christian families are able to witness to the life-giving quality of the reign of the God who is *agape*, the truly self-transcending love first embodied in the person of Jesus and now embodied in the family of his disciples. In the midst of a culture that pursues self-indulgent "feels good" individualism, the Christian family is called to bear prophetic witness to a mystery that is as much "stumbling block" (1 Cor 1:23) to many today as it was in the early years of Christianity, the mystery of the cross of Christ. The crossing of lives, self and other, in covenant-love is both demanding and life-giving. To bear witness to that scandalous mystery is perhaps the essence of the Christian family's service to the world in the new millennium.

Notes

1. Stephanie Coontz, *The Way We Really Are: Coming to Terms With America's Changing Families* (New York: Basic Books, 1997), 39. See also her earlier *The Way We Never Were: American Families and the Nostalgia Trap* (New York: Basic Books, 1992). Nostalgia for the supposed "ideal" family life of a former era is hardly new. Historians of the ancient world have identified similar sentiments in ancient Rome. In her discussion of "the myth of the archaic Roman family," Suzanne Dixon observes that the Roman discourses, like the modern, often blame women and children for the moral decline of the family, faulting in particular their departure from their "traditional" roles within the family. See Suzanne Dixon, *The Roman Family* (Baltimore: Johns Hopkins University Press, 1992), 19–24. For an example of the "in the good old days" rhetoric, see Tacitus, *Dialogus* 28.

2. Concern for the family and for the values of contemporary American society is hardly the exclusive preserve of Christians. Many Americans of diverse religious affiliation as well as secular humanists are troubled by the deterioration of the moral fabric of our country. Unfortunately, however, the term "family values" has become a partisan term, defined primarily by the Christian Right and its agenda. There are, in fact, diverse advocates of family in contemporary America, many of whom would contest the Christian Right's diagnosis of the causes of the current crisis as well as its proposed solutions. Throughout this essay, however, the term "family values" refers to the campaign and rhetoric of the Christian Right which frequently cites the Bible as divine warrant for its views.

3. Anthropologists once thought that the family consisting of a man, a woman, and their children was a universal phenomenon. The research of Claude Levi-Strauss

indicated otherwise, concluding that humans universally construct relationships with those to whom they are related by birth and marriage but "family" is constructed differently in different cultures; see "The Family," in *Man, Culture, and Society*, H. Shapiro, ed. (London: Oxford University Press, 1971). Numerous historical and anthropological studies attest that patterns of family life are various and changing; furthermore, that the nuclear, so-called "traditional," family promoted by sitcoms of the nineteen fifties and valorized by contemporary family values advocates is a product of the industrial revolution, hence, a modern development. For a brief review of historical and anthropological studies, see Joan Kelly, "Family and Society," in her *Women, History and Theory: The Essays of Joan Kelly* (Chicago: University of Chicago Press, 1984), 110–55. On "family" in Christian history and the American context, see Rosemary Ruether, *Christianity and the Making of the Modern Family: Ruling Ideologies, Diverse Realities* (Boston: Beacon Press, 2000). On religion and family in America, see in this volume Charles L. Harper, "Religion and Family in America: A Sociohistorical Reconnaissance." On the social and cultural construction of family with application to the New Testament and early Christianity, see Halvor Moxnes, "What is Family? Problems in Constructing Early Christian Families," in *Constructing Early Christian Families. Family as Social Reality and Metaphor*, H. Moxnes, ed. (London/New York: Routledge, 1997), 13–41.

4. On the claim that the biblical family is "natural," Rodney Clapp observes, "We must resist the hasty and careless blurring of such words as traditional, natural, and biblical. Such blurring has created the impression that those who would question aspects of the industrial, middle-class family are disputing Scripture and departing from a way of life that is thousands of years old, even based on the order of nature itself" (*Families at the Crossroads: Beyond Traditional and Modern Options* (Downers Grove, IL: InterVarsity, 1993), 16.

5. Joseph A. Fitzmyer, *Scripture, the Soul of Theology* (New York: Paulist, 1994).

6. E.g., Jesus cites Gen 1:27 and 2:24 in support of his prohibition of divorce (Mark 10:6–8) and the fifth commandment in his criticism of those neglecting filial obligations (Mark 7:10). For additional New Testament examples of the citation of biblical texts to support teachings, see Stephen C. Barton, "Biblical Hermeneutics and the Family," in *The Family in Theological Perspective*, Stephen C. Barton, ed. (Edinburgh: T. & T. Clark, 1996), 3–23, esp. 3.

7. The language of war is prominent in recent publications by family values advocates; e.g., James Dobson and Gary Bauer, *Children at Risk: The Battle for the Hearts and Minds of Our Kids* (Dallas: Word, 1990); Tim LaHaye, *The Battle for the Family* (Old Tappan, NJ: Revell, 1982); a chapter entitled "The Assault on the

Family," in Pat Robertson, *The New Millennium* (Dallas: Word, 1990). See also Brigitte and Peter Berger, *The War Over the Family: Capturing the Middle Ground* (Garden City: Doubleday, 1983). The choice of the war metaphor indicates the intensity of the perceived threat. It also suggests that ideological interests are at stake. As Stephen Barton notes, "Whenever there is a 'war over family,' we need to exercise a hermeneutic of suspicion in order to try to discern whether the family is being used as a weapon to serve the interests of a broader (and sometimes hidden) agenda; e.g., a conservative agenda to maintain or re-establish a desired status quo of (androcentric and patriarchal) "family values" and free-market economics; or a liberal agenda to do with social reform aimed at protecting the rights of the individual; or a feminist agenda to do with changing the social status quo in the interests of women's liberation; and so on." See his "Towards a Theology of the Family," *in Christian Perspectives on Sexuality and Gender*, E. Stuart and A. Thatcher, eds, (Grand Rapids: Eerdmans, 1996), 451–52.

8. For family values advocates, the Genesis creation account determines not only the normative family form (man, woman, children) but the gender roles within the family as well. Specifically, the curses meted out for the sin of the first couple (Gen 3:1–24, esp. 16–19) are read as justification of a patriarchal arrangement: the male as head of household, laboring to feed the family; the woman cursed by the painful labor of childbirth and required to submit to her husband's authority. For Christians to interpret the text in this way is theologically problematic. In the Genesis account, these gender roles are the result of "the fall." According to Christian theology, however, the coming of Christ has reversed the fall and worked a restoration of creation. In the light of the incarnation, creation redeemed and transfigured, gender roles within Christian families should no longer reflect the cursed fallen state with its hierarchy of dominance and submission.

9. Bill Bright and John N. Damoose, *Red Sky In the Morning: How You Can Help Prevent America's Gathering Storms* (Orlando: New Life, 1998), 142. Bright is founder of Campus Crusade for Christ; Damoose is a Christian broadcaster.

10. I use "partial" here in two senses of the word, "only part of "and "partial to," the latter suggesting partisan and taking sides.

11. In referring to biblical families and "the first family" I do not mean to suggest that all families portrayed in the Bible, including "the first family" in Gen 1–4, were actual historical persons or, even for those who were, that the details of their stories are historically accurate. Although as a biblical scholar I am ordinarily interested in determining the historicity of events portrayed in biblical texts, there is no need to do so here since "the Bible tells me so" approach generally does not raise the question of the historicity of biblical accounts.

12. Although these letters bear the apostle's name, a majority of New Testament scholars believe that they were not written by Paul but by later Pauline disciples; hence, their designation as Deutero-Pauline tradition rather than Pauline.
13. The "household code" or *Haustafel* is a literary form that prescribes the proper roles and conduct of three key pairs in the ancient household—husband and wife, father and children, master and slave. In addition to its multiple occurrences in the Deutero-Pauline texts cited above, the form also appears in 1 Pet 2:18–3:7. On the household code, see esp. David L. Balch, *Let Wives Be Submissive. The Domestic Code in 1 Peter* (Atlanta: Scholars, 1981).
14. Paul's comments in 1 Cor 7 are hardly an enthusiastic endorsement of marriage. Warning of the anxieties and distractions that marriage causes (7:28, 32–35), he recommends marriage only as a prophylactic for those whose lust could lead to immorality (7:2, 5, 8–9). It should be noted, however, that Paul's attitude toward and counsel regarding marriage is conditioned by his conviction of the imminence of the End or *eschaton* (7:26, 29, 31). As will emerge in the discussion of Gospel traditions below, Jesus operated out of an eschatological consciousness that relativized marital and blood kin ties in view of the imminent End. Apparently Paul "inherited" Jesus' eschatological consciousness; thus, it is unsurprising that one finds in Paul's letters a relativization of marital and blood kin ties similar to that found in Gospel traditions (see below).
15. On family and families in the New Testament and early Christianity, see esp. Halvor Moxnes, ed., *Constructing Early Christian Families: Family as Social Reality and Metaphor* (London/New York: Routledge, 1997); Carolyn Osiek and David L. Balch, *Families in the New Testament World: Households and House Churches* (Louisville: Westminster/John Knox Press, 1997); Carolyn Osiek, "The Family in Early Christianity: 'Family Values' Revisited," *Catholic Biblical Quarterly* 58 (1996): 1–24; "The New Testament and the Family," *Concilium* 4 (1995): 1–9; Stephen C. Barton, *Discipleship and Family Ties in Mark and Matthew* (Cambridge: Cambridge University Press, 1994); Will Deming, *Paul on Marriage and Celibacy: The Hellenistic Background of 1 Corinthians 7* (Cambridge: Cambridge University Press, 1995); O. Larry Yarbrough, *Not Like the Gentiles. Marriage Rules in the Letters of Paul* (Atlanta: Scholars, 1985); Lisa S. Cahill, "Family Bonds and Christian Community: New Testament Sources," in *Family: A Christian Social Perspective* (Minneapolis: Fortress Press, 2000), 18–47; Joseph Hellerman, *The Ancient Church as Family* (Minneapolis: Fortress, 2001). The Jewish and Greco-Roman cultures provided the social and cultural patterns of families reflected in New Testament texts; hence, New Testament scholarship is informed by research on families in ancient Israel, Greece, and Rome. On families in ancient Israel, see Leo G. Per-

due, Joseph Blenkinsopp, John J. Collins, and Carol Meyers, *Families in Ancient Israel* (Louisville: Westminster/John Knox, 1997); Shaye J.D. Cohen, *The Jewish Family in Antiquity* (Atlanta: Scholars, 1993). On families in ancient Greece and Rome, see esp. Suzanne Dixon, *The Roman Family* (Baltimore: Johns Hopkins University Press, 1992); Jane Gardner, *Family and "Familia" in Roman Law and Life* (New York: Clarendon Press, 1998); Keith R. Bradley, *Discovering the Roman Family* (New York: Oxford University Press, 1991); Richard P. Saller, *"Familia, Domus,* and the Roman Conception of the Family," *Phoenix* 38 (1984): 336–55; Cheryl Cox, *Household Interests: Property, Marriage Strategies and Family Dynamics in Ancient Athens* (Princeton, NJ: Princeton University Press, 1998).

16. Osiek, "The Family," 9–11. In the study of family in the Bible, the problem of "native" terminology is also encountered in relation to the term "father." Hebrew, Aramaic, Greek, and Latin all have words that are translated "father" in English, but each has a different semantic range. On this point see K. C. Hanson, "Kinship," in *The Social Sciences and New Testament Interpretation*, Richard Rohrbaugh, ed. (Peabody, MA: Hendrickson, 1996), 65.

17. Aka the absolute nuclear family. Social scientists have identified a typology of seven basic family forms found throughout the world; for a brief overview of types, with application to the biblical world, see K. C. Hanson and Douglas E. Oakman, *Palestine in the Time of Jesus: Social Structures and Social Conflicts* (Minneapolis: Fortress, 1998), 20–23.

18. The sentimental notion of the family home as a refuge or haven is part of the nostalgia surrounding the so-called "traditional" family of the nineteen fifties; see Clapp, *Families,* 31. Separation of life into compartments of public and private occurred with the rise of industrialization; on this, see Clapp, *Families,* 48–66; also Kelly, "Family and Society," esp. 125–40.

19. Aka the endogamous community family, the family form most common in ancient Israel and Roman Palestine; on this point, see Hanson and Oakman, *Palestine,* 22.

20. For New Testament and other ancient evidence of households headed by women and for evidence of houses owned by brothers, presumably each with his dependents, see Osiek, "The Family," 11, ns. 24–25.

21. On kinship and marriage practices in the ancient Mediterranean, see Bruce J. Malina, *The New Testament World. Insights From Cultural Anthropology,* revised edition (Louisville: Westminster/John Knox, 1993), 117–48. Persons in the ancient Mediterranean were not individualists; socially and psychologically, they were embedded in the family. On the first-century personality, see Malina, *New Testament World,* 63–89.

22. The loss of a female through marriage required compensation in the form of a bride-price; see Bruce J. Malina and Richard L. Rohrbaugh, *Social Science Commentary on the Synoptic Gospels* (Minneapolis: Fortress, 1992), 290; on the perception of limited good in the ancient world, see Malina, *New Testament World*, 90–116.
23. Abraham had children by both his wife Sarah and her maidservant Hagar (Gen. 16; 21); Jacob married both Rachel and Leah (Gen. 29–30); the numbers of children fathered by various judges presupposes multiple wives (Judges); David and Solomon had multiple wives as well as concubines (1 Chr 3:1–9; 1 Kgs 11:3).
24. On levirate marriage, see Ronald Simkins, "Competing Portraits of the Israelite Family," in this volume.
25. The image of Donna Reed vacuuming the family home in high heels and pearls comes to mind; see Coontz, *Way We Never Were*, esp. ch. 1, "The Way We Wish We Were. Defining the Family Crisis," and ch. 2, " 'Leave It to Beaver' and 'Ozzie and Harriet': American Families in the 1950s"; also Ruether, *Christianity*, 132–39.
26. Feminist biblical scholarship has drawn attention to the ways in which the patriarchal structure of family life presumed in these texts contributes to the manipulative conduct on the part of women. See e.g., Esther Fuchs, "Who is Hiding the Truth? Deceptive Women and Biblical Androcentrism," in *Feminist Perspectives on Biblical Scholarship*, Adela Yarbro Collins, ed. (Chico, CA: Scholars, 1985), 137–44.
27. It is worth noting that the Gospels are silent about Jesus' interaction with his father Joseph and about Joseph's and Mary's interaction with one another.
28. Cited by Ruether, *Christianity*, 3.
29. Throughout this discussion I speak of the "Jesus of the Gospels" or the "Gospel Jesus" rather than the Historical Jesus. Because of the complex tradition and composition history of the four canonical Gospels, biblical scholars do not assume that everything contained in the Gospels represents the actual words and deeds of Jesus; thus, ordinarily, a distinction is made between the Historical Jesus and Jesus as he is portrayed in the Gospels, i.e., the Gospel Jesus. However, because the "the Bible tells me so" approach that informs family values discourse is interested simply in what the Bible tells us about what Jesus said and did and does not see any need to determine the historicity of Gospel accounts, there is no need to do so for the purposes of my argument here. In using the term "the Gospel Jesus" or "the Jesus of the Gospels" throughout this essay, I am not making a judgment for or against the historicity of any of the gospel traditions under discussion here.
30. Familial strife and division were traditionally associated with the time before the coming of the Messiah (Mic 7:6; Jub 23:16, 19; 1 En 100:2); on this point, see Bar-

ton, *Discipleship*, 112, 176. Throughout this essay, biblical quotations are from the *New American Bible*.

31. Similarly, Luke 21:16: "You will even be handed over by parents, brothers, relatives, and friends, and they will put some of you to death." In his reference to coming tribulations, Matthew omits the reference to betrayal by family members; see Matt 24:9–13.

32. Jesus' parable of the great feast (Luke 14:15–24), in which the feast is symbolic of the messianic, eschatological banquet, implies that marital ties are a potential obstacle to one's participation in the eschatological salvation that the reign of God will bring. In the parable, the excuse offered by one invitee—"I have just married a woman, and therefore cannot come" (14:20)—is rejected by the host, resulting in exclusion from the feast.

33. Scholars have sought to understand Jesus' radical call of disciples to abandon their families and property to follow him by analogy to, e.g., the rabbi-disciple relationship or the conversion to philosophy in Greco-Roman sources. Martin Hengel has argued, to my mind persuasively, that Jesus' action in this regard is to be interpreted in terms of his messianic vocation as proclaimer of the reign of God; see his *The Charismatic Leader and His Followers* (Edinburgh: T. & T. Clark, 1981).

34. On fishing in the first century Palestinian economy, see Hanson, *Palestine*, 106.

35. Exod 20:12; Deut 5:16; Prov 23:22–25; Tob 5:1; Sir 3:1–16, esp. v. 16. Men who did not remain home to protect their women and family honor as well as the family's precious resources were considered shameless; see Malina, *Social-Science Commentary*, 212–13.

36. Gerd Theissen, *The Shadow of the Galilean* (Philadelphia: Fortress, 1987), 71. Elsewhere she reports the bitter complaint she made to her son and his response: "What you're doing is immoral. We're getting old. We've brought up you children. And now you leave us in the lurch. Do you know what he said to me? Someone once came to his master wanting to follow him, but first he had to bury his father. Jesus said, 'Let the dead bury their dead' and told the man to follow him immediately. Isn't that inhuman? Aren't parents worth anything any more? Are we parents worth no more than animal corpses, that one need not bury?" (*The Shadow*, 72).

37. The costliness of an itinerant lifestyle in the ancient context is further suggested by Jesus' sobering statement to a would-be disciple: "Foxes have holes, and birds of the air have nests, but the Son of Man has nowhere to lay his head" (Matt 8:20). Barton notes that the disciples' renunciation of household ties (Mark 1:16–20) corresponds with the mission instruction to renounce possessions and depend upon others' hospitality (Mark 6:7–13); see *Discipleship*, 63.

38. D. M. May, "Mark 3:20–35 from the Perspective of Shame/Honor," *Biblical Theology Bulletin* 17 (1987) 83–87; see 85.
39. Significantly, the Gospel of John corroborates the Synoptic evidence, remembering Jesus' brothers as unbelievers (John 7:3–5). Thus, two independent streams of gospel tradition, the Synoptic and the Johannine, cohere in their image of Jesus' strained relations with his own blood kin, including his mother and brothers.
40. Also worth noting is the Johannine account of the crucifixion according to which Jesus, from the cross, entrusts his widowed mother to the care of the so-called "beloved disciple", thereby doing his filial duty by providing for her care (John 19:25–27).
41. Rightly noted by Stephen Barton, "Living as Families in the Light of the New Testament," *Interpretation* 52 (1998): 130–44; on this point, see 138.
42. Barton observes that Jesus' declaration, "Whoever loves father or mother *more than me* is not worthy of me, and whoever loves son or daughter *more than me* is not worthy of me" (Matt 10:37), suggests that the issue is not one of social policy but of ultimate allegiance (*Discipleship*, 177).
43. See Barton, *Discipleship*, 217–18.
44. Given the centrality of kinship relations in the ancient Mediterranean, Jesus' relativization or de-prioritization of blood kinship ties was undoubtedly troubling to his contemporaries. However, it is not without precedent in the ancient context. Recent studies of family in the New Testament identify Greco-Roman and Jewish precedents for Jesus' attitude and conduct; on this, see esp. Barton, *Discipleship*, 23–56.
45. The relativization of blood kin ties accompanied by redefinition of family is further attested in Luke. To the woman in a crowd who called out to him, "Blessed is the womb that carried you and the breasts at which you nursed" (Luke 11:27), Jesus replies, with words reminiscent of Mark 3:34–35, "Rather, blessed are those who hear the word of God and observe it" (Luke 11:28). A similar pattern may be observed in Pauline tradition. In 1 Corinthians, Paul clearly discourages believers in Corinth from marriage or re-marriage in view of the imminent End (7:26, 29, 31) and in his references to marital sexuality makes no reference to procreation; yet he counsels against an unrealistic sexual abstinence between spouses (7:1–5) and also prohibits divorce except when an unbelieving spouse demands it (7:10–16). Thus, according to Paul, marital life is no longer the ultimate priority, but he gives it a degree of support.
46. "Fictive kinship" or pseudo-kinship, a term used by social scientists, refers to the ways in which societies link people who are not blood relatives into family-like relations.

47. Women's abandonment of domesticity is frequently cited by family values advocates as the cause of family breakdown. Feminists in particular, branded "feminazis" in the rhetoric, are demonized for inspiring such conduct. Evidence suggests, however, that it is women who continue to carry most of the responsibility for child- and eldercare; on this, see Mary Stewart Van Leeuwen, "Re-Inventing the Ties That Bind: Feminism and the Family at the Close of the Twentieth Century," in *Religion, Feminism, and the Family*, Anne Carr and Mary Stewart Van Leeuwen, eds. (Louisville: Westminster/John Knox, 1996), 33–52. It should be noted that, contrary to the caricature of feminists in family values discourse, feminists are not of one mind on family. Although early feminist theory emphasized the disadvantages to women of the patriarchal nuclear family, hence, the need for its rejection, during the last thirty years feminist thought on family has become increasingly diverse and now includes a concern to retrieve and preserve the positive features of the nuclear (not patriarchal) family. On this, see esp. Carr and Van Leeuwen; Susan F. Parsons, "Feminism and the Family," *The Family in Theological Perspective*, 273–90; Linda Woodhead, "Faith, Feminism and the Family," *Concilium* 4 (1995): 43–52.
48. E.g., the essay by Simkins in this volume examines the way in which Israel's transition from a tribal society to a monarchical state involved shifts in the mode of production that in turn impacted family form.
49. This is not to say that the nuclear family consisting of spouses and their biological and/or adoptive children should not enjoy normative status. Given the demands that responsible child-rearing entails, surely there is wisdom to the two-parent family. This does not mean, however, as family values advocates contend, that "any other formula leads to broken hearts and broken homes," thus, that single-parent families are automatically defective. In addition, it is important to distinguish between a nuclear family and a patriarchal nuclear family. In the view of many, including feminists, it is not the nuclear family that is problematic but the patriarchal nuclear family. Hence, an increasing number of spouses in nuclear families are currently seeking to create more egalitarian and mutual patterns of marital and familial relations.
50. The allegedly "golden age" of American families in the nineteen fifties had a shadow side that, in its hostility to people defined as "other," resulted in racial and political repression; on this, see Coontz, *The Way We Really Are*, 39.
51. Family values discourse routinely privileges the second creation account (Gen 2) and the New Testament household codes, treating them as a "canon within the canon" on the subject of family. In doing so, however, it fails to articulate a rationale that explains why these particular texts should enjoy greater authority than other others on the subject.

52. On the distinction between "what the Bible says" and "how the Bible speaks," see Barton, "Biblical Hermeneutics," 6; also Sally Purvis, "A Question of Families," *Interpretation* 52 (1998): 145–60, esp. 152–56.
53. E.g., some might well be tempted to read the Gospels' picture of Jesus' iconoclastic behavior as an earlier and more authentic rendering of the nature of discipleship, in which case the later Deutero-Pauline household codes are adjudged concessions to the status quo of the patriarchal family, thus, a degenerative stage. Others, preferring the less radical and more conventional household codes, might argue that the later traditions are the more authoritative, assuming the ongoing inspiration of the Spirit in the life of the church. In view of the temptation to proof-texting by Christian readers of every denomination and of every ideological camp, Barton calls for the development of what he terms a theological-ecclesial hermeneutic. He also provides an insightful critique of the limitations of the historical critical method of reading the Bible. For both discussions, see Barton, "Living as Families."
54. On covenant love (*agape*) in family life, see Michael G. Lawler and Gail S. Risch, "Covenant Generativity: Toward a Theology of Christian Family," *Horizons* 26 (1999), 7–30, esp. 18–20; also Michael G. Lawler, *Family American and Christian* (Chicago: Loyola, 1998), esp. 162–65; "Marriage in the Bible," in *Perspectives on Marriage. A Reader*, second edition, Kieran Scott and Michael Warren, eds. (New York: Oxford University Press, 2001), 7–21, esp. 18–19. According to Purvis, *agape* functions as a norm *within* families and as a norm *for* families; see "A Question," 157.
55. One thinks, for example, of news reports of the discussions of welfare reform that took place shortly after the seating of the new Congress in 1994. The rhetoric of the Christian Coalition in its lobbying for various legislative proposals in the Republican "Contract with America" rationalized its call for severe cuts in welfare programs with equally severe moral judgments regarding, for example, the high incidence of "children having children" in America's inner-cities. What was troubling in these discussions was not the call for welfare reform but the rhetoric in support of it, which, in its focus on the conduct of inner-city youth and families, appeared mean-spirited, even racist. On the politics of the Christian Right in relation to family issues and policies, see Sara Diamond, *Roads to Dominion: Right Wing Movements and Political Power in the United States* (New York: Guilford, 1995), esp. ch. 10, "Undaunted Allies: The Christian Right in the 1980s," 228–56; also Michael Lienesch, *Redeeming America: Piety and Politics in the New Christian Right* (Chapel Hill: University of North Carolina Press, 1993), esp. ch. 2 on "Family," 52–93.

An Early Christian Debate on Marriage and Family: *The Jovinianist Controversy*[1]

DAVID G. HUNTER

In the later years of the fourth century, a worried Pope Siricius wrote a letter to his fellow bishops in Italy. Reporting the results of a recent synod, Siricius informed the Italian bishops that a monk named Jovinian and eight followers had been condemned as "the authors of a new heresy." Siricius did not describe any of Jovinian's teaching in detail; he simply stated that Jovinian had claimed that married Christians and celibate Christians were equally deserving of honor. In other words, Jovinian denied that the celibate life was intrinsically superior to the married life, and this, to Siricius' mind, was heresy.[2]

Siricius' letter was only the beginning of what was to become a significant controversy in the Western church. Christian leaders, such as the bishops Ambrose of Milan and Augustine of Hippo, soon weighed in with their own condemnations of Jovinian's "heresy." The most extensive contribution came from the prominent biblical scholar, Jerome, who had recently withdrawn to a monastic retreat in Bethlehem. Jerome sent to Rome two volumes attacking Jovinian that were so hostile to marriage that many Christians believed Jerome himself had fallen into heresy by opposing Jovinian too strongly. Jerome's closest friends at Rome rebuked him and even tried discretely to withdraw his treatise from circulation.[3]

The controversy surrounding Jovinian provides a fascinating glimpse into the development of Catholic traditions on marriage and celibacy. It marked the first time that the superiority of celibacy over marriage was officially defined as Christian doctrine and that its denial was labeled as "heresy." My aim here is to explore the reasons behind Jovinian's condemnation, especially by his three chief opponents, Pope Siricius, Am-

247

brose, and Jerome. Each of these church leaders had his own particular reasons for opposing Jovinian. These three men did not always agree with each other; as we will see, they did not even like each other. Nevertheless, they agreed in their rejection of Jovinian's teaching. Their agreement, I will argue, had as much to do with issues of authority and power in the Church—specifically the authority of the clergy—as it did with the theological merit of Jovinian's arguments.

The Teaching of Jovinian

In his two volumes, *Against Jovinian*, Jerome preserved numerous fragments of Jovinian's writings. In one place, for example, he provided the following summary of Jovinian's views in four propositions:

1. Virgins, widows, and married women who have once been washed in Christ are of the same merit, if they do not differ in other works.
2. Those who have been born again in baptism with full faith cannot be overthrown by the devil.
3. There is no difference between abstinence from food and receiving it with thanksgiving.
4. There is one reward in the kingdom of heaven for all who have preserved their baptism.[4]

It is clear from Jerome's excerpts that baptism was a central category in Jovinian's thought. For Jovinian, baptism was the fundamental basis of Christian salvation. Since baptism was the ritual by which a person was freed from sin and incorporated into the body of Christ, Jovinian argued, baptism provided Christians with equal access to the kingdom of God. Therefore, he concluded, distinctions based on ascetic practice, whether celibacy or fasting, should not be considered relevant in this life or the next.[5]

We know from other passages of Jovinian's writings that he also emphasized that all Christians shared equally in the presence of God and Christ. For example, in his comments on a series of passages from the Gospel of John, Jovinian stressed that Christ dwells in all Christians alike. He cited John 6:56, "Those who eat my flesh and drink my blood abide in me and I in them," which Jovinian observed does not speak of different degrees of Christ's abiding. Therefore, he concluded, "Just as Christ does not abide in us in varying degrees, so there are not varying degrees of our abiding in Christ."[6]

Besides the equality of God's presence in all of the redeemed, Jovinian also emphasized the unity of all Christians within the one body of Christ. Drawing on the ancient metaphors of the Church as the Body of Christ, Jovinian used the image to defend his view of the equal merit of married and celibate Christians. For example, alluding to the Pauline teaching on Christians as the limbs or members of Christ, Jovinian wrote:

> We love all the members alike, and do not prefer the eye to the finger, nor the finger to the ear. The loss of any single one means that all the members share the same sorrow. We all alike come into this world, and we all alike depart from it.[7]

For Jovinian, the incorporation of all Christians into the one body of Christ by virtue of their one baptism meant that all share the same salvation.

These various theological positions—the focus on baptism, the emphasis on God's indwelling all of the faithful, and the stress on the unity of the Church—all point to the centrality of ecclesiological concerns in Jovinian's theology. As Jerome's most recent biographer J. N. D. Kelly has observed, what gave a theological basis and inner cohesion to Jovinian's views was "his stress on the element of faith in baptism and his conviction that the transformation effected by it not only rescued a man from the power of sin but created a unified, holy people in which considerations of merit were irrelevant."[8] According to Jovinian, a hierarchy based on the superiority of celibacy over marriage fractured the unity of the Church. It introduced invidious distinctions and fostered arrogance and elitism. As Jovinian remarked in one passage quoted by Jerome: "I do you no wrong, Virgin. You have chosen a life of chastity on account of 'the present distress.' You wished to be 'holy in body and spirit.' Be not proud! You and your married sisters are members of the same Church."[9]

At this point, I should stress that Jovinian had nothing against celibacy in itself. He was a celibate monk himself, and Jerome tells us that many of Jovinian's supporters were also celibate monks or priests.[10] What Jovinian objected to was the fact that in the late fourth century celibacy had become a divisive factor in the Church. Celibacy had become an essential element in the construction of hierarchy. Like different variations on the same theme, the notion of hierarchy could be invoked in different ways: widows over married women, virgins over widows, and the celibate clergy over the married laity. The central theme, however, was always the same: not to have sex was always better than to have sex.

Against this view Jovinian objected that the very notion of a hierarchy based on sexual renunciation was faulty. It implied that sex was somehow sinful or defiling. Jovinian believed that the Bible itself spoke otherwise. From the ancient blessing at creation to "increase and multiply" to the apostle Paul's advice that the bishop should be "a man of one wife" to the presence of married men among the apostles, Jovinian cited an array of biblical passages attesting to the goodness of sexual activity, even to its place in the divine plan of salvation. Ultimately, Jovinian argued, those who denigrated sexuality and marriage in favor of celibacy were guilty of the same heresy that had afflicted the Church since its beginning: the rejection of creation espoused by Marcion, the Encratites, and the Manichees.[11]

We have to keep in mind this idea of hierarchy when we come to examine Jovinian's opponents. Pope Siricius, Bishop Ambrose, and Saint Jerome all rejected Jovinian's views and endorsed some form of hierarchy based on sexual renunciation. But each one had a different view of what the celibate life meant (or, better, how it was to function) in the establishment of order and authority in the Church. For Pope Siricius the issue of the celibacy of the clergy loomed large and seems to lie behind his rejection of Jovinian. For Bishop Ambrose the consecration of women as virgins in the Church took center stage, along with the image of the Virgin Mary. For Jerome, the focus was on women and men living in monastic community. But despite their differences, all three men embraced celibacy as a strategy for creating hierarchy and for enhancing their own authority in the Church.

Pope Siricius

At first sight it is surprising to find Siricius engaged in the fight against Jovinian. Since becoming bishop of Rome late in 384, Siricius had been decidedly lukewarm in his response to the ascetic movement. For example, one of his first acts in office was to preside over the trial and expulsion of Jerome from the city in the spring of 385. The details are sketchy, but it is clear from Jerome's own letters that he was put on trial by an assembly of the Roman clergy and forced to leave the city. The charge seems to have involved improper relations with some of his female associates, in particular the noble widow Paula. Jerome says that the accusation was not substantiated, and it probably was politically motivated. Jerome had severely criticized the luxurious lifestyles of the Roman clergy, and as soon as his patron and protector, Pope Damasus, died, the clergy under Siricius moved to get rid of him.[12]

Another example of Siricius' ambivalence about asceticism is a series of letters he wrote to various Western churches attempting to restrict the entry of monks into the clergy. Siricius was not opposed to the monastic life itself, but he felt very strongly that monks should not be ordained priests or bishops without spending adequate time in the lower orders of the clergy. For example, in the earliest document of his pontificate, a letter to the Spanish bishop Himerius of Tarragona, Siricius argued that monks "should not ascend to the lofty dignity of the episcopate at a single leap."[13] He insisted that monks must follow the same course of preparation as other candidates: those under the age of thirty could be admitted only to the lower ranks of lector, acolyte, and subdeacon; after the age of thirty, one could become a deacon; after five years of acceptable service as deacon, one could advance to the presbyterate; only after ten years as presbyter, could a man advance to the "episcopal chair."[14] Siricius' aim clearly was to reinforce the structure of the clergy and to enhance its authority in relation to the new monastic asceticism.[15]

Despite his ambivalence about monasticism, Siricius was a strong proponent of one ascetical practice: clerical celibacy, that is, celibacy as a requirement for the higher ranks of the clergy: deacons, presbyters, and bishops. In fact, the decretal letters of Siricius are the earliest evidence we have of a bishop of Rome trying to require celibacy of the clergy in the Western church.[16] In his letters Siricius argued that celibacy was essential to the performance of priestly ministry. Likening the role of the priest in baptism or eucharist to that of the Old Testament priests in the Jewish Temple, Siricius argued that sacred rituals required ritual purity. For example, in his *Letter to the Bishops of Africa*, Siricius wrote:

> Let priests and Levites have no intercourse with their wives, inasmuch as they are absorbed in the daily duties of their ministries. Paul, when writing to the Corinthians told them: "Leave yourself free for prayer" (1 Cor 7:5). If lay people are asked to be continent so

that their prayers are granted, all the more so a priest who should be ready at any moment, thanks to an immaculate purity, and not fearing the obligation of offering the sacrifice or baptizing. Were he soiled by carnal concupiscence, what could he do? Would he excuse himself? With what shame, in what state of mind would he carry out his functions?[17]

Similarly, in his *Letter to the Bishops of Gaul*, Siricius cited the same passage from 1 Cor 7:5 and commented: "If intercourse is defiling (*si commixtio pollutio est*), it is obvious that the priest must stand ready to carry out his heavenly duty, since he must supplicate on behalf of the sins of others, so that he himself is not found to be unworthy."[18] Since sexual relations caused "pollution" and rendered the priest "unclean," the daily duties of priestly service, in Siricius' view, required sexual abstinence.

Siricius' sense of the importance of celibacy for the clergy must have been one of the factors that led to his rejection of Jovinian. For if, as Jovinian argued, celibacy did not make a Christian holier (that is, if sex did not make a person "unclean"), then the very basis on which Siricius justified the requirement of clerical celibacy was removed. Siricius, by contrast, envisioned celibacy as the way to create a priestly *persona* that would define the unique status of the clergy. As Peter Brown has observed, in the West at this time celibacy was emerging as a way to make the existing clergy an acceptable "middle party" somewhere between the radical renunciants, on the one hand, and the "worldly" laity, on the other: "Priests and bishops who were continent by that strict, if narrow, definition could stand between the shrill ascetics and the new men of power, grossly stained by the world."[19] Celibacy of the clergy, as Siricius articulated it, was essential to the construction of the authority of that "middle party" in the Western church.

Ambrose of Milan

Ambrose brought a unique perspective to the controversy because he discussed one of Jovinian's ideas that was not mentioned by Siricius or Jerome. According to Ambrose, Jovinian denied that Mary the Mother of Jesus had remained always a virgin.[20] It is important to be clear about Jovinian's position here. Jovinian did not deny that Mary had conceived Jesus virginally; nor did he claim, as some Christians before him had done, that Mary and Joseph produced additional children after the birth of Jesus. Rather, Jovinian argued that Mary could not have remained physically a virgin in the process of giving birth to Jesus. The issue, from Jovinian's perspective, was not sex, but the reality of the Incarnation. To claim that Jesus did not have a normal human birth was to deny that he was really human and this, in Jovinian's view, was heresy.

Ambrose, by contrast, was an enthusiastic proponent of Mary's perpetual virginity—before, after, and during Jesus' birth. More than any of his contemporaries, Ambrose took the idea of Mary's perpetual virginity and made it the center of his theology of Christ, salvation, and the Church. For Ambrose the virginity of Mary was a powerful symbol of purity and holiness in the midst of a corrupt and sinful world. As Peter Brown has described it, Mary's virginal integrity "stood for all that was unbroken and sacred in the world."[21] Mary's virginity meant so much to Ambrose because it embodied (quite literally) his own vision of the Church, an oasis of purity and calm, ringed around with impenetrable boundaries, shut tight against the formless, disruptive forces of "the world."

We see this idea at work in Ambrose's earliest treatise, *Concerning Virgins*, based on a set of sermons in which he first developed the idea of Mary as a "type" or symbol of the Church, using the image of virginal purity:

> The Church is unstained by intercourse (*immaculata coitu*), and yet she is fruitful in childbirth. She is a virgin because of her chastity and a mother because of her offspring. She brought us into life, conceived not of man but of the Holy Spirit, in a birth free of bodily pain and full of the joy of angels.[22]

This assimilation of the Church and the virgin Mary was a persistent theme in Ambrose's writings. Eventually, he added bridal imagery from the Song of Songs. Ambrose found special significance in the words of the bridegroom from Song 4:12: "A garden enclosed is my sister, my bride; a garden enclosed, a fountain sealed up." According to Ambrose, Christ spoke these words prophetically to the Church, "which he wishes to be a virgin, without stain, without wrinkle" (cf. Eph 5:27).[23]

At this point it is clear how differently Ambrose and Jovinian viewed the nature of the Church and the significance of virginity. Both men appealed to the image of the Church as the virginal bride of Christ. For Jovinian, however, the virginity of the Church signified the holiness that belonged to the entire Christian community. For example, Jerome reported that one of the many biblical texts cited by Jovinian was 2 Cor 11:2 ("I espoused you to one husband, that I might present you as a chaste virgin to Christ"). According to Jerome, Jovinian took the text to refer to "the whole church of believers."[24] In another excerpt from Jovinian's writings cited by Jerome we find the following:

> Call the Church what you will: Bride, Sister, Mother. She is the gathering of one Church, which is never without her Bridegroom, Brother, or Son. She has one faith and is not defiled by a variety of doctrines or divided by heresies. She remains a virgin.[25]

For Jovinian, the image of the Church as Virgin and Bride stood for all baptized Christians as one holy community of the redeemed. Ambrose, by contrast, tended to see the virginity of the Church and of Mary in terms of its exclusivity. The idea of virginity as exclusion was the basis of his view of hierarchy.

Another unique feature of Ambrose's ascetic perspective (one directly linked to his view of Mary and the Church) was his focus on a particular category of celibate person. In most of his ascetical writings Ambrose is concerned not with the celibacy of priests or with those who have adopted the monastic life. Virtually all of his focus is on the sexual purity of young women consecrated to a life of perpetual virginity. In this case there was a specific liturgical ritual behind Ambrose's view, the *velatio*, or veiling of a virgin. This was a practice that had begun only in the fourth century and only in the west.[26] Ambrose, in fact, was one of the major promoters of the practice. The ritual of veiling was a ceremony modeled after a Roman wedding, but in this case the bride was married to Christ. According to Jerome, the ritual involved the bishop placing a veil over the head of the virgin, while reciting the words of the apostle Paul: "I wish to present you as a chaste virgin to Christ" (2 Cor 11:2). The ceremony may also have included the antiphonal chanting of verses from the Song of Songs.[27]

Given his strong interest in the idea of absolute virginity and the symbolic resonance that the liturgy of the veiling of virgins would have provided, we can easily understand bishop Ambrose's desire to foster the cult of female virginity and, hence, his opposition to the views of Jovinian. But there may have been another factor at work as well. Like Pope

Siricius, Ambrose was not unconcerned about the authority of the clergy, especially the bishop. The ritual of the *velatio*, as Ambrose promoted it, was itself a decidedly *episcopal* event. According to Ambrose, it was the bishop who decided at what age a girl could take the veil and whether she had the necessary virtues. The bishop customarily presided at the ceremony, bestowed the veil, pronounced the marriage blessing, and delivered a sermon of exhortation. The bishop also continued to supervise the consecrated virgin after her veiling and sometimes took responsibility for her welfare if her parents died.

Ambrose's emphasis on the prominent role of the bishop in the recruitment, veiling, and supervision of consecrated virgins, suggests that the ritual of veiling may have functioned as a way of enhancing episcopal authority, much as clerical celibacy did in the perspective of Pope Siricius. If this is so, then Ambrose had even more reason to oppose the views of Jovinian. By challenging the elevated status of the consecrated virgins, Jovinian would have appeared (to Ambrose, at least) to be undermining one of the central pillars of episcopal authority, namely the bishop's role in consecrating the bride of Christ.

Saint Jerome

Although Jerome was far removed from Rome at the time of Jovinian's appearance, it is clear that he was quite eager to involve himself in the controversy. Jerome saw much at stake in the arguments for and against marriage, and he was intent on getting his own voice heard in the Roman debate. I would like to suggest that Jerome's engagement with Jovinian, though no doubt motivated by his sincere support for celibacy, also was strongly influenced by his own troubled history with the Roman clergy, as well by his difficult relations with both Pope Siricius and Bishop Ambrose. Jerome desperately needed to rehabilitate his own reputation, especially after his disgraceful exit from Rome eight years earlier. He also wanted to state, in no uncertain terms, how his own view of the ascetic life differed from that of Siricius and Ambrose. Jerome's treatise, *Against Jovinian*, was written, therefore, not merely to refute Jovinian, but also to reestablish Jerome's own authority in Rome as an ascetic teacher.

There are several reasons for interpreting Jerome's entry into the controversy at least partly as an act of literary self-promotion. Shortly before Jovinian's condemnation, that is, about the year 391, Jerome had composed a book titled, *On Illustrious Men*, a sort of handbook of Christian teachers. The aim of the book had been to demonstrate that the Church had produced its own philosophers and men of learning. With characteristic immodesty Jerome included himself prominently in the list of literary notables; his is the final (and lengthiest) entry among the contemporary authors.[28]

Even more telling is the fact that "On Illustrious Men" included the following entry on Bishop Ambrose, which can only be explained as a sign of strained relations between the two men:

> Ambrose, bishop of Milan, at the present time is still writing. I withhold my judgement of him, because he is still alive, fearing either to praise or to criticize him. If I praise him, I will be blamed for flattery; if I criticize him, I will be blamed for telling the truth.[29]

Jerome's hostile treatment of Ambrose indicates, at the very least, that relations between the two men were not entirely friendly at the time Jerome wrote *Against Jovinian*. One explanation of Jerome's hostility to Ambrose may be that Ambrose had failed to intervene and defend Jerome when he had been accused before the Roman clergy in 385.

Other writings of Jerome, however, indicate that there may also have been a kind of literary competition between the two men and that Jerome was out to discredit Ambrose. For example, about the same time that he wrote "On Illustrious Men," Jerome had translated a set of homilies on the Gospel of Luke written by the Greek scholar, Origen of Alexandria. In the preface to his translation Jerome said that he had translated Origen's homilies primarily to expose a certain unnamed plagiarist, whom he described as a croaking black bird who adorned himself with colored feathers pilfered from others.[30] Jerome was referring to Ambrose's own homilies on Luke, which had been largely lifted (without acknowledgment) from the homilies of Origen. A few years earlier Jerome had stated similar accusations in the preface to his translation of a treatise *On the Holy Spirit*, written by a Greek theologian, Didymus the Blind. Here, too, Jerome's translation had been undertaken expressly in order to expose Ambrose's treatise *On the Holy Spirit* as a plagiarism of Didymus' work.[31]

There may have been additional reasons for rivalry between Ambrose and Jerome, besides these literary quarrels. In his treatise *Against Jovinian* Jerome had complained that men were often elected bishops simply because they were wealthy, educated, or powerful. Ambrose's election to the bishopric of Milan was a prime example of the sort of procedure that incensed Jerome. At the time of his election Ambrose was a provincial governor, and not even a baptized Christian. In one week he was baptized, passed through all of the lower clerical ranks, and was consecrated bishop. Jerome seems to have always resented Ambrose's accession to the episcopacy, even though he occasionally praised his writings on virginity. For example, in a letter written a couple of years after *Against Jovinian*, Jerome wrote disparagingly about the elevation of a worldly man to the clergy in terms that point unmistakably to Ambrose:

> There is someone who yesterday was a catechumen, and today is a bishop; yesterday in the amphitheatre, today in the church; in the evening at the circus, in the morning at the altar; just a little while ago the patron of actors, now the consecrator of virgins![32]

Jerome's personal and professional hostility to Ambrose has here fused with his convictions about clerical office. This letter shows that Jerome was still deeply resentful of Ambrose's accession to the episcopate. Perhaps Jerome's resentment also betrays some jealousy. Ambrose had acquired a position of moral and intellectual leadership in the western Church to which Jerome continued to aspire, and to which he could only aspire.

A similar point can be made about Jerome's relations with Pope Siricius, although here the rivalry had a somewhat different character. As I noted earlier, Siricius was the Roman bishop who had presided over the trial and expulsion of Jerome from the city in 385. Obviously, this action, even if only approved and not actually instigated by Siricius, would have cast a lasting shadow over relations between the two men. If we add to this the fact that Jerome may once have been considered a likely successor to Pope Damasus (at least Jerome says so in one of his letters), then Jerome would have had even further reasons for resenting Siricius.[33]

But the conflict between Jerome and Pope Siricius was not merely a personal one. They also differed significantly from each other in their views of asceticism and the recruitment of the clergy. I have already noted Siricius' reluctance to accept monks into the episcopacy unless they had spent time in the lower ranks of the clergy. Jerome, by contrast, was a strong proponent of a monastic clergy. He often criticized Christians (and their clergy) for preferring to elect bishops from the ranks of married men, rather than from the monastic life. In his treatise *Against Jovinian* Jerome directly attacked the Roman church (and its bishop, Siricius) for electing clergy who had once been married. Jerome acknowledged that the apostle Paul had once said that a bishop should be "a man of one wife." But, Jerome added, when Paul said this he was deliberately diluting the requirements for the episcopacy in order to attract Gentile converts. The election of married men to the episcopacy, Jerome insisted, was a regrettable necessity caused by the lack of virgins.[34]

It is clear from Jerome's comments in *Against Jovinian* that he did not enter the Jovinianist controversy merely to refute Jovinian. Jerome had bigger fish to fry. Having once been driven from Rome in disgrace, he now seized the opportunity to reassert himself as a player in the competitive world of fourth century ecclesiastical and literary politics. This also meant inserting himself into the ongoing discussion of asceticism and clerical authority. Pope Siricius, and the Roman church as a whole, seems to have preferred a more traditional model of clerical authority, what has sometimes been described as the "post-marital" celibacy of the traditional married householder.[35] That is to say, the preferred candidate for the clergy was still a married man, who had decided (usually late in life) to put aside sexual activity and enter the service of the Church. Jerome, by contrast, had little respect for this degree of renunciation. Fully embracing the ascetical hierarchy, Jerome argued on behalf of a clerical order that was fully monastic, both in regard to celibacy and in regard to other ascetic practices.

Conclusion

I have suggested here that the controversy around Jovinian was not so much about the Christian family itself, as about the use of celibacy to construct hierarchy and, specifically, clerical authority in the late fourth century. But there were implications in the debate for a Christian view of the family. Celibacy had always been a prominent feature of the early Christian movement, but during the first two centuries the presence of married Christian householders—especially in positions of authority, such as bishop and elder—had helped to maintain a balance between the call to abandon the world and the necessity to remain within it. As Christianity grew in strength and numbers, and especially after it became officially sanctioned in the fourth century, the need arose for new and more prominent boundaries between the Church and the world, for new and more potent markers of holiness, if you will. Celibacy performed the function of creating and maintaining identity and of generating clerical authority, but it did so at a significant cost. What was lost was the sense of the full participation of the Christian family in the life of holiness, even in the life of the Church. The repercussions of this ancient debate are still with us today, as the Catholic Church faces renewed calls for the introduction of a married priesthood. Perhaps a renewed discussion of the nature of clerical authority in the Church will lead to a rediscovery of the value of the Christian family—or vice-versa.

Notes

1. I wish to express my appreciation to John J. O'Keefe, chair of the Department of Theology at Creighton University, for extending to me the kind invitation to participate in the Religion and Family symposium, and to Ronald A. Simkins, Director of the Center for the Study of Religion and Society, for his generous hospitality and support of my participation. A more extensive version of this paper appeared in *Re-Reading Late Ancient Christianity*, Dale Martin and Patricia Cox Miller, eds., *The Journal of Medieval and Early Modern Studies* 33 (2003), 453–70.
2. Siricius, *Letter 7 To Various Bishops*, 2 (*Patrologia Latina* [hereafter PL] 13, col. 1171). All translations of the ancient sources are my own, unless otherwise noted.
3. Further background on the Jovinianist controversy can be found in J. N. D. Kelly, *Jerome. His Life, Writings, and Controversies* (New York: Harper and Row, 1975), 179–194. See also my two articles, "Resistance to the Virginal Ideal in Late-Fourth-Century Rome: The Case of Jovinian," *Theological Studies* 48 (1987), 45–64; "Helvidius, Jovinian, and the Virginity of Mary in Late Fourth-Century Rome," *Journal of Early Christian Studies* 1 (1993), 47–71.
4. Cited in Jerome, *Against Jovinian* I. 3 (PL 23, col. 224).
5. The significance of baptism in Jovinian's theology was first recognized by Francesco Valli, *Gioviniano. Esame delle fonti et dei frammenti* (Urbino: Università di Urbino, 1953). See also the useful theological appreciation of Jovinian by Allan J. Budzin, "Jovinian's Four Theses on the Christian Life: An Alternative Patristic Spirituality," *Toronto Journal of Theology* 4/1 (1988), 44–59, especially 52–55.
6. Cited in Jerome, *Against Jovinian* II.19 (PL 23, col. 327).
7. Cited in Jerome, *Against Jovinian* II.20 (PL 23, col. 328).
8. Kelly, *Jerome*, 181.
9. Cited in Jerome, *Against Jovinian* I.5 (PL 23, col. 228).

10. Jerome stated this in his *Letter 49 to Pammachius* 2 (*Corpus scriptorum ecclesiasticorum latinorum* [hereafter CSEL] 54, 352).
11. In *Against Jovinian* I.5 (PL 23, col. 225–227) Jerome summarized Jovinian's appeal to the Bible, which culminated in Jovinian's statement: "All this makes it clear that you are following the teachings of the Manichees, who prohibit marriage and the eating of foods which God has created for our use." Much of Jerome's treatise, *Against Jovinian*, consisted of his responses to Jovinian's biblical arguments.
12. Most of the evidence is found in Jerome's *Letter 45 to Asella*. There is a good account of the events surrounding Jerome's departure in Kelly, *Jerome*, 112–15.
13. *Letter 1 to Himerius* 13.17 (PL 13, col. 1144).
14. *Letter 1 to Himerius* 9.13 (PL 13, col. 1142–43).
15. Similar concerns are voiced elsewhere in Siricius' letters. For more on this topic, see Philip Rousseau, *Ascetics, Authority, and the Church in the Age of Jerome and Cassian* (Oxford: Oxford University Press, 1978), 129–30.
16. Three letters of Siricius addressed the celibacy requirement: *Letter 1 to Himerius*, *Letter 5 to the Bishops of Africa*, and *Letter 10 to the Bishops of Gaul*.
17. *Letter 5 to the Bishops of Africa* 3 (PL 13, col. 1160–61); translated in Christian Cochini, S.J., *Apostolic Origins of Priestly Celibacy* (San Francisco, CA: Ignatius Press, 1990), 11 (slightly altered).
18. *Letter 10 to the Bishops of Gaul* 6 (PL 13, col. 1186).
19. Peter Brown, *The Body and Society. Men, Women, and Sexual Renunciation in Early Christianity* (New York: Columbia University Press, 1988), 358. For a similar development of this theme, see my essay, "Clerical Celibacy and the Veiling of Virgins: New Boundaries in Late Ancient Christianity," in *The Limits of Ancient Christianity. Essays on Late Antique Thought and Culture in Honor of R. A. Markus*, William E. Klingshirn and Mark Vessey, eds. (Ann Arbor: The University of Michigan Press, 1999), 139–52.
20. This information is found in Ambrose, *Letter 42 to Siricius*, a report from the synod at Milan that condemned Jovinian after his condemnation at Rome. The letter has been edited as *Epistula 15 Extra Collectionem* in the latest edition of Ambrose's letters: CSEL 82/3, 302–11.
21. Brown, *Body and Society*, 354.
22. Ambrose, *Concerning Virgins* I.31 (PL 16, col. 208).
23. *Letter 63 to the Church at Vercelli* 36 (CSEL 82/3, 253–54). Elsewhere I have explored the different readings of the image of the Virgin Bride in Ambrose and others: "The Virgin, the Bride, and the Church: Reading Psalm 45 in Ambrose, Jerome, and Augustine," *Church History* 69 (2000), 281–303.
24. Cited in Jerome, *Against Jovinian* I.37 (PL 23, col. 275–76).

25. Cited in Jerome, *Against Jovinian* II.19 (PL 23, col. 328).
26. For the ceremony of virginal consecration, see R. Metz, *La consécration des vierges dans l'église romaine* (Paris, 1954); and R. D'Izarny, "Mariage et consécration virginale au ive siècle," *La Vie Spirituelle*, Supplément, 6, 24 (1953), 92–107.
27. Jerome, *Letter 130 to Demetrias* (CSEL 56, 176–77). For the argument on the chanting of the Song of Songs, see Nathalie Henry, "The Song of Songs and the Liturgy of the velatio in the Fourth Century: From Literary Metaphor to Liturgical Reality," in *Continuity and Change in Christian Worship: Papers Read at the 1997 Summer Meeting and the 1998 Winter Meeting of the Ecclesiastical History Society*, R. N. Swanson, ed. (Woodbridge: Boydell, 1999), 18–28.
28. *On Illustrious Men* 135; text in E. C. Richardson, *Hieronymus. Liber de viris illustribus* (Leipzig, 1896), 55.
29. *On Illustrious Men* 124 (Richardson, 53).
30. Jerome, *Preface to the Homilies of Origen on the Gospel of Luke* (*Sources Chrétiennes* 87, 94). Jerome's nemesis, Rufinus of Aquileia, identified Ambrose as the object of Jerome's attack: *Apology against Jerome* II.22–23.
31. Jerome, *Preface to the Book of Didymus of Alexandria on the Holy Spirit* (PL 23, col. 107–10); discussed in Rufinus, *Apology against Jerome* II.24–25.
32. *Letter 69 to Oceanus* 9 (CSEL 54, 698).
33. Jerome, *Letter 45 to Asella* 3 (CSEL 54, 325).
34. Jerome, *Against Jovinian* I.34 (PL 23, col. 268–70).
35. The expression is taken from the discussion in Peter Brown, *Body and Society*, 377–78.

Faith, Praxis, and Practical Theology: *At the Interface of Sociology and Theology*

MICHAEL G. LAWLER

This essay is an exercise in practical theology, the "theological discipline which is concerned with the Church's self-actualization here and now—both that which *is* and that which *ought to be*."[1] Practical theology is the *theological* reflection arising out of and in response to the Church's actual situation. It does not simply explain from deductive theological principles the Church's actual situation, but reflects critically on the actual situation to test it for relevance and significance in light of the gospel and the socio-historical conditions of the time. Practical theology grows out of the relationship between *theoria* and *praxis*, which, for the Church, is the relationship between *faith* and *praxis*. To recognize scientifically the Church's actual situation and to perform the required theological reflection, Rahner argues, "practical theology certainly requires sociology."[2]

I explore, therefore, the relationship between practical theology and sociology. Specifically, I examine the theological realities, *sensus fidei* and *reception*, and explore their relationship to the data of sociological research. The exploration is concretized by a consideration of the sociological data and theology of the Catholic moral doctrine about the regulation of births. A *theological* reflection on the actual situation of the doctrine and a *sociological* consideration of the data suggest that a dramatic development and re-reception[3] of the doctrine is under way and that the development is in line with previous dramatic developments of doctrine in the Church.

Development of Doctrine

The development in the doctrine about the regulation of births can be detected in what may be called the High Tradition, comprised of believers whose grasp of the philosophical precision of the language in which Catholic doctrine is articulated enables them to understand the meanings embedded in doctrine, and the popular Low Tradition, comprised of believers who do not understand the language and, therefore, more often than not, misunderstand doctrine. There is an important and theologically legitimate distinction in the High Tradition between the Magisterium, whose task is to speak *from* and *for* the Church, and theologians, who speak only *from* the Church. Because the theologian's role is to speak *from* the actual faith situation of the Church, not only to hand on traditional doctrine but also to test and retest it for relevance and significance in the present situation, sociology, which explores and manifests the present situation of doctrine, can be an ancillary tool for theological reflection as important as philosophy and history.

No Catholic theologian would deny that ecclesial faith is the primary source for theological reflection, but that faith, as the New Testament consistently teaches, always includes *praxis* or action. The Letter of James is usually advanced as *the* foundation for the Catholic claim that faith includes *praxis*. "What does it profit, my brethren," James asks, "if a man says he has faith but has not works? Can his faith save him? . . . If a brother or sister is ill-clad and in lack of daily food, and one of you says to them, 'Go in peace, be warmed and filled,' without giving them the things needed for the body, what does it profit? So faith by itself, if it has not works, is dead" (2:14–17). James, of course, was regretted by the Reformers, to preserve intact their slogan of "justification by faith alone," but he is far from the only New Testament book connecting faith and *praxis*. His text, indeed, reverberates with loud echoes of Matthew. From his Sermon on the Mount, "You will know them by their *fruits*" (7:16) and "not everyone who says to me 'Lord, Lord,' shall enter the kingdom of heaven, but he who *does* the will of my Father who is in heaven" (7:21) to the great parable of the last judgment, Matthew is clear. Genuine faith includes the good fruit of action. In the parable of the last judgment, the Judge separates people "as a shepherd separates the sheep from the goats" (25:32). "Come, O blessed of my Father," he says to those on his right hand, "inherit the kingdom prepared for you from the foundation of the world; for I was hungry and you gave me food, I was thirsty and you gave me drink, I was a stranger and you welcomed me, I was naked and you clothed me" (25:35–36). The question is posed when had they seen him hungry, thirsty, naked, or a stranger, and the Judge replies with the punch-line of the parable: "Truly, I say to you, as you did it to one of the least of these my brethren, you did it to me" (25:40).

Both Paul and John reiterate this judgment. "The fruit of the Spirit," Paul teaches, "is love, joy, peace, patience, kindness, goodness, faithfulness, gentleness, self-control" (Gal 5:22–23). He prays that the Philippians be "filled with the fruits of righteousness, which come through Jesus Christ to the glory of God" (Phil 1:11). The Colossians are "to lead a life worthy of the Lord . . . bearing fruit in every good work" (Col 1:10). "If anyone has the world's goods and sees his brother in need, yet closes his heart against him," John asks, "how does God's love abide in him?" (1 John 3:17; cp. 4:20). These texts are not proof texts for any position, but they reveal a pattern that pervades the New Testament and establish the connection between faith and action as a long-standing Catholic position. One can conclude from the presence of genuine faith to appropriate *praxis*; conversely one can conclude from *praxis* to the faith that sustains it. Sociology can play an important part in that process by illuminating action, making it possible for theologians to conclude to the faith behind the *praxis*.

The Second Vatican Council taught, "in pastoral care sufficient use should be made, not only of theological principles, but also of the findings of secular sciences, especially psychology and sociology." The Council goes on to assert, "in this way the faithful will be brought to a purer and more mature living of the faith."[4] The empirical principle is clear, "there are no true factual judgments without a foundation in relevant data,"[5] and I suggest the actual faith of the Church in its present situation can best be uncovered by sociological analysis. Relevant data, required to achieve true knowledge of any kind, are required to achieve true knowledge of what the Church believes. The intersection of empirically demonstrated faith-*praxis* and faith-seeking-understanding or theology is a nodal point at which Berger's judgment is verified. "*Methodologically*, in terms of theology as a disembodied universe of discourse, sociology may be looked on as quite harmless—*existentially*, in terms of the theologian as a living person with a social location and a social biography, sociology can be a very dangerous business indeed."[6] My claim in this essay is that, however dangerous to apparently settled theological positions, sociology has an important part to play in manifesting and interpreting what the Church *actually* believes and *ought to* believe in both faith and *praxis*. I will return to an important distinction between *faith* and *belief* later in the discussion.

Reception

Reception is an ecclesial process by which virtually[7] all the members of the Church assent to a teaching presented them as apostolic truth and ecclesial faith, thereby assimilating the doctrine into the life of the whole Church.[8] The teaching may come to them internally from their own Church, for instance, from an ecumenical council or a decision of the Magisterium, or it may come to them externally from the decision of another religious community. In either case, though it is not what makes the teaching true, reception confirms that the teaching or decision is good for the whole Church and is in agreement with the apostolic tradition on which the Church is built up. It is important to be clear from the outset that reception effects, not the truth or validity of a teaching, but its efficacy in the life of the Church. A non-received teaching is not thereby false or invalid; it is simply irrelevant to the life of the Church. As culture, time, and place necessarily inculturated the gospel, the good news of what God has done in Jesus the Christ, they also inculturate every doctrine and every reception of doctrine.[9] The act of reception, therefore, cannot and does not receive the tradition of the past unchanged; the past is always re-appropriated or re-received in the present.[10] There are many examples in Catholic history of both reception and non-reception.

Already in the New Testament, both Jesus and those he sends are to be received (Matt 10:40–41; Mark 6:11; Luke 9:5). This underscores a theological truth that should never be forgotten, namely, reception in the Christian Church is primarily the reception of a *person*, never simply the reception of words or doctrines about that person. The word of God is also to be received (Mark 4:20), as is the message of Jesus (Matt 19:11–12; John 3:11; Rev 2:41) and the gospel (1 Cor 15:1; Gal 1:9–12), leading Alberigo to define the Church as "the communion of those who receive the gospel."[11] The implication is always that without reception the person, and the word the person speaks, is ineffective (see Luke 4:16–29). The technical meaning of *reception*, however, came into existence in relation to the Councils of the Church and their doctrinal teaching. Extraordinary reverence and authority are given especially to the first Ecumenical Council of Nicaea (325) and its Christological confession, but it was not always so. A few months after the Council, some bishops withdrew their reception of its dogma about the divine sonship of the Word, leading to the situation described by Jerome: "the whole world woke from a deep slumber and discovered that it had become Arian."[12] It was not until the Nicene Creed was officially received by, first, the Council of Constantinople (381) and, then, the Council of Chalcedon (452) that it became the foundational confession of the Christian Church.[13] Zizioulas summarizes the importance of reception in the Church when he comments that "the Church was born out of a process of reception and has grown and existed through reception."[14]

There are many classic examples of non-reception in history. The Councils of Lyons (1274) and Constance (1439) both produced decrees of union to heal the rift between the churches of the East and West, but both came to nothing when the people and clergy of the Eastern churches refused to receive them. Closer to modern times there are four classic examples of non-reception leading to dramatic development of Catholic teaching. The first of these is the doctrine on usury. Between 1150 and 1550 the Church taught that "seeking, receiving, or hoping for anything beyond one's principal—in other words looking for profit—on a loan constituted the mortal sin of usury."[15] The Council of Vienna (1311–12) condemned the taking of interest in the most severe terms: "If anyone should fall into that error of pertinaciously persisting to affirm that interest taking is not a sin, we declare he should be punished as a heretic."[16] This doctrine, which forbade usury as contrary to the natural law, Church law, and the gospel, was taught by the ecumenical councils, Lateran II (1139)[17] and Lateran III (1179),[18] and by Popes and theologians unanimously. Its reception was altered by the historic rise of capitalist economies and the approval of interest by lay and clerical believers alike.

The second example is slavery. As late as 1860, the Church "taught that it was no sin for a Catholic to own a human being; to command the labor of that other human being without paying compensation . . . to sell him or her for cash."[19] In 1866, the Holy Office, formerly the Holy Inquisition and now the Congregation for the Doctrine of the Faith, issued an instruction about slavery: "Slavery itself, considered as such in its essential nature, is not at all contrary to the natural and divine law, and there can be several just titles of slavery."[20] Gradually, however, as modern European cultures came to value the uniqueness of the human person, the reception of this teaching changed to non-reception and it was abandoned in the nineteenth century.

The third example has to do with the teaching on religious freedom. From the middle of the fourth to the middle of the twentieth century, a 1600 year tradition, the Catholic Church taught that only Christian faith had the right to freedom of expression and worship, and that those who did not share that faith could be punished, even by death, for their false belief. In 1864, Pius IX condemned "that erroneous opinion, most fatal in its effects on the Catholic Church and the salvation of souls, called by our predecessor Gregory XVI *insanity*, namely, that freedom of conscience and worship is each man's personal right which ought to be proclaimed and asserted in every rightly constituted society."[21] Against the loud objections of a vocal Vatican minority, this tradition was un-received by the Second Vatican Council and re-received in a way that affirmed as a sacred religious right the freedom to believe as one freely chooses. Tierney comments that to argue that this shift in Church teaching is not a correction of a past error but a simple development of what was already implicit in the tradition is "to strain human credulity too far," and that anyone "who believes that will believe anything."[22]

The fourth example of non-reception is a crucial doctrinal example. From the Council of Trent in the sixteenth century to the Second Vatican Council in the twentieth, non-Catholic Christians were held to be excluded from the Body of Christ. The Council, again over the objections of a vocal Vatican minority that held such a traditional doctrine could not be abandoned, un-received this teaching and re-received it as "all who have been justified by faith in baptism are incorporated into Christ; they therefore have a right to be called Christians, and with good reason are accepted as brothers by the children of the Catholic Church."[23] All four of these examples illustrate what theologians call *non-reception* of a traditional teaching that leads to dramatic development and re-reception. These cases will be exemplary when we consider what the Church might learn from the sociological data about artificial contraception.

Orsy's description of the process of the reception of law is paradigmatic of all reception. He distinguishes two stages in the life of a law. In the first stage, the actor is the legislator, who conceives, formulates, and promulgates the law. In the second stage, the actors are the subjects of the law, who must understand the meaning and value of the law, decide to implement it, and then affirm it by observing it or, by not observing it, bring to the attention of the legislator the difficulty of the law. "When this process is completed and the law is observed throughout the community, its reception is achieved; it has become a vital force that shapes the life of the church."[24] Orsy points out that all this must be done under the umbrella of communion.

Margaret Farley asserts, correctly, that this two-stage process is not only useful but also actually *needed* in the case of moral norms. "This is because understanding of moral choices cannot come merely from receiving laws or rules. It entails at the very least a discernment of the meaning of laws and rules in concrete situations."[25] Such discernment and understanding require reflection on human experience, personal, social, and religious, and the social sciences throw revealing light on that experience. I agree wholeheartedly with Farley's further assertion that "it is inconceivable that moral norms can be formulated without consulting the experience of those whose lives are at stake."[26] It is equally inconceivable that doctrines can be formulated without consulting the faith of the whole Church that is articulated in them. Even Pius XII, before he defined the dogma of the Assumption of Mary, surveyed the bishops of the world to find out whether or not their various churches received the doctrine. It never occurred to him to define the dogma without consulting "the Church." All of which leads us into the consideration of another ecclesiological concept related to reception, namely, *sensus fidei*.

Sensus Fidei

Sensus fidei is a theological concept that denotes "the instinctive capacity of the whole Church to recognize the infallibility of the Spirit's truth."[27] It is a spiritual charism of discernment, possessed by the whole Church, which recognizes and receives a teaching as apostolic truth and, therefore, Church faith. The idea of *sensus fidei* was focused for moderns by John Henry Newman's essay *On Consulting the Faithful in Matters of Doctrine*, though he erroneously restricted *faithful* to laity rather than to the whole body of believers. He suggested that *sensus fidei* was "a sort of instinct, or *phronema*, deep in the bosom of the Mystical Body of Christ," and cited with approval Moehler's opinion that the Spirit of God arouses in the faithful "an instinct, an eminently Christian tact, which leads it to all true doctrine."[28]

The theological concept of *sensus fidei*, however, is much older than Newman and the nineteenth century. Vincent of Lerins formulated the ancient rule of faith in the fifth century: *quod ubique, quod semper, quod ab omnibus creditum est*, "what is believed everywhere, always, and by all."[29]

Aquinas explained *sensus fidei* in scholastic language. The faithful understand a teaching *per modum connaturalitatis*, that is, they incline naturally in faith to adhere to what is in harmony with the true meaning of the word of God.[30] Christian apostolic faith connaturally recognizes a truth that belongs to it. Bellarmine added his opinion that "what all the faithful hold as a matter of faith is necessarily true and of faith."[31] In every development of doctrine that has taken place in the Church, and there have been many, Lerins' rule was the essential factor in the reception or non-reception of a doctrine as the faith of the universal Church. Thus, Pius XII surveyed all the bishops of the world before he defined the doctrine of the Assumption of Mary in 1950, as I noted above.

One of the sub-texts at the Second Vatican Council, and in the theological developments that followed it, was a debate over who precisely were the *all* in Lerins' rule of faith—everywhere, always, and *by all*. Vatican theologians argued that it was only the *Magisterium* who determined doctrine and that they, therefore, were the *all*, a claim that had become common since the definition of papal infallibility by the First Vatican Council in 1870. Conciliar bishops and theologians responded with the more historically accurate claim that the Church's faith was preserved in the faith of *all* the faithful, lay and clerical together. They argued that, although the Magisterium ultimately spoke *for* the Church, it was also obliged to speak *from* the Church and that, when it structured doctrine along only magisterial lines, ignoring a clear *sensus fidei* in the whole Church, it was being unfaithful to the Church's primary rule of faith. The Vatican I Constitution *Pastor Aeternus* made it clear that, even on those rare occasions when he speaks infallibly, the Pope does not create faith *ex nihilo* but judges and declares what already is the faith of the Church and only when he does so does he enjoy "that infallibility the Redeemer willed his Church to have in defining doctrine on faith and morals."[32] At Vatican II, the position of conciliar bishops and theologians prevailed.

The Council taught that the doctrine of the Catholic Church is preserved by the Holy Spirit in all the faithful, laity and hierarchy together. "The body of the faithful *as a whole*, anointed as they are by the Holy One (cf. 1 John 2:20; 2:27), cannot err in matters of belief [they are infallible]. Thanks to a supernatural sense of the faith (*sensus fidei*) which characterizes the people *as a whole*, it manifests this unerring quality when, 'from the bishops to the last of the faithful,'[33] it manifests universal agreement in matters of faith and morals."[34] John Paul II adds his authority, teaching that the discernment of the full dignity of marriage "is accomplished through the *sensus fidei,* and is therefore the work of the *whole Church* according to the diversity of the various gifts and charisms."[35] He cites the above text from *Lumen Gentium* and 1 John 2:20 in support of this teaching. John could not be clearer: "You, no less than they, are among the initiated; this is the gift of the Holy One and by it you *all* have knowledge" (1 John 2:20). He is even clearer a few verses further on: "The anointing which you have received from him abides in you, and you have no need that anyone should teach you, as his anointing teaches you about everything, and is true, and is no lie" (1 John 2:27). Catholic tradition enshrines this belief in the doctrine that the Spirit of God is gifted to the whole Church.

These texts make two things clear. First, *sensus fidei* of virtually the whole Church is a gift of grace; its source is the Spirit of God. Second, this gift of grace is given to the *whole Church,* laity and clergy alike; it is not a gift given only to a hierarchical few. "The entire People of God is the subject that receives."[36] The Church has always been convinced that authentic *sensus fidei* and reception require *universalis ecclesiae consensione* (consent of the whole Church),[37] *totius mundi reverentia* (the reverence of the whole world),[38] *universalis ecclesiae assensus* (the assent of the whole Church),[39] and that this reverence and assent is a sign of the presence of the Spirit in the whole Church.[40]

The following sentence in the passage from *Lumen Gentium* cited above introduces another consideration. "By this appreciation of the faith . . . the People of God, guided by the sacred teaching authority (*Magisterium*), and obeying it (*cui fideliter obsequiens*), receives . . . truly the word of God." The Latin word *magister,* the root of *magisterium,* literally means *master,* schoolmaster, ship's master, master of an art or a trade. In the medieval Church, it came to mean one who has authority deriving from mastery of a subject. Thomas Aquinas, for whom the symbol of genuine authority was the *cathedra* or chair, distinguished two kinds of *magisterium*: that of a bishop, *magisterium cathedrae pastoralis,* and that of a theologian, *magisterium cathedrae magistralis.* The former derives from ordination as a bishop, the latter from mastery of the theological tradition. In the Catholic Church of the past two hundred years, *Magisterium* has come to be restricted exclusively to the teaching authority of bishops.[41]

Flannery's translation of the sentence from *Lumen Gentium* cited above underscores the attitude Vatican theologians demand of believers toward the ecclesial Magisterium: the People of God are to be guided by the Magisterium and are to *obey* it.[42] The translation of the Latin *obsequium* by the English *obedience*, however, is seriously doubtful. In the official English translation of the *Code of Canon Law*, *debitum obsequium* is translated as *due respect* (Can 218), and *religiosum obsequium* as *religious respect* (Can 752 and Can 753). There is a wide gulf between obedience and respect, and Flannery's translation tendentiously and falsely bridges the gulf in favor of passive obedience rather than respectful dialogue. Sullivan's reading of *obsequium* is more accurate. "As I understand it, then, to give the required *obsequium religiosum* to the teaching of the ordinary *magisterium* means to make an honest and sustained effort to overcome any contrary opinion I might have, and to achieve a sincere assent of my mind to this teaching."[43] In a Church that is communion, any effort to evaluate a magisterial teaching will include open dialogue, uncoerced judgment, and free consensus. That is the way genuine reception happens and authentic *sensus fidei* is formed.

Reception is understood in the Church, then, as a matter of either fiat or dialogue. Vatican theologians seek to reduce it to magisterial fiat and believers' obedience, in keeping with the hierarchical model of church still favored by them, "a wholly pyramidal conception of the Church as a mass totally determined by its summit."[44] In the communion model of Church re-introduced into the Catholic world by the Second Vatican Council,[45] reception requires active dialogue, judgment, and consensus among the virtually whole body of the communion's faithful. Reception "is not a matter of blind obedience to formal authority, but of the divinely-assisted recognition of the truth of what is taught."[46] Congar points out that obedience is called for "if the church is conceived as a society subject to monarchical authority," and dialogue and consensus are required "when the universal church is seen as a communion of churches." "It is certain," he continues, "that this second conception was the one that prevailed effectively during the first thousand years of Christianity, whereas the other one dominated in the West between the eleventh-century reformation and Vatican II."[47] Kilmartin agrees, emphasizing that the patristic and medieval notion of reception was "a tributary of the dominant ecclesiology of that age: a communion ecclesiology."[48]

Reception of doctrine is not the task of the Magisterium alone but "of the *whole* people . . . from the bishops to the last of the faithful."[49] In the case of infallible statements, "the assent of the Church can never be lacking to such definitions on account of the same Spirit's influence, through which Christ's *whole* flock is maintained in the unity of the faith and makes progress in it."[50] If "Christ's whole flock" is involved in receiving *infallible* teaching, it is a safe theological conclusion that the whole flock is involved also in the process of receiving non-infallible teaching. The instances of dramatic development to be noted in the next section suggest one obvious reason why this must be so: authoritarian pronouncements do not necessarily assure correct understanding or freedom from error.

Sociology

The two most influential theologians in the Latin Church used Greek philosophy as a tool to construct their theologies. Augustine used Plato to further the understanding of the biblical God and God's world, and Aquinas used Aristotle. Aquinas' Aristotelianism, initially condemned by the Church, eventually developed into the Scholastic theology that dominated Catholic thought in the nineteenth and early twentieth century. "The outstanding event in the Catholic theology of [the twentieth] century is the surmounting of [this] Scholasticism."[51] Scholasticism sought to construct a systematic theology that provided a timeless norm for a timeless Church. The twentieth century judged that norm to be just too timeless; it could not stand as the theology of a church that, far from being timeless, is inescapably time-conditioned.[52] Vatican II demanded that Christians scrutinize "the signs of the times" and interpret them "in the light of the gospel,"[53] and scholastic theology, with its ahistorical conceptual system, could not stand up to such scrutiny and gave way. The question continues to be "gave way to what?" The partial answer of this essay, founded in the teaching of Vatican II noted earlier that "in pastoral care sufficient use should be made, not only of theological principles, but also of the findings of secular sciences, especially psychology and sociology,"[54] is that, when theologians seek to understand *what* is actually received and believed, sociological research is as indispensable a tool as Greek philosophy was for Augustine and Aquinas.

The Catholic Church praises sociological research, teaching that "methodical research in all branches of knowledge . . . can never conflict with the faith, because the things of the world and the things of faith derive from the same God."[55] It asks its theologians "to seek out more efficient ways . . . of presenting their teaching to modern man: for the deposit and the truths of faith are one thing, the manner of expressing them is quite another."[56] John Paul II teaches, "the church values sociological and statistical research," but immediately adds the proviso that "such research alone is not to be considered in itself an expression of the *sensus fidei*.[57] The Pope is correct. Empirical research neither creates nor expresses *sensus fidei*, but it does manifest *what* is actually believed. As noted earlier, only when he received a virtually unanimous affirmative response to his quasi-sociological survey about whether the local churches believed that Mary was assumed into heaven, did Pius XII define in infallible judgment that Mary's Assumption was a universal belief, and therefore a dogma, of the Catholic Church. Though he did not consult *all* the faithful, from the bishops to the last of the faithful, it still never occurred to him, with all his papal authority, to define the dogma on his own without somehow seeking to determine the universal *sensus fidei*.

How could Lerin's rule of faith, everywhere, always, and by all, ever be determined without sociological survey? Of course, such survey does not create faith, which is a gift of God; neither does it express faith; but it does manifest *what* is actually believed. "Doctrines," Martin reminds us, "do not land like meteorites from outer space but grow organically where they have a supporting, fertile niche or cranny."[58] Without sociological survey to illumine the niches and crannies and the doctrines that grow in them, the work of theologians tends to appear, at best, as no more than interesting speculation or, at worst, as abstract anachronism. Gill offers a judgment that theologians of all stripes should heed. Christian ethicists, he complains, have been "reluctant to admit that sociology has any constructive role to play in their discipline. It is rare to find a Christian ethicist prepared to examine data about the moral effects of church-going. Instead Christian communities have become far *too idealized*."[59] What Gill asserts about ethicists I assert here about the Magisterium, which tends to talk about faith and beliefs as they *ought* to be, rather than as they *are*. If "the body of the faithful as a whole cannot err in matters of belief,"[60] however, they must be infallible in the beliefs they actually believe. It is that actual belief that is illuminated by sociological survey.

John Paul's words cited above are intended to suggest that the *theological* reality, *sensus fidei*, is not reached solely by demonstrating sociologically majority reception or non-reception of a teaching or decision. The Church, as has so often been pointed out, is not a political democracy in which majority head count controls reality. Neither, however, is it a monarchy. The Church is, rather, a communion of faithful who accept the apostolic faith handed down to them in a tradition that stretches back to the story of Jesus of Nazareth recorded in their scriptures. Those very scriptures or, more precisely, the way Christians read them, illustrate why majority rule can never be the sole rule of faith. The authentic Catholic approach to reading the scriptures today is an historical-critical approach, the literal meaning of the texts is the meaning intended by the writers at a particular time, place, and culture.[61] The approach of a large majority of Christians, Catholic and Protestant alike, is different; the literal meaning of the text is the meaning they find in and through modern language translations, ignoring the time, culture, and place of the writer. Interpreting documents written in another time and another culture is always a difficult task, requiring competence in languages, cultures, social rules, and histories that are not one's own. It would be disastrous to permit anyone unskilled in these specialties to judge what the gospel writers did and did not mean. Only those believers who understand the specialties involved are qualified to be judges. A majority opinion that results from a lack of education, incompetence, and ignorance can never be permitted to be the exclusive rule of faith.

The same argument applies to Church doctrines. Such doctrines, which are always not only ends but also beginnings of theological developments,[62] are articulated in concise, technical language: *homoousios*, *hypostasis* (incorrectly equated with the English *person*), substance, accident, transubstantiation. They are best understood by believers who grasp the philosophical and theological precision of the language of the ecclesial High Tradition, and are more often than not misunderstood by believers of the popular Low Tradition who do not understand either the language or its precision. Theological doctrines and their meanings can be properly evaluated only by believers who understand the historical, philosophical, and theological competencies involved. Dulles argues that, to determine *sensus fidei*, "we must look not so much at the statistics, as at the quality of the witnesses and the motivation for their assent."[63] I agree. *Sensus fidei*, the connatural capacity to discern the truth into which God as Spirit is leading the Church, must itself be carefully discerned by all who are competent. John Paul II is correct: a simple head count does not necessarily express the faith of the Church. A count, however, which includes virtually *all* the faithful, including virtually *all* the theologically-competent faithful, most certainly manifests the actual faith of the whole church. What sociology can and does show is that, in the case of the moral doctrines related to divorce and remarriage without annulment and birth control, the contemporary *sensus fidei* of both competent and non-competent faithful shows a dramatic development and is virtually at one.

I return now to what I promised earlier, namely, the distinction between *faith* and *belief*. It is impossible to read the New Testament and not be impressed by its insistence on faith as a means of salvation. Jesus complained frequently and insistently of the absence of faith. Paul passionately defended the necessity of faith against the legalism of the Judaizers. The Council of Trent, while rejecting Luther's claim that *faith alone* was required for salvation, still underscored the importance of faith in the process of salvation. It taught, "we may be said to be justified through faith, in the sense that faith is the beginning of man's salvation . . . without [faith] it is impossible to please God (Heb 11:6) and to be counted as his sons."[64] Alfaro defines that faith: It "includes knowledge of a saving event, confidence in the word of God, man's humble submission and personal self-surrender to God, fellowship in life with Christ. . . Faith is man's comprehensive 'Yes' to God's revealing himself as man's savior in Christ."[65]

Faith is a personal *process*, a comprehensive 'Yes" to God; belief is a *product* of intellectual reflection on that process, an intellectual assent to propositional formulae, or doctrines, about God that we accept in faith. Catholics and Lutherans now agree that genuine faith yields good fruits in the social world, having laid to rest the polemical and false debate between them about faith and good works. "We confess together," they declared, "that good works—a Christian life lived in faith, hope, and love—follow justification and are its fruits. When the justified live in Christ and act in the grace they receive, they bring forth, in biblical terms, good fruit."[66] Genuine Christian faith, as I explained earlier, always includes action in accord with faith.

Many sociological research projects inform us about the faith-praxis of Catholics in the United States.[67] I cite only three, and focus only on data related to contraception. D'Antonio and his colleagues conducted three surveys among American Catholics, in 1987, 1993, and 1997. They report increasing agreement on the following statement: a person can be a good Catholic without obeying the Church hierarchy's teaching on birth control. For the three studies, the level of agreement increased from 66% to

73% to 71%. The authors comment that the majority of American Catholics saw this item as neither "defining a good Catholic today" nor "definitive of a good Catholic." A 1996 Gallup study replicated the data: 89% believed that Catholics who use birth control are still good Catholics.[68]

D'Antonio and his colleagues note a "shift from 1987 to 1999 [that] depicts a trend from conformity to autonomy."[69] This trend is confirmed by the responses to a question about the locus of moral authority. In 1999, only 10% assigned the authority for practicing contraceptive birth control to Church leaders, while 62% assigned it to the individual.[70] Hoge and his colleagues also document this trend from conformity to authority. In their study, 73% of Latinos and 71% of non-Latinos agreed that, in morality, the final authority on good and bad is the individual's informed conscience. They comment, "this reliance on the individual authority is the same found in past research on Catholic young people."[71] It is also found in other sectors of the Church besides America. Though such data are far from expressions of the faith of Catholics, they do two important things: they manifest what their belief actually is and how it is at variance with the belief proposed by the Magisterium. This data cannot be ignored by theologians who wish to be taken seriously in the public arena, where claims about "what the Church believes" are so easily contradicted by the data of sociological research. I propose now, as concrete examples of *sensus fidei* and reception in the contemporary Church, to examine the data of sociological research with respect to birth control, and to ask what that data might mean theologically.

Procreation, Interpersonalism, and Contraception

In the 1960s, the Second Vatican Council sought to discern the "signs of the times" with respect to marriage and family, following John XXIII's instruction that there was a difference between the substance of Catholic faith, which would remain stable always, and the forms in which that faith was expressed, forms which had changed before and could change again in new historical and cultural times. One outcome of the Council, achieved largely by diocesan bishops and theologians over the loud objections of Vatican functionaries,[72] was a re-reception of Catholic theology about marriage which altered its teachings as surely as capitalist theories altered its teaching on usury and personalist teachings altered its teaching on slavery.

The exclusive model of marriage and of sexuality in Catholic thinking from the third century onwards was a biologically procreative model, which focused on bodily organs and their functions: the purpose of male and female sex organs and of the acts associated with them was procreation. Any use of the organs that was not biologically procreative was held to be sinful. In the twentieth century, as Western societies came to value the human person more, this biologically procreative model was re-received in a new, interpersonal form which focused on human persons, not their bodies and organs, and in which the mutual love and communion of the spouses was acknowledged as a purpose of marriage, at least, equal to biological procreation.

In the biologically procreative model, procreation was held to be the *primary* purpose of marriage, and all other purposes were held to be *secondary*. Despite insistent demands by the minority at the Council to continue to receive exclusively that model, because it was the tradition of the Church, the Council refused to do so. It taught that marriage and conjugal love "are by their very nature ordained to the generation and education of children" but that "does not make the other ends of marriage of less account."[73] To underscore the change and so that its words would not be misunderstood, the Preparatory Theological Commission, which submitted documents to the full Council for debate and vote, appended a note to this text which explained that it did not "suggest [a hierarchy of ends] in any way." Any doubt about this was removed by the publication of the new Code of Canon Law in 1983 which prescribed that marriage "is by its nature ordered toward the good of the spouses and the procreation and education of offspring" (Can 1055), with no suggestion of any hierarchy of ends.

In the modern Western world, social scientific research shows that sexual intercourse is no longer viewed exclusively as being for biological procreation: 82% of young adult Americans now see it as for *making love*, not necessarily for making babies.[74] That meaning is replicated in the contemporary Catholic scene via another datum of research: 75–85% of Catholics, who consider themselves good Catholics, approve a form of contraception forbidden by the Church.[75] Speaking of the situation in England, sociologist Hornsby-Smith notes that "the evidence we have reviewed suggests . . . that lay people . . . have largely made up their own minds on this matter, and now regard it as none of the business of the clerical leadership of the Church."[76] The theologian seeking factual judgment founded in empirical data has to ask whether or not such sociological data tell us anything about the truth of things?

Archbishop Bernardin of Cincinnati spoke at the 1980 Synod for the interpersonal procreative model of marriage and sexuality, arguing that the Church needed a more positive theology of sexuality, situated not in bodily organs and their acts, but in the human person and the meanings persons find in those acts. Archbishop Angelo Fernandes of New Delhi made a plea for the millions of families in his diocese living in ignorance and destitution who have no realistic hope of ever exercising responsible parenthood or achieving the dignity of a true marriage. Bishop Jullien of Beauvais, France, presented the theological argument. The essentials of human, and therefore of marital, life and love are of the spirit, not of the body which is but an organ of the spirit; the quality of a couple's Catholic commitment is of their spirit, not of their body and its acts. Cardinal Hume of Westminster added that, if the Christian family was to exercise the "prophetic mission" assigned to it by the synodal working paper, the Church's pastors had better pay attention to the *sensus fidei* expressed in the results of pastoral, or social scientific, consultations around the world. That mind, he continued, was a theological source for doctrinal awareness.[77]

The question of birth control became a major moral question in the Catholic Church with the appearance of the female cycle-regulating pills (still referred to today as "The Pill," as if there was only one). It became clearly focused in 1968 with the publication of Paul VI's encyclical *Humanae Vitae*, which emerged from the traditional biologically procreative model of marriage and prescribed that "each and every marriage act (*quilibet matrimonii actus*) must remain open to the transmission of life."[78] Paul VI took this statement from the Minority Report of the Commission he had set up to research and discuss the question of birth control. The Majority Report from the Commission argued, from the new interpersonal procreative model of marriage, that it is marriage itself (*matrimonium ipsum*), not "each and every marriage act," that is to be open to the transmission of life. It asserted, "human intervention in the process of the marriage act *for reasons drawn from the end of marriage itself* should not always be excluded, provided that the criteria of morality are always safeguarded."[79] The differential in the two positions was precisely the differential created by adherence to two different models of sexuality and marriage. The Minority Report followed the traditional biologically procreative model; the majority report followed the re-received procreative model in its interpersonal-union form that emerged from the Second Vatican Council.

The judgment of the majority of the competent, High Tradition faithful on the papal commission continues to be the judgment of the majority of Catholic theologians of the High Tradition and the vast majority of Catholic couples in the Low Tradition. They do not receive the prescription that every act of intercourse must be open to new life, because they do not receive the biologically procreative model, and therefore the arguments, on which it is based. Rather, they re-receive the interpersonally procreative model on which the majority report was based. Their non-reception does not make the traditional teaching necessarily false; it does, however, make it irrelevant to the life of the whole Church. Thirty-five years after the publication of *Humanae Vitae*, despite a concerted minority effort to make adherence to it a litmus test of authentic Catholicity, the debate between the biologically procreative and interpersonally procreative models continues tenaciously in the Church. Magisterial efforts to silence key voices in the theological debate, efforts that totally ignore the documented majority *sensus fidei* in both the theological High and popular Low Traditions, have not succeeded in silencing the debate. They have, however, succeeded in creating a loss of respect for Church law in general and Church law about sex in specific.[80]

The clear, scientifically documented non-reception of *Humanae Vitae* and the nuanced re-reception of the procreative model in its interpersonal form, among both those expert in theology and those expert in marriage, suggest a contemporary example of re-reception and dramatic development of doctrine in the Church, in line with the developments that took place in the doctrines on usury, slavery, religious freedom, and membership in the Body of Christ. Sociological research further suggests that dramatic development is now well under way. It shows that the assertion, "the Church believes that each and every marriage act must be open to the transmission of new life," is not true today for the vast majority of Catholics. Theologians cannot be comfortable with any statement of belief that can be shown empirically to be untrue. At the very least, the data suggest a development that the whole Church, of both High and Low Traditions, "from the bishops to the last of the faithful,"[81] is called to faithfully discern in order to judge whether it is or is not an authentic example of re-reception of the apostolic truth toward which the Spirit of truth is constantly impelling the Church.

Conclusion

This essay is an exercise in practical theology, "the theological discipline which is concerned with the Church's self-actualisation here and now—both that which *is* and that which *ought to be*."[82] That exercise includes exploration of the theological realities of reception and *sensus fidei* and of their connection to the data of sociological research. It demonstrates that both reception, a process by which virtually all the members of the Church assent to as apostolic truth and ecclesial faith a teaching or decision offered to them, and *sensus fidei*, a charism of discernment, possessed by the whole Church, which recognizes and receives a teaching or decision as apostolic truth and, therefore, ecclesial faith, are matters for the whole church and not just for a hierarchical few. The exploration focuses the questions of reception and *sensus fidei* on the Catholic doctrine of contraception, and demonstrates that contemporary sociological research documents a re-interpretation and re-reception of the doctrine in a way that illuminates a dramatic development of doctrine in the Church in line with others that have happened in history.

Though both reception and *sensus fidei* can appear as abstract realities, of concern only to professional theologians, the doctrine about contraception touches the most practical and intimate daily lives of believers. That alone is enough to demonstrate that questions about it are of concern to practical theology and have practical pastoral consequences. I conclude this essay by suggesting that the sociological evidence is clear: what *is* in virtually the whole Church is a re-reception of the doctrine about contraception. It is past time to acknowledge and magisterially teach that re-reception as not only what *is* but also what *ought to be* the belief of the Church. As the *Tablet* of London opined: "There is danger of a division between the institutional Church and a popular Church going its own way . . . The Mystical Body is rent."[83] It is time, yet again, for dialogue and consensus and the ancient rule of faith: *quod ubique, quod semper, quod ab omnibus creditum est*.

Notes

1. Karl Rahner, "Practical Theology Within the Totality of Theological Disciplines,"

Theological Investigations, IX (London: Darton, Longman, and Todd, 1972), 102. Emphasis in original.
2. Ibid., 105.
3. See John E. Thiel, *Senses of Tradition: Continuity and Development in the Catholic Faith* (New York: Oxford University Press, 2000), 100–28.
4. *Gaudium et Spes*, 62. All references to documents of the Second Vatican Council are taken from *The Documents of Vatican II*, Walter M. Abbott, S.J. ed. (New York: America, 1966).
5. Bernard J. F. Lonergan, "Moral Theology and the Human Sciences," *Method: Journal of Lonergan Studies* 15 (1997), 5–20.
6. Peter L. Berger, "Sociological and Theological Perspectives," in Robin Gill, ed., *Theology and Sociology: A Reader* (London: Cassell, 1996), 97. Emphasis in original.
7. In this essay, I embrace the ambiguity of the word *virtual*, and argue that it can be specified only by dialogue and consensus in the Church. I have no doubt that 86% of any population is virtually all of it, but is 80% or 75% or 68%? Only dialogue and consensus can decide.
8. The foundational work on reception was done by Yves Congar, "La réception comme réalité ecclésiologique," *Revue des Sciences Philosophiques et Théologiques* 56 (1972), 369–403, and Alois Grillmeier, "Konzil und Rezeption: Methodische Bemerkungen zu einem Thema der ökumenischen Discussion der Gegenwart," *Theologie und Philosophie* 45 (1970), 321–352. See additional bibliography in Richard R. Gaillardetz, *Teaching with Authority: A Theology of the Magisterium in the Church* (Collegeville: Liturgical, 1997), 252–253.
9. See Second Vatican Council, *Dogmatic Constitution on Divine Revelation*, nn.11–20; Congregation for the Doctrine of the Faith, *Mysterium Ecclesiae*, 5, *Acta Apostolicae Sedis* 65 (1973), 402–3; John Zizioulas, "The Theological Problem of Reception," *Centro Pro Unione*, 26 (Fall 1984), 6.
10. Herman J. Pottmeyer, "A New Phase in the Reception of Vatican II: Twenty Years of Interpretation of the Council," in *The Reception of Vatican II*, Giuseppe Alberigo, Jean-Pierre Jossua, and Joseph A. Komonchak, eds. (Washington: Catholic University of America Press, 1987), 27–43.
11. Giuseppe Alberigo, "The Christian Situation after Vatican II," in *The Reception of Vatican II*, 3.
12. Jerome, *Dialogus Contra Luciferianos*, 19, *Patrologia Latina* (hereafter PL) 23, 172.
13. Yves Congar lists a whole series of examples of reception in his classic essay, "Reception as an Ecclesiological Reality," in *Election and Consensus in the Church*, Giuseppe Alberigo and Anton Weiler, eds., *Concilium* 77 (1972), 45–58.

14. Zizioulas, "The Theological Problem of Reception," 4.
15. John T. Noonan, Jr., "Development in Moral Doctrine," *Theological Studies* 54 (1993), 662.
16. H. Denzinger and A. Schoenmetzer, eds., *Enchiridion Symbolorum Definitionum et Declarationum de Rebus Fidei et Morum* (Freiburg: Herder, 1965), 906. Cited hereafter as DS.
17. DS 716.
18. DS 753.
19. Noonan, "Development in Moral Doctrine," 664.
20. Cited in Charles E. Curran, "Authority and Dissent in the Roman Catholic Church," in *Vatican Authority and American Catholic Dissent*, William W. May, ed. (New York: Crossroad, 1987), 29.
21. Pius IX, *Quanta Cura*, in Claudia Carlen Ihm, *The Papal Encyclicals 1740–1878* (Raleigh: McGrath Publishing, 1981), 383.
22. Brian Tierney, *Origins of Papal Infallibility 1150–1350: A Study on the Concepts of Infallibility, Sovereignty, and Tradition in the Middle Ages* (Leiden: Brill, 1972), 277.
23. *Unitatis Redintegratio*, 3.
24. Ladislas M. Orsy, "Reception of Law," in *Encyclopedia of Catholicism*, Richard P. McBrien, ed. (San Francisco: Harper Collins, 1995), 1082.
25. Margaret A. Farley, "Moral Discourse in the Public Arena, " in *Vatican Authority and American Catholic Dissent*, 177.
26. Ibid.
27. Thiel, *Senses of Tradition*, 47.
28. John Henry Newman, *On Consulting the Faithful in Matters of Doctrine* (New York: Sheed and Ward, 1961). 73.
29. Vincent of Lerins, *Commonitorium Primum* 2, PL 50, 640.
30. *Summa Theologiae*, IIa-IIae, 2, 3, ad 2. See J. de Guibert, "A propos des textes de Saint Thomas sur la foi qui discerne," *Revue des Sciences Religieuses* 9 (1919), 30–44; C. H. Joyce, "La foi qui discerne d'apres Saint Thomas," *Revue des Sciences Religieuses* 6 (1916), 433–55.
31. Cited in Avery Dulles, "*Sensus Fidelium*," *America* (November 1, 1986), 240.
32. DS 3074.
33. Augustine, *De Praed. Sanct.*, 14, 27, PL 44, 980.
34. *Lumen Gentium*, 12. Emphasis added.
35. *Familiaris Consortio*, 5. Emphasis added.
36. Pottmeyer, "A New Phase in the Reception of Vatican II,"30.
37. Augustine, *De Baptismo*, VII, 53, PL 43, 243.
38. Pope Leo the Great, *Epist*. 14, 2, PL 54, 672.

39. Pope Gelasius, *Epist. XIII*, PL 59, 63.
40. See Gerard Bartelink, "The Use of the Words *Electio* and *Consensus* in the Church (Until about 600)," *Concilium* 77 (1972), 147–54.
41. See, for instance, DS 3011 and 3065; *Lumen Gentium* 18, 22, 25.
42. Austin Flannery, *Vatican Council II: The Conciliar and Postconciliar Documents* (Collegeville: Liturgical Press, 1992), 363.
43. Francis A. Sullivan, *Magisterium: Teaching Authority in the Catholic Church* (Dublin: Gill and Macmillan, 1985), 164.
44. Yves Congar, "Reception as an Ecclesiological Reality," *Concilium* 77 (1965), 60.
45. See, for example, Jean-Marie R. Tillard, *Church of Churches: The Ecclesiology of Communion* (Collegeville: Liturgical, 1992); Michael G. Lawler and Thomas J. Shanahan, *Church: A Spirited Communion* (Collegeville: Liturgical, 1995); Dennis M. Doyle, *Communion Ecclesiology* (Maryknoll: Orbis, 2000).
46. Sullivan, *Magisterium*, 112.
47. Congar, "Reception as an Ecclesiological Reality," 62.
48. Edward Kilmartin, "Reception in History: An Ecclesiological Phenomenon and Its Significance," *Journal of Ecumenical Studies* 21 (1984), 34.
49. *Lumen Gentium*, 12.
50. Ibid., 25.
51. Walter Kasper, *Theology and Church* (New York: Crossroad, 1989), 1.
52. See Congregation for the Doctrine of the Faith, *Mysterium Ecclesiae*, 5, in *Acta Apostolicae Sedis* 65 (1973), 402.
53. *Gaudium et Spes*, 4.
54. Ibid., 62.
55. Ibid., 36.
56. Ibid., 62.
57. Pope John Paul II, *Familiaris Consortio*, 5 (Washington, DC: United States Catholic Conference, 1982), 3–4.
58. David Martin, *Reflections on Sociology and Theology* (New York: Oxford University Press, 1997), 69.
59. Robin Gill, *Churchgoing and Christian Ethics* (Cambridge: Cambridge University Press, 1999), 1. Emphasis added.
60. *Lumen Gentium*, 12.
61. Pius XII, *Divino Afflante Spiritu*, *Acta Apostolicae Sedis* 35 (1943), 297–325; Pontifical Biblical Commission, *Instructio De Historica Evangeliorum Veritate*, *Acta Apostolicae Sedis* 56 (1964), 712–18; Second Vatican Council, *Dogmatic Constitution on Divine Revelation*, in *Vatican Council II: The Conciliar and Postconciliar Documents*, Austin Flannery, ed. (Collegeville: Liturgical, 1992), 750–65; Pontifical Bib-

lical Commission, *The Interpretation of the Bible in the Church, Origins* (January 6, 1994).

62. See Karl Rahner, "Current Problems in Christology," *Theological Investigations, I* (London: Darton, Longman, and Todd, 1965), 150.

63. Avery Dulles, "*Sensus Fidelium,*" *America* (November 1, 1986), 242.

64. DS 1532.

65. Juan Alfaro, "Faith," *Sacramentum Mundi: An Encyclopedia of Theology* (New York: Herder, 1968), II: 315.

66. *Joint Declaration on the Doctrine of Justification* (Strasbourg: Institute for Ecumenical Research, 1997), 61.

67. Patrick H. McNamara, *Conscience First: Tradition Second* (Albany: State University of New York Press, 1992); Robert A. Ludwig, *Reconstructing Catholicism for a New Generation* (New York: Crossroad, 1995); William V. D'Antonio, James D. Davidson, Dean R. Hoge, Ruth A. Wallace, *Laity American and Catholic: Transforming the Church* (Kansas City: Sheed and Ward, 1996); James D. Davidson, Andrea S. Williams, Richard A. Lamanna, Jan Stenftenagel, Kathleen Maas Weigert, William J. Whalen, and Patricia Wittberg, *The Search for Common Ground: What Unites and Divides Catholic Americans* (Huntingdon: Our Sunday Visitor, 1997); William V. D'Antonio, James D. Davidson, Dean R. Hoge, and Katherine Meyer, *American Catholics: Gender, Generation, and Commitment* (Lanham: Rowman and Littlefield, 2001); Dean R. Hoge, William D. Dinges, Mary Johnson, and Juan L. Gonzales, Jr., *Young Adult Catholics: Religion in the Culture of Choice* (Notre Dame: University of Notre Dame Press, 2001).

68. George H. Gallup, Jr., *Religion in America 1996* (Princeton: Princeton Religion Research Center, 1996), 44.

69. D'Antonio et al., *American Catholics*, 43.

70. Ibid. 76.

71. Hoge et al., *Young Adult Catholics*, 59–60.

72. See Giuseppe Alberigo, ed., *History of Vatican II*, 3 volumes, English version edited by Joseph A. Komonchak (Maryknoll: Orbis, 2000).

73. *Gaudium et Spes*, 50.

74. William V. D'Antonio et al., *Laity: American and Catholic*, 79. Corroborating evidence is supplied by Davidson et al., *The Search for Common Ground*, 47.

75. See Andrew M. Greeley, William C. McCready, and Kathleen McCourt, *Catholic Schools in a Declining Church* (Kansas City: Sheed and Ward, 1976), 35; D'Antonio et al., *Laity: American and Catholic*, 140; Davidson et al., *The Search for Common Ground*, 131.

76. Michael Hornsby-Smith, *Roman Catholicism in England: Customary Catholicism*

and Transformation of Religious Authority (Cambridge: Cambridge University Press, 1991), 177.
77. The foregoing information may be found in more detail in Murphy, "Of Sex and the Catholic Church," 49–52.
78. Pope Paul VI, *Humanae Vitae*, 11 (Washington, DC: United States Catholic Conference, 1968), 7.
79. Cited in Clifford Longley, *The Worlock Archive* (London: Chapman, 2000), 233. Emphasis added.
80. See, for example, George Gallup, Jr. and Jim Castelli, *The American Catholic People: Their Beliefs, Practices, and Values* (New York: Doubleday, 1987); Andrew M. Greeley et al. *Catholic Schools in a Declining Church*.
81. Augustine, *De Praed. Sanct.*, 14, 27, *PL* 44, 980. See also *Lumen Gentium*, 12.
82. Rahner, "Practical Theology," 102.
83. "Viewpoint," *The Tablet* (9 January, 1993), 30.